Department of the Environment

LEEDS METROPOLITAN UNIVERSITY

vital and viable town centres:
meeting the challenge

Urban and Economic Development Group (URBED)

in association with: Comedia, Hillier Parker, Bartlett School of Planning University College London, and Environmental and Transport Planning.

London: HMSO

1994.

Cover photographs:
The refurbished Lewisham Centre: Lewisham
Gentleman's Walk: Norwich
New shops on the edge of the town centre: Witney
A symposium on the future of Birmingham City Centre

Inside cover photograph: Festival time: Bradford

foreword by Rt Hon. John Gummer MP
Secretary of State for the Environment

I welcome this report, which represents a major contribution to our understanding of town centres. It will help local authorities, property owners, retailers and local people to determine the action they need to take to achieve vital and viable town centres. It should provide a major impetus towards the implementation of our policy, set out in PPG6.

That policy is intended to help foster town centres which serve the whole community. Town Centres should provide a focus for retail development where competing businesses are near enough for shoppers to compare prices and benefit from competition. They should be places in which a wide variety of different uses are encouraged. In that way town centres will be attractive to local residents, shoppers and visitors, because they have lively restaurants and cafes, culture and entertainment, as well as interesting shops.

Improving the quality of our towns means encouraging new shopping development to locations where it can reinforce the town centre. We may also need to discourage development on green field sites on the edge of cities, where it would result in an unacceptable impact on a town centre. Those messages in PPG6 have been widely welcomed - by the retail industry and by the public at large. We expect local authorities to act on them.

The liveliness that we want to see in town centres cannot be achieved in an atmosphere of decline. We now have an economy which is clearly growing. We want to encourage growth, but manage it, so that it brings life back to our town centres - places where people can live and work and shop and play.

Local authorities should not be afraid of such a vision. They should be positive in their approach to planning and managing their town centres. They should be imaginative in enabling things to happen. However, they also need the help and support from all those who have an interest in the quality of our town centres. This report will help to stimulate that interest and provide inspiration.

contents

Study team

Project Director: Dr Nicholas Falk, Urban and Economic Development Group

Project Manager: Simon Quin, Urban and Economic Development Group

Core Team: Charles Landry, Comedia
Dr Brian Raggett, Hillier Parker
Dr Russell Schiller, Hillier Parker
Dr Carmen Hass-Klau, Environmental and Transport Planning
Alan Penn, Bartlett School of Planning
Dr James Simmie, Bartlett School of Planning

DoE Nominated Officer: Chris Pagdin

Thanks are also due to:

URBED: Kate Bambridge, Johnny Burton, Helen Preston, and Khoria Stewart
Comedia: Liz Greenhalgh and Ken Worpole
Hillier Parker: Jonathan Baldock and Stuart Lloyd
Bartlett: Amanda Sutcliffe

Photographs by URBED unless otherwise credited. Report designed by URBED, Graham Whatley and Melissa Readings

The views and recommendations expressed in this report are those of URBED and the study team and should not be taken to represent the views or opinions of the Department of the Environment

executive summary

Whereas in the 1980s most British towns expected their shopping centres to grow, many now feel threatened, and there are widespread signs of decline. The challenge stems not just from the recession and competition from other towns, but from social and economic changes. In particular, local authorities have to reconcile growing pressures for dispersal, as a result of rising car usage, with improvements to the environment for the many who value the mix of functions that town centres provide.

The new emphasis on positive planning, reflected in PPG6 and ministerial statements, recognises the threat to sustainability posed by excessive dispersal. It also encourages those with an interest in a town to work together to devise and implement strategies for improvement. This report, therefore, draws together information on trends, as well as experience in this country and abroad, to enable local authorities and others to make the most of their town and city centres.

Report structure

The report is the result of a year's work by the Urban and Economic Development Group (URBED), and a multi-disciplinary team of consultants and researchers. It is in three main parts. The first part deals with the challenges. It draws on fresh analyses of employment and population trends in 32 towns by the Bartlett School of University College London, and includes reviews of shopping and leisure trends by Hillier Parker and Comedia, and of transport by Environmental and Transport Planning. It considers alternative futures, based on American or Continental models. An assessment is made of the impact of different policies.

The second part then considers the responses local authorities can make, both in assessing vitality and viability and in devising town centre strategies. A series of indicators for both performance and the underlying components of a healthy town centre are put forward. The report sets out a sequential approach for drawing up a strategy. It also differentiates between the main types of town centre in terms of the particular problems and opportunities they face.

The final part deals with good practice. It is based on responses to a survey from 335 district and borough councils (85% of all such local authorities in England and Wales) and a number of case studies, as well as on visits, interviews and an analysis of the extensive literature. The section sets out some basic guidelines, with illustrations from the five basic types of town (and the report includes over 50 boxed examples). Appendices provide further information on measuring retail performance, undertaking a health check, and a list of examples of good practice, followed by a bibliography.

Underlying trends

Many town centres, in expanding market towns as well as contracting old industrial areas, feel they are declining. Chapter 2 argues that while the most obvious threat to town centres has come from out-of-town shopping and new forms of retailing, there are deeper trends towards dispersal. These are causing the population of larger towns to change and contract, although there is a slight increase in the numbers living near the town centre. The wide variation in employment trends between different town centres, suggests that there is a range of possible futures. However, with the growth of business parks on the periphery of towns, there is a danger of functions other than just shopping drifting away.

The underlying causes lie in the shift towards a service-based economy, and one where most people increasingly rely on cars to get around from one centre to another. Most towns were not built with cars in mind and reconciling the individual desire for personal mobility with collective desires for an attractive town centre depends on investment and good urban design. Major retailers and financial institutions who have invested heavily in the expansion of town centres, are in many cases now finding it more profitable to move out of town, where access by car is far easier.

Chapter 3 considers how towns have evolved and looks at possible alternative futures. It suggests one possible scenario is for British towns to follow the North American example, where retailing is no longer concentrated in town centres, and as a result many have contracted and gone 'down market'. Another is to become more like Continental towns, where a high density of population, good public transport and attractive streets keep the centres strong and popular.

Chapter 4 examines the impact of public policies. While the situation varies around the country, in general public policies are not checking dispersal or ensuring that enough investment is going into making centres competitive, although there are some promising examples of what could be achieved. The danger arises when dispersal has gone too far, and the response of 'beautification' may be like putting cosmetics on a corpse.

Positive planning

Chapter 5 deals with the meaning of vitality and viability, and how to assess them. The organic nature of town centres makes them hard to reduce to a few figures, and this is made more difficult by the lack of data on retail turnover. Nevertheless, reasonably reliable information is available on a number of factors that can be used to assess whether a town centre is healthy or at risk. Vitality refers to how busy the town is at different times, and information can be collected on pedestrian flow or footfall, as it is already for major shopping malls, to show trends and also areas of weakness. Viability refers to the capacity to attract ongoing investment, and here we suggest looking at town centres through the eyes of investors by using information on retail property yields and rentals. In each case, information is available which can also be analysed in terms of trends over time and comparable areas.

The strengths and weaknesses of town centres should also be analysed systematically. We propose that local authorities undertake "health checks", where possible in association with local businesses, to look in turn at how well the centre is performing in terms of attractions, accessibility, amenity, and action (the four `A's). A series of concepts such as diversity, linkages, identity and organisational capacity can be helpful, and these are described and illustrated.

Chapter 6 outlines a process for drawing up town centre strategies. Towns vary enormously, but success usually depends on a process that gives the centre the attention it needs and ensures the right strategic choices are taken. Success is helped by a realistic vision that draws the support of key interests, plus a strategy and action programme that mobilises resources, and effective management to maintain improvements.

Strategic differences

Chapter 7 deals with how to classify town centres. The most valid comparisons are not with the town down the road, but with similar types of town in terms of their wider function, not just their role as shopping centres. We have identified a number of archetypes that reflect different kinds of centre. The basic categories we propose are Market Towns, Industrial Towns, Suburban Centres, Metropolitan Cities, and Resorts and Historic Towns. The latter have been combined as they share a number of characteristics and problems.

Chapters 8 to 12 describe the common features and examples of good practice in each of the different types of town centre in turn. Although they perform eight or nine different functions, it is vital that they do not lose their retail function which still underpins the use and value of most British town centres. The town centres most at risk are the industrial and suburban centres, as these both face a drop in purchasing power and strong competition from all sides. Many market towns are also vulnerable from the development of too many out-of-town food superstores if their centres are not sufficiently attractive to compete. Seaside resorts face a special problem, having lost their traditional economic base, but could look to follow the example of historic towns, most of which have prospered. The Metropolitan city centres have made the greatest strides to match their Continental rivals and many are now vibrant.

After the collapse of the property boom, with less finance for major redevelopment schemes, priority is switching to schemes that improve the centre as a whole. As standards rise and retail requirements change, local authorities need to work with local businesses and other key interests to assess how well their centres match up to competition, and what can practically be done to improve their attractions, accessibility and amenity.

Attractions

In smaller towns, empty space can sometimes be used to improve the retail mix, while planning briefs can secure appropriate development on the edge of the town centre, including housing as well as space for food stores. In larger towns, imaginative refurbishment of redundant buildings can help to create places where arts, culture and entertainment thrive. Mixed uses can also revitalise quarters on the edge of metropolitan cities. In some cases activities such as education and health uses can be important. Many major cities have also shown how to use events to bring places to life and promote a positive image. Though most centres cannot survive on residents alone, successful town centres tend to have people living in or around them, and there is great scope for expanding their populations once again, as on the Continent.

Accessibility

The stronger the attractions, the more effort people will make to get to town, but with much more choice it is vital that trips are a pleasure and not a chore. In market towns this may mean having free short stay parking close to the centre. In many larger towns the answer lies in making the bus system as attractive to use as the car, or through park and ride or rapid transit systems. As most towns cannot expect to compete with the convenience and parking availability of out-of-town centres they must take care not to lose customers. The relative success of historic towns provide much of the inspiration on how to create walkable cities. Walking must feel attractive and safe at all times, and this means more than an isolated pedestrian precinct. Many towns could do much more to improve their gateways, such as bus stations, and the linkages between car parks and the shops. Traffic calming provides an attractive option to total exclusion of cars in some situations.

Amenity

The main priority for amenity, or the appearance of the town, is to ensure that it looks well cared for, so that people feel welcome to explore and linger. Security is an increasing concern, and towns have to match standards set by managed shopping centres. However, the future of town centres lies in emphasising their distinct identity as real places whose bustle comes from a mix of functions, such as housing and entertainment. Towns also need to make people feel safe through good maintenance and lighting. Instead of copying fads, towns need to undertake environmental or urban design audits to establish what makes them special, and then to invest in quality. While historic towns provide a useful model, the message is that good design pays.

Action

The final and perhaps most important element of a successful town is the capacity to turn visions into results or action. Successful towns are enterprising towns. This is mainly about organisation, with the different public and private agencies working together for the good of the town, and involving the business community on an ongoing basis so there is a sense of partnership. Town centre management involves much more than simply giving an officer the title of town centre manager. However, action also depends on money, and as businesses often believe they are already paying for local services through the business rate, there is a need to review the mechanisms for resourcing the improvement and maintenance of town centres.

Recommendations

A number of conclusions, leading to nine principal recommendations are put forward in Chapter 13. Local government should adopt a town centre focus, devise town centre strategies, implement town centre management, take initiatives on key sites through positive planning, and work with public transport operators to make alternatives to the car more attractive. The process of revitalising town centres should be supported with technical assistance, local business involvement, and measures to create a positive climate of investment and to introduce new resourcing mechanisms.

introduction

- This research programme arose from the need to assist local authorities with improving town centres and in dealing with 'out-of-town' planning applications.

- The research approach combined a survey of local authorities, analysis of census and employment trends, and a series of case studies, with inputs from a multi-disciplinary team of consultants.

- The report is divided into three parts, the challenges facing town centres, techniques for assessing performance and devising town centre strategies, and good practice in terms of possible initiatives.

'There exists a lack of comprehensive, consistent and timely local knowledge on retail change... The end result can be likened simply to a series of matches being struck to illuminate conditions in a range of places at various points in time. There have been few flashlights in use.'

'The Effects of Major Out of Town Retail Development', DoE.

1.01 Town centres, like society as a whole, cannot stand still. Their continuing survival and success is largely bound up with their capacity to recognise and adapt to change. The fundamental reason for focussing on the future of town centres at the present time lies in the long-term impact of a continuing dispersal of their traditional activity on their capacity to be self-sustaining. (Exhibit 1.1) The primary impetus for change comes from increased personal mobility. This has prompted developments 'out-of-town' and on the 'edge-of-town', often facilitated by the availability of sites as a result of industrial closures or new roads. Dispersal applies to all kinds of activity, residential, leisure and business as well as retail.

1.02 At the same time a consumer revolution combined with new technology has led to the growth of service employment and the decline of traditional manual jobs. With more women out at work during the day, many people are using cars to do bulk shopping once a week, often when town centre shops are closed. For some, non-food shopping has become a leisure activity as people 'shop around', perhaps by visiting historic towns for specialist purchases and a pleasant day out.

1.03 The resulting shifts in purchasing power, aggravated by the recession and unemployment, are putting pressures on many centres that may have taken their futures for granted. For in addition to growing competition from other towns, they also face the challenges of new forms of retailing, from retail parks and warehouse clubs to what some newspapers have called 'store wars', as superstores battle for larger sites with dedicated surface parking. Many centres are now showing signs of neglect.

1.04 Our survey of local authorities showed that a significant number of town centres are regarded as declining and only a

Signs of neglect... **1.1**

Vacant premises: Margate

Traffic Dominant: Sleaford (Before 1993 by-pass)

Unfriendly streets: Woolwich

few vibrant. Many local authorities are worried about what they should be doing under pressure from both local traders and citizens concerned about growing levels of vacancy. The ultimate fear is that some of our towns could end up like many American town centres, where the bulk of retail spending has gone out-of-town (Davies 1988). There the loss of trade has led to disinvestment, and many can no longer maintain or sustain their centres. However, there are other models, and a growing number of British town centres are now looking to continental towns for inspiration, as well as to British success stories.

Brief

1.05   This year-long research study was commissioned by the Department of the Environment to throw light on the challenges facing town centres, how they can best be tackled, and to highlight effective approaches and examples of good practice. The study arose from ongoing work which has given rise to the new Planning Policy Guidance note 6 (DoE 1993) and policies to make development sustainable. It was also prompted by the literature review of the *Effects of Major Out-of-Town Retail Development* (DoE 1992a) which suggested the need to learn from the experience of contrasting 'winners and losers'.

1.06   The objectives as set out in the brief were:

a) to define the concepts of viability and vitality in relation to town centres, establish the major factors that contribute to these two qualities and indicate how these qualities might be measured for the purpose of policy evaluation and impact assessment

b) to establish the nature, strength and cause of trends, including private sector investment patterns, which have influenced the viability, vitality and role of town centres over the last 20 years

c) to consider whether these past trends are likely to continue, and to identify what new trends might influence the viability, vitality and the role of town centres in future years

d) to identify and assess the effectiveness and impact of plans, policies and actions of the public sector on the viability, vitality and role of town centres

f) to identify appropriate planning and planning-related approaches to encourage private sector investment and to ensure the future viability and vitality of town centres as places to shop, work, visit and live.

Research approach

1.07   Because the subject is so complex, and hard information is still very scarce, the team of consultants led by the **Urban and Economic Development Group** (URBED) sought to take a multi-disciplinary and holistic approach. Considerable use has been made of existing literature and reports, and the bibliography in *The Effects of Major Out-of-Town Retail Development* provided an excellent starting point. The cultural planning specialists **Comedia** investigated the range of possible indicators and the different dimensions of a healthy town centre. Leading retail and property consultants **Hillier Parker** provided advice on how to assess the performance of town centres from a property investment perspective as well

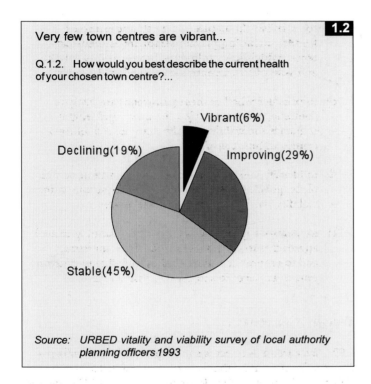

Very few town centres are vibrant... 1.2

Q.1.2.   How would you best describe the current health of your chosen town centre?...

Vibrant(6%)

Declining(19%)

Improving(29%)

Stable(45%)

Source: URBED vitality and viability survey of local authority planning officers 1993

as influencing the team's thinking on the changing nature of retailing. The **Bartlett School of Planning at University College London** analysed demographic and employment trends to establish how far dispersal is taking place, as well as providing input on the subject of accessibility within town centres. **Environmental and Transport Planning** provided advice on transport policy and ways of reconciling traffic and pedestrians.

1.08   The research has drawn heavily on advice from a wide range of experts in different fields and regular input from members of the study Steering Group. In addition seminars were held in Woolwich, Bradford and Worcester. These examined the basic ideas arising from the research with practitioners in the public and private sectors. We are most grateful to all who helped our deliberations.

1.09   A multiple-choice questionnaire, devised and distributed with the help of the Royal Town Planning Institute, and sent to local authority chief planning officers, produced an 85% response and 335 usable replies. This survey gives a picture of both the state of town centres and initiatives planned or underway. The results were subsequently analysed to provide the first comprehensive view of the health of town centres and what is happening in them around the country (Exhibit 1.2)

1.10   A series of case studies of different types of town and city centres allowed us to test a number of hypotheses concerning what leads to successful places. They also helped, along with visits to many other places, to generate a 'menu' of ways in which town centres can be strengthened and improved. The case studies confirmed that because centres are so complex there is no simple formula or quantitative measure that can be used to judge a town's capacity to survive the impact of out-of-town competition. Instead each town has to be considered on a number of dimensions, which involve qualitative assessments against standards which are continually changing.

1.11   The team has benefited from comparing the situation in Britain with experience in both North America and the Continent, particularly Germany and Belgium. Reports and visits provided some useful models for understanding the nature of town centres and the processes of urban change.

Taken together, they provide some real warnings of what can happen through neglect, but also offer considerable inspiration for how town and city centres could enjoy a renaissance.

Key issues and methodology

1.12   The complex nature of town centres and the limited data generally available raised a number of methodological problems. First, was how to define the **town centre**. There is a tendency to see town centres simply as places to shop whereas their functions and significance are wider. We sought, therefore, to consider the full range of functions in reviewing trends. We defined the town centre as not just the central shopping core, where the national multiples tend to congregate, but also the secondary areas where there is a continuing retail frontage usually occupied by independent businesses (see PPG6 for a useful glossary of terms). Retail and leisure development has, in many cases, also taken place outside this continuing frontage, but still within a few minutes walk of the centre. This we have considered as **edge-of-centre** or **fringe**. Developments outside this area we consider **out-of-centre** or **out-of-town**, and these are usually most accessible by car. The wider central area, including the fringes, can be defined by the central wards to provide statistical information. This equates to the US downtown and is referred to here as the **centre of town**.

1.13   The second problem relates to measuring vitality and viability. In the absence of information on turnover and investment within the town centre, which could be compared with the surrounding area, we have sought a few key indicators that can be used to judge whether a town is `at risk (though interpretation will always require judgment and wider knowledge). We have suggested ways of comparing centres

with each other and over time, using information which can be obtained fairly readily. The proposed indicators are broadly consistent with the way that local authorities think town centres should be evaluated, with the difference that most put more emphasis on vacancy, which we see as potentially misleading for reasons that are explained later.

1.14   This method, however, can only give a broad indication of how a centre ranks and does not say anything about the underlying components of a healthy centre. We, therefore, devised a **health check** or series of tests, which emerged from the factors our survey of local authorities found to be generally important. They were refined through the case studies, which we used to verify ideas from the team on what makes town centres healthy. In a number of instances we sought to compare pairs of towns which were basically similar, but where one was generally considered to be doing better than the other.

1.15   In assessing trends, we focussed on analysing population and employment trends between the last censuses, and also reviewed longer term economic trends for towns as a whole. We utilised data on employment available through NOMIS, the National On-line Manpower Information System, a Government on-line statistical service. This necessitated using a definition of town centres based on wards, which has a number of drawbacks, but should not affect the overall con clusions.

1.16   Because towns differ so, we spent considerable time on the best way of classifying them to reflect their problems and opportunities. The conventional classification into regional and district centres, which is based on shopping provision, is over simple when looking at centres as a whole, and excludes qualitative differences. It is also not universally understood.

Methods based on catchment characteristics can be over complex. Furthermore, while there are regional differences, there are perfectly successful centres in what are considered poor areas and vice versa. We, therefore, went for a compromise which involved classifying towns into five **archetypes** in terms of their history, location and population, and this system was used in analysing different types of information. While any one town may want to consider itself in several categories, clear differences emerge both through the response to the survey, and in terms of statistical data. The approach, which was tested out on a panel of experts, appears to be sufficiently robust for policy purposes.

Structure of the report

1.17   The first part of this report considers the main challenges affecting the future of town centres. It looks at demographic and economic trends, and then at the impact of private and public policies. The second part puts forward a framework for analysing vitality and viability, and the components of a healthy town centre, and outlines how to devise town centre strategies. The final part considers good practice, and deals in turn with the five main types of town centres that the research showed faced different problems and opportunities: Market Towns, Industrial Towns, Suburban Centres, Metropolitan Cities, and Resorts and Historic Towns.

1.18   Appendices provide additional material, including our analysis of town centres from an investment point of view, a health check questionnaire with some sources of information, and a list of places that illustrate good practice. Examples are used throughout to highlight what can be done to improve town centres, given the will (Exhibit 1.3).

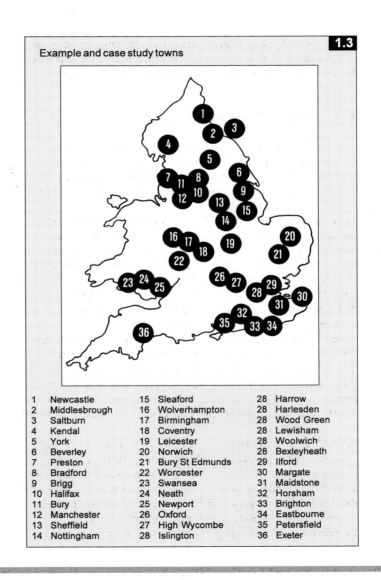

1.3

Example and case study towns

1	Newcastle	15	Sleaford	28	Harrow
2	Middlesbrough	16	Wolverhampton	28	Harlesden
3	Saltburn	17	Birmingham	28	Wood Green
4	Kendal	18	Coventry	28	Lewisham
5	York	19	Leicester	28	Woolwich
6	Beverley	20	Norwich	28	Bexleyheath
7	Preston	21	Bury St Edmunds	29	Ilford
8	Bradford	22	Worcester	30	Margate
9	Brigg	23	Swansea	31	Maidstone
10	Halifax	24	Neath	32	Horsham
11	Bury	25	Newport	33	Brighton
12	Manchester	26	Oxford	34	Eastbourne
13	Sheffield	27	High Wycombe	35	Petersfield
14	Nottingham	28	Islington	36	Exeter

PART ONE • CHALLENGES

2 social and economic trends

- Town centres perform an organic mix of functions, including acting as a shopping centre and market place, an arts, cultural and entertainment venue, a business centre, a transport hub, and increasingly as a place to live and visit, as well as potentially a place for educational and health services.

- Their role has been affected by the dispersal of population and employment, though the population of many town centres is beginning to rise again.

- The pressures come from increased personal mobility and the move towards a service or 'self service' economy, with resulting changes in working patterns.

- Retailers are responding by expanding out-of-town, where access by car is easier and where there are larger sites available at lower cost allowing space for adjacent parking.

- Some leisure activities are also following suit, with cultural losses and entertainment dispersal.

- Private investment is now dominated by financial institutions, motivated by expectations of rental growth.

'Sprawl is economically foolhardy, too. We have been squandering a massive share of our available national capital recreating, on the metropolitan periphery, what already exists in our cities - road and bridge systems, universities and hospitals, retail facilities, office and sports complexes...'

Neil Pearce, US National Council for Urban Economic Development

2.01   What really are town centres? How well are they
doing? Who shapes their future? Where are they going and
how can we influence their development? These are some of
the key questions addressed by this research project. We start
with an appreciation of the mix of functions in a town centre,
then examine the trends in dispersal and mobility, the 'retailing revolution' and changing leisure patterns, before considering the implications for private investment.

A changing mix of functions

2.02   Most people's idea of a town centre is a place that
enables a wide range of needs to be met through one trip;
town centres are places that provide a broad range of facilities
and serve as a focus for the community and public transport.
There are about 1,000 centres in Great Britain which are large
enough to attract national multiple retailers and 1,200 justify
a plan of their shops being published (Goad 1994). Over 400
are of interest to institutional investors (Hillier Parker 1991a).
Most local authority districts have several significant centres,
some of which directly compete with one another. Their
continuing health essentially depends on being able to attract
enough people to spend time and money in the heart of the
town. However, there is growing competition which calls
into question what functions town centres will be performing
in future.

2.03   All town centres are multi-functional, which is what
most distinguishes them from out-of-town developments,
but many of these functions are changing (Exhibit 2.1).
Their fundamental or primary role currently, and the one that
occupies the bulk of the ground floor space, is as a **market
place** for **retailing**. It is usual to distinguish between

comparison shopping, where the emphasis is on choice, such
as fashion or electrical appliances, and **convenience** shopping
where the emphasis is on time and perhaps value, such as
food or toiletries (Davies 1989). Comparison shopping is
vulnerable to competition from retail parks and in some
places regional shopping centres; convenience shopping is
often competing with out-of-town superstores.

Town centres have a range of functions...   `2.1`

- **Market places:** retailing forms the heart of most centres
  including comparison, convenience and specialist

- **Business centres:** providing workspace and employment in
  financial and business services, administration and perhaps
  manufacturing and distribution, as well as sometimes the
  'incubators' for new enterprise

- **Educational, health and fitness resources:** most centres
  have schools, colleges, training centres and there are universities in larger centres as well as doctors, dentists, clinics and
  hospitals, gyms, sports clubs, swimming pools and health clubs

- **Meeting places:** whether in the open air or in pubs, cafes,
  restaurants, clubs of all kinds or more formally in societies,
  conferences, community or religious groups

- **Arts, culture and entertainment zones:** with libraries, museums, galleries, theatres, cinemas, concert halls, amusement
  venues and stadia, possibly supported by a series of festivals
  or other events

- **Places to visit:** often having historic or specialist buildings,
  unique views or well known sites or events

- **Transport hubs:** providing interchange and connections to local,
  regional, national and in some cases international services

- **Residential areas:** with town centre accommodation often
  most suited for students and single people or for the elderly
  or the transitory

Jean Carr, a marketing consultant, argues that shopping performs a wider social role than simply stocking up with goods:

> 'Shopping is an important source of ideas and information and indeed education... secondly shopping is an outlet for self-expression... the way shops themselves look and equally important the people you see in them send out messages to shoppers about who they might be... Thirdly, while shopping is a social activity for everyone by its very nature, the social interaction it provides is particularly important and valued by certain groups of people. For many elderly people living on their own a trip to the local shops is the only source of contact they may have with other people in the course of the week. For mothers with young children shopping presents a real reason for getting out of the house and a change of scene. ...The fourth important social aspect of shopping is as a form of recreation. ...People have always shopped for pleasure but never so frequently or for so long as they do now.'

Jean Carr (1990), Out of Town Shopping: Is the Revolution Over?, Royal Society of Arts Symposium

2.04   Town centres, however, offer far more than just a variety of shops and services. They are also **business centres**, with a range of offices and other workspace, providing an important source of employment and training. However, telecommunications improvements are making it less necessary for office workers to occupy central locations near each other. New business parks off ring roads and motorways are providing good quality space for many firms; for some, working from home is becoming a viable option. But town centres still act as incubators for small businesses, and play a role in disseminating new ideas and services.

2.05   Many centres, particularly the larger cities, function as **arts, culture and entertainment zones or venues**. Here too there has been some dispersal away from traditional centres, with, for example, the growth of home entertainment and out-of-town multi-screen cinemas and bowling alleys. The heritage of buildings and open spaces in many cases creates **places to visit**, and probably affects how most people feel about the wider town (including influencing whether they want to live in the area). Some parts act as **meeting places** or specialist centres, for groups such as mothers, the unemployed and the elderly during the day and largely for the young at night. Town centres are therefore particularly important to the least mobile sections of the population. A number of secondary areas have found a specialist niche in serving a particular ethnic group.

2.06   One of the original roles of a town centre was as a **transport hub**. Located at points of relatively high accessibility, town centres have flourished in the past because they could be easily reached. Although in most larger towns this is still the case, it is a role that is increasingly vulnerable to declining usage of buses and to insufficient investment in making public transport competitive with cars. Yet in the longer term this transport role will be vital, if the aims of PPG13 are to be realised (DoE 1994).

2.07   Two other roles could become increasingly important. The first is as a **housing** location, particularly for the growing numbers of single people and those without children, such as young professionals or 'empty nesters' whose children have grown-up. The second, drawing on the experience of US downtowns, is as centres for **education and health services**, where personal contact is required (sometimes called 'hi-touch' as opposed to 'hi-tech').

'Towns are an efficient form of organising our lives and can be a very positive element in the environment as a whole. By concentrating development they help preserve the wider landscape, and can make travel distances shorter and sustain better public transport. And by concentrating demand for services, they offer economies of scale which can help measures such as recycling'.

This Common Inheritance: Britain's Environmental Strategy.

2.08   The wheel of the post-industrial revolution may have come full circle, as the environment of most city centres looks far cleaner and healthier than it has ever been. The loss of industry and the contraction of many centres means that there is also space available to house a new 'urban renaissance' in terms of housing or education if we were to want it enough (DoE 1980). It is this combination of roles and function which generates the excitement or vitality that characterises what could be called 'real' town centres. Together they form a hub that helps hold our society together. Town centres therefore provide an important degree of continuity, as well as a series of social and environmental benefits that contribute to sustainability.

Dispersal and counter-urbanisation

2.09   The over-riding trend for British towns in this century has been dispersal or counter-urbanisation, that is the growth and spread of activity away from the traditional centres (Hall 1973). Dispersal has affected not only housing, with the growth of outer suburbs, but also employment, shopping, and even entertainment. In Britain the population of cities of over 500,000 has been declining steadily for over 30 years, though this trend may be bottoming out. At the same time, smaller towns have been expanding. Thus the metropolitan counties and Greater London lost 900,000 people between 1981 and 1991, while the non-metropolitan counties gained the same number. The fact that in many cases the more affluent moved means that the shift in purchasing power from the centre to the periphery must have been greater still.

2.10   A key issue in the research has been how far the current trends towards dispersal are draining town centres of

life and investment. There is a danger that some town centres could go into a 'vicious circle' or spiral of decline, most obvious in what are called inner city areas. The pattern is for local employment to decline and for the environment to decay. A threshold may be crossed where the centre is no longer able to attract enough private investment to maintain buildings in use. Over time those who can leave do so, and those who take their place may not have the skills required to secure employment, thus further reducing their purchasing power.

2.11   **Population shifts:** The size and make-up of the local population heavily influences the amount of purchasing power available for a town or city centre. These are subject to a number of long-term trends. The overall population is rising gradually, and ageing. According to the General Household Survey the most common household now is a couple with no children (36% of households). For many of these people the facilities offered by a town centre can be a considerable attraction and they may choose to live within walking distance or a short bus ride away.

2.12   A further factor has been the changing ethnic mix in many urban areas, which was highlighted in the seminars in Woolwich and Bradford, where it emerged that the surrounding population had changed, while the shops in the centre had largely remained the same. Nationally ethnic minorities have higher proportions of young people, those under 16 make up 34% of the ethnic minority population compared with 19% of the total population, (Simmie 1993). Population changes are thus creating demands for new services as well as often providing the people to run them.

2.13   The changes in population, however, vary greatly between different places. There are far more older people in resorts, for example, while ethnic minorities are concentrated

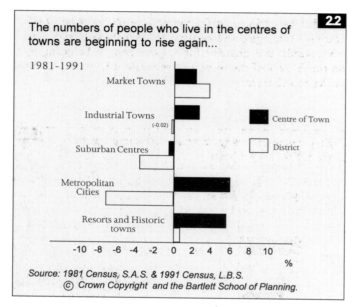

The numbers of people who live in the centres of towns are beginning to rise again...

1981-1991

Market Towns

Industrial Towns
(-0.02)

Suburban Centres

Metropolitan Cities

Resorts and Historic towns

■ Centre of Town

☐ District

-10 -8 -6 -4 -2 0 2 4 6 8 10
%

Source: 1981 Census, S.A.S. & 1991 Census, L.B.S.
© Crown Copyright and the Bartlett School of Planning.

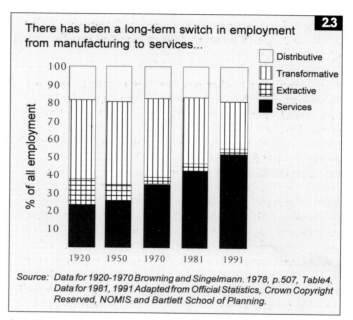

There has been a long-term switch in employment from manufacturing to services...

☐ Distributive
▥ Transformative
▦ Extractive
■ Services

% of all employment

1920 1950 1970 1981 1991

Source: Data for 1920-1970 Browning and Singelmann. 1978, p.507, Table4.
Data for 1981, 1991 Adapted from Official Statistics, Crown Copyright
Reserved, NOMIS and Bartlett School of Planning.

in metropolitan cities and some industrial towns - making generalisations difficult. There are also changes taking place within districts, as land comes up for development or changes use. To find out what was happening we analysed population and employment changes in the central area of 32 towns, using wards for which data is available from both the Census of Population and NOMIS, which records employment (Exhibit 2.2). The figures showed that for these towns there was a growth in population in the centre of town over the period 1981-91 of 3.5% on average compared with a decline of 2.6% for the districts as a whole. A few places, such as Middlesbrough and Birmingham, seemed to be countering the trend, but in general, population was more likely to have fallen in a centre where population in the district had also

fallen. Industrial towns and suburban centres are now not only facing greater competition, but are also suffering in many cases from a loss of population and spending power.

2.14 We also compared the centres of towns that were generally considered to have been relatively successful with similar towns that had lagged behind. The population of the five successful towns selected rose by on average 10%, whereas the five other towns fell by 3%. We may conclude that while it is desirable to increase the number of people living near town centres, this may well be an effect of successful town centres rather than a cause. What this means is that if the town centre loses its attractions, it may be harder to persuade people to live nearby, particularly if the surrounding district is also declining. As Aristotle is sometimes quoted as having said "people move to cities to live; they stay for the sake of the good life".

2.15 **Employment changes:** Population changes are often thought to be linked to employment changes. To understand the trends in employment, we had to find a way of breaking down what is a very complex pattern into a number of elements. An American approach, pioneered by Browning and Singelmann, was used, which breaks employment into six sectors, extractive (or primary), transformative (which includes manufacturing) and four types of service (distributive, producer, social and personal) (Browning 1978). This break-down is valuable because of the predominant importance of the service sector today, which now far outstrips manufacturing as a source of employment and, some argue, the basis of our economy. Over a 70 year period the percentage of the labour force employed in producer and social services rose dramatically, whereas distributive services (including retailing) have grown slowly and personal services have actually declined. This could favour some town centres by strengthening their role as business or educational centres (Exhibit 2.3). Even over the 20 year period 1971 to 1991 there has been a marked shift, with producer services, such as finance, up from 5.6% to 14.6%, while social services rose from 19.4% to 27.5% as a proportion of total jobs.

2.16 Our analysis of employment changes found that though employment in some centres had increased by more than in the districts as a whole there were some very wide variations which were unrelated to the type of district. In general, however, employment growth in town and city centres tended to lag behind the district as a whole

(Exhibit 2.4). Some of the extreme results may be due to boundary changes, and because the figures analysed came from wards, it is possible for employment to be going up on the fringes of the town centre while it is going down in the actual centre.

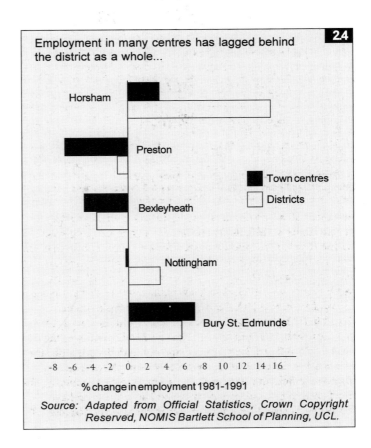

24

Employment in many centres has lagged behind the district as a whole...

■ Town centres
□ Districts

Horsham

Preston

Bexleyheath

Nottingham

Bury St. Edmunds

-8 -6 -4 -2 0 2 4 6 8 10 12 14 16

% change in employment 1981-1991

Source: Adapted from Official Statistics, Crown Copyright Reserved, NOMIS Bartlett School of Planning, UCL.

2.17   A breakdown of employment into different sectors and also into different types of retailing has not so far revealed a discernible pattern, except in the wide variations that occur between apparently similar towns. Nor was there any relationship between changes in employment and changes in population. This suggests, along with evidence from the case study towns, that it is possible for towns to pursue distinct economic strategies. Many of the changes, for example growth in population due to new housing, reflect the efforts of local authorities working together with other partners.

2.18   The analysis generally bore out the idea that dispersal was taking place and affecting larger towns most (though problems in obtaining data for the core of the town as well as occasional changes in definitions means that too much weight should not be placed on individual figures). The situation has certainly not reached crisis point and in many cases there are

encouraging counter trends. However, when taken together with the empty space available in out-of-town business parks, and major employers, such as banks, closing high street branches, reducing employment, and relocating staff to peripheral locations, the trends need to be watched.

Increased personal mobility

2.19   **The impact of the car:** Dispersal is related to, and accelerated by, other trends such as the growth in the use of private cars, and the emergence of a 'post industrial' or service based economy (though self-service may be closer to the truth). The number of cars has risen from just under 2 million in 1950 to ten times that number by 1991 and it has been predicted that it could rise by another 70% over the next 30 years (National Road Traffic Forecast 1989). Two thirds of households now own a car, though there are major differences between urban and non-urban areas and between women and men. Distances that people commute by car are growing to levels that may be environmentally unsustainable. The distance travelled by car, taxi and van rose from 27% of total miles travelled in 1952 to 86% in 1993 while the distance travelled by bus fell by a half (Exhibit 2.5). Overall, the distance travelled by the average Briton has risen by a fifth in the last five years to nearly 6,500 miles per person per year.

2.20   While increased car ownership has expanded mobility for many, it has not helped the accessibility of town centres. Town centres were generally not built with cars in mind, and capacity will always be less than potential demand (MoT 1963). This in turn gives rise to congestion and pollution, making it less pleasant for walking and cycling. Both activities have declined in recent years. Overall, walking distance per

---

2.5

Cars have come to dominate passenger transport...

**PASSENGER TRANSPORT
BY MODE 1952-1992
Mode (Billion passenger land km/percentage)**

Year	Car/Van		Bus/ Coach		Rail		Cycle	
	km	%	km	%	km	%	km	%
1952	58	27	92	42	39	18	23	11
1962	171	57	74	25	37	12	9	3
1972	327	76	60	14	35	8	4	1
1982	406	81	48	10	31	6	6	1
1992	585	86	43	6	38	6	5	1

Source: The Department of Transport (1992 Figures Provisional)

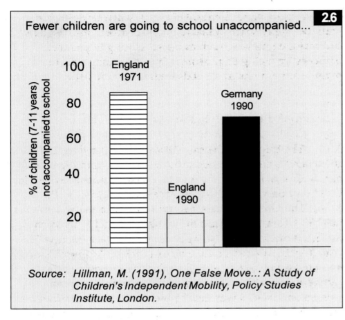

Fewer children are going to school unaccompanied... `26`

% of children (7-11 years) not accompanied to school

England 1971

Germany 1990

England 1990

Source: Hillman, M. (1991), One False Move..: A Study of Children's Independent Mobility, Policy Studies Institute, London.

'Development plans should aim to reduce the need to travel, especially by car'

PPG13

person fell by 4% between 1975/6 and 1989/91, though there has been little change in short distance walking. There has, however, been a 20% decline in distance walked by children aged 5-10 and a 13% decline for those aged 11-15 in this period (Hillman 1991) (Exhibit 2.6). This is due in part to more children being driven to school or to other activities; it probably reflects perceptions of safety, as well as higher levels of car ownership. Cycling has declined even further, despite the fact that the number of cycles owned per head has doubled in the period. Cycle mileage has dropped 19%, with a drop of about one third to and from schools over the fifteen years. The biggest fall was for those aged 5-10.

2.21   Increased congestion and pollution also deter people from shopping in town centres, and encourage people to want to move out. Continental experience suggest these can only be counteracted if other transport modes are sufficiently attractive to make a switch to bus or cycle easily accom-plished. Congestion charging and traffic management, while important, may not be enough on their own. The policies that came out of the Rio Summit require a shift to more environmentally benign forms of transport. They also favour compact cities with the concentration of development along corridors that can be served efficiently by public transport. (DoE 1992c, DoE 1994).

2.22   **The self-service economy:** The switch to a service based economy has had a marked impact on how people spend time. It is not just Britain, but all advanced economies that have been going through an economic transformation, with the loss of traditional 'working-class' jobs in manufacturing and utilities, and the growth of white collar employment in the service sector. Thus, over the last decade the European Community as a whole has lost 3 million manufacturing jobs, but gained 14 million service jobs. Many of these have been taken by women, often returning to work after having children. As women still do most of the shopping, these changes are having profound implications for traditional use patterns of town centres. Some consequences are late opening of supermarkets and the pressures for Sunday trading.

2.23   Increased car ownership, refrigerators and deep freezes have allowed many families to stock up, and have given them more freedom over where to shop. Instead of buying fresh food each day, families shop once a week. They frequently go to where it is easiest to park, the 'one-stop-shop' offering the widest choice, best value for money, and open outside working hours.

Home entertainment and rising expectations also drain purchasing power away from town centres. Together they can make 'going to town' seem a chore rather than the pleasure it perhaps once was (Marks and Spencer 1992).

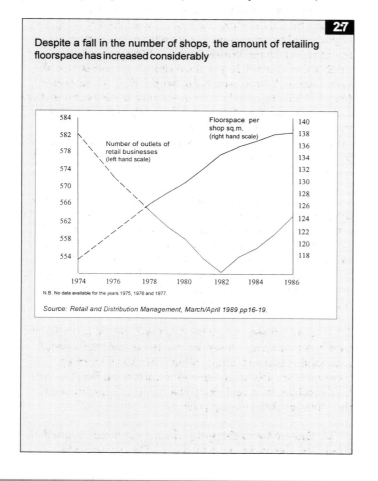

2·7

Despite a fall in the number of shops, the amount of retailing floorspace has increased considerably

N.B. No data available for the years 1975, 1976 and 1977.

Source: Retail and Distribution Management, March/April 1989 pp16-19.

The retailing revolution

2.24   Faced with a combination of strong private trends towards dispersal, and relaxed public policies towards town and city centres, it is not surprising that private investment in both businesses and property is increasingly going out-of-town in search of profit. To understand what is happening, planners need to understand the retailing revolution that has taken place over the last two decades (e.g Kay 1987, Guy 1994). There are also similar trends in leisure and entertainment and business location, which are leading towns to feel less lively and secure.

2.25   Until about a decade ago, the private sector was broadly content to support town centres as the principal places in which to invest and trade. The expansion of offices and retailing (with the exception of supermarkets) was concentrated in the top 200 - 300 town centres of Britain. There was widespread agreement that the town centre was the right place to locate most forms of offices, commercial services and shopping, together with the employment and the development that went with it.

2.26   During the last ten years this mood of certainty has been lost. The more relaxed planning regime of the second half of the 1980s and the pressure of rising car use, seem to be leading towards increasing decentralisation. Offices began moving to business parks and retailers increasingly adopted out-of-town centre formats, either on retail parks or in stand-alone locations, to run alongside their town centre operations.

2.27   **Retail concentration:** Britain has a remarkably successful and efficient retail industry. Productivity and investment have risen steadily over the past thirty years. Whilst the number of individual shops has nearly halved since 1950, the amount of retail floor space has risen by 30% in the last 20 years (Institute for Retail Studies 1991) (Exhibit 2.7). Whilst the number of workers in retailing has remained on a slow downward trend, inflation-adjusted retail sales rose at an annual rate of 2.2% between 1955 and 1987.

2.28 Productivity, measured in terms of real sales per employee (expressed in terms of full-time equivalents) is estimated to have increased by 5% a year throughout the last three decades. High levels of productivity are particularly marked in the leading chains of national multiples, which enjoy sales per member of staff at a level more than twice those of smaller independents. The result has been a growing concentration of retailing into the hands of a few dozen multiples with nationally-known names. These multiples dominate the centres of the top 300 towns of Britain to an extent unmatched in France, Germany or America.

2.29 Until the last decade, and again with the exception of the supermarkets, the expansion of the multiples has been concentrated in town centres, which have experienced high levels of investment as a result. A study by the National Economic Development Office in 1988 showed that investment in retail business had increased between 1955 and 1986 at a consistently faster rate than the economy as a whole (NEDO 1988). Much of this investment consisted in the expansion and modernisation of the existing shop premises occupied by these multiples in town centres. Marks and Spencer, for example, increased their branch network from 251 in 1974 to 262 in 1984, an increase of only 11. During that same period, however, their sales area rose from 5.5 million to 7 million square feet. In other words, up until the mid-1980s they increased their floorspace mainly in the town

centres where their branches were already located. But the position, even for Marks and Spencer, is changing as we explain below.

2.30 **Shopping malls:** In order to accommodate this pressure from expanding multiples, there was a rapid growth of purpose-built shopping centres within town centres. A recent report by the British Council of Shopping Centres (BCSC) shows that 950 managed shopping centres or malls have been built in Britain so far, with 59% in town centres (BCSC 1993). In no other major country in the world is there such a concentration of covered shopping centres within traditional town centres as in Britain. There is scarcely a major town in the country whose centre does not include a purpose-built shopping centre which has been developed in the last 25 years.

2.31 The unusual concentration of modern retailing (and the property development it caused) within British town centres has been both a liability and an asset. One result of town centre redevelopment has been a loss of individuality. In many towns traditional streets were cleared. The modern replacement tends to emphasise the similarity between towns, with the same shop names appearing in each town, a fact often commented on by observers.

2.32 But in return for paying this price, British town centres have accommodated within them some of the world's most successful modern retailing. With rising car ownership, consumers are able to go where the choice and facilities are best, resulting in much greater competition between centres than five, let alone twenty years ago.

2.33 **Out-of-town shopping:** Rising car ownership and usage, and the consequent problems of congestion and

'We're facing an American-style future of faceless malls. These places are economic blackholes on our doorstep. And, more than that, they are sterile from an architectural point of view. If we keep allowing them, Britain will look and feel increasingly narrow and uniform'

'The supermarkets that are eating up Stroud' - President of local Chamber of Trade, quoted in The Independent, Glancey

parking, are widely seen by the private sector as the main problems besetting town centres (Powell 1987). America shows the impact that high car ownership can have on town centre retailing. It has only taken two or three decades for the towns to lose their retail role almost completely. For example, in Atlanta the city centre attracted 26.4% of all retail sales in the metropolitan area in 1958. By 1972 this share had fallen to only 7.4% and the pattern is repeated in other cities. (See **para 3.11** for more discussion on this point).

2.34   Most British multiples hope that such rapid decline can be avoided, but they are nevertheless aware of the pressure exerted by the car-using shopper. A good example is Marks and Spencer. In 1985 they announced an agreement with Tesco to develop joint sites in edge-of-town locations. The year before, in the 1984 Annual report, the Chairman issued the following warning;

> 'The use of family cars for shopping has increasing importance to our customers. Where local authorities have recognised this need and worked with retailers to improve parking facilities and good access roads, the public continue to prefer to shop in the High Street. Unfortunately, the response by some local authorities to the requirement of the car-shopping public is inadequate. Unless there is a change of attitude by some local authorities, the importance of the High Street in some localities will decline. When considering future store development plans, the Company will have to review what steps are necessary to ensure that our investment is directed to locations where our customers will prefer to shop'.

2.35   Whilst Marks and Spencer have continued to affirm their commitment to town centres, since 1984 they have

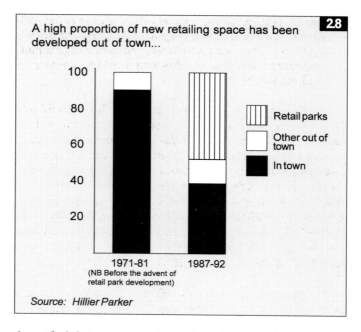

2.8

A high proportion of new retailing space has been developed out of town...

Retail parks
Other out of town
In town

1971-81
(NB Before the advent of retail park development)

1987-92

Source: Hillier Parker

diversified their expansion into edge-of-town and neighbourhood food stores, as well as town centres. Commenting on the selling space added in the UK in 1992, the Chairman stated:

> 'A large proportion of this footage expansion was for edge-of-town locations. In addition we have a first-class property portfolio in town centre locations which we continually upgrade and expand. Where we have large stores in both high street and edge-of-town locations, such as Newcastle, sales show that both types of outlet are complementary and wanted by consumers - there is substantial business to be done in both. Our commitment to town centre trading is further demonstrated by the full

part we play in the commercial part of the towns and cities where we trade. The Company has taken a lead in developing town centre management and improving the shopping environment and is now being supported by a number of local authorities'.

2.36   The lead given by Marks and Spencer has been followed by many retailers with the result that commitment to and expansion within town centres has run in parallel with the development of out-of-town retailing and shopping centre developments. During the development boom of 1987-90, there was a rise in the number of town centre shopping schemes opened, but there was a far more dramatic rise in the number of out-of-town shopping centres (Exhibit 2.8).   34% of the shopping centre floor space opened in that period was in town centres, compared to 66% out-of-town, of which no less than 51% was in retail parks (Hillier Parker 1991b).

2.37   The emergence of retail parks has been a major event in retail development. Consisting mainly of retail warehouses of over 20,000 square feet, dominated by DIY, and discount furniture, carpets and electrical goods, retail parks grew from under one million square feet in 1985 to over 25 million by the end of 1990. Retail parks take less time to develop than town centre schemes, so that with the coming of the recession, retail park openings fell more sharply. In 1991 and 1992, therefore, the balance swung back with towns centre taking 73% of shopping floor space opened. But retail park development activity recovered at the end of 1993, and it is likely that the town centre share of shopping centre development will drop back to below 50% in the next few years because fewer schemes are starting.

2.38   **Retail decentralisation:** Retail warehouses form the second of what are sometimes referred to as three waves of decentralisation in retailing (Schiller 1986). The first was food and involved the moving out-of-town of supermarkets in the period following the mid-1970s. The effect of this has been to reduce the amount of food sold in many town centres. The second wave involved bulky goods and occurred during the 1980s. The third wave included durable goods and followed the announcement by Marks and Spencer in 1984. Some decentralisation of durable retailing has occurred in new regional shopping centres, such as Brent Cross, and four of these have opened in recent years. Much of it, however, consists of free-standing development, such as the stores belonging to Toys 'R' Us and Boots' Childrens World.

2.39   The first wave did little harm to major town centres. Commonly known as **regional town centres**, these are characterised by the presence of variety and department stores, such as Marks and Spencer and Debenhams, typically trading on several levels. Retailing is dominated by durable goods, such as fashion or jewellery, and the loss of food sales from these centres was generally held to have had little impact.

2.40   It also had little impact on **district centres**, the smaller town centres which mainly serve the weekly family shopping trip, combining both food and other more routine types of shopping. These towns were considered to be too small to justify out-of-town superstore development. In recent years, this picture has changed and supermarkets have begun to open on the edge of towns as small as Godalming, Cirencester and Sevenoaks. There is now a danger that the smaller supermarkets, which served to anchor these district centres, could be vulnerable from out-of-town supermarket competition. If they close, the role of these town centres could contract to the extent that they would no longer be viable.

2.41 The second wave of decentralisation, which involved the rapid increase of retail warehouses and retail parks, is also considered to have had little impact on town centres. DIY largely replaced goods sold by builder's merchants and therefore took little from town centres. Retailers of furniture and other bulky goods have difficulty in finding adequate accommodation in town centres. There has been a fall in furniture retailing in town centres, but otherwise there is little evidence of retail parks having a harmful effect as yet. However, some retailers are concerned about what would happen if these retail sheds were allowed to sell a wider range of goods, a potential 'time bomb' as one put it.

2.42 The effect of the third wave could be the most significant. Durable goods, such as clothing are central to town centre retailing, and their importance increases amongst the larger cities. The level of decentralisation in this area so far is small. Marks and Spencer, for example, as yet have little more than a dozen edge-of-town stores out of a total of some 300 branches, though they expect to be able to reach a significant share of the market from them. In other areas, for example toys, the effect has been far more significant. There are also a number of other new forms of retailing, from factory shops to manufacturer's outlets, car boot sales to festival market places, and catalogues to mail order or television shopping whose impact has yet to be fully appreciated. Overall the third wave of decentralisation is undoubtedly working against the interests of preserving durable retailing at the heart of British town centres.

Competing leisure attractions

2.43 **Leisure shopping:** Changes are also taking place in the way people occupy their leisure time 'out of hours' which are having an impact on the role of town centres (Comedia 1991). The growth of home-based entertainment, with television, videos, computers and takeaway and delivered food, is providing strong competition for the 'leisure pound'. However, shopping itself is increasingly becoming a leisure activity for the more affluent. With basic shopping out of the way, many people are using some of the time saved to travel to other places, (Exhibit 2.9) and the total amount of time spent by women on shopping and

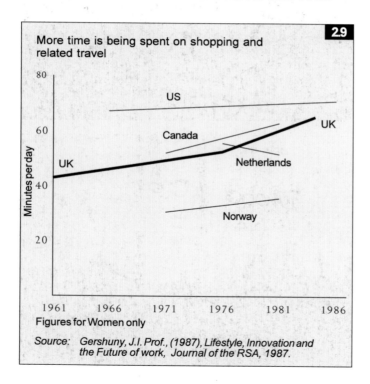

2.9

More time is being spent on shopping and related travel

US

Canada

UK

UK

Netherlands

Norway

Minutes per day

80

60

40

20

1961 1966 1971 1976 1981 1986

Figures for Women only

Source: Gershuny, J.I. Prof., (1987), Lifestyle, Innovation and the Future of work, Journal of the RSA, 1987.

Waves of Dispersal - shopping and leisure is moving out-of-town

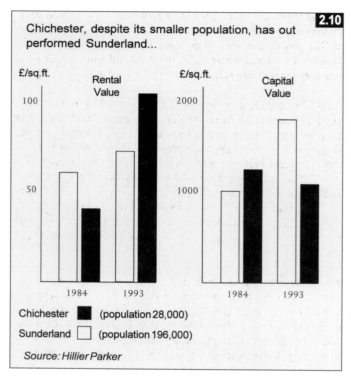

Chichester, despite its smaller population, has out performed Sunderland...

£/sq.ft. — Rental Value

£/sq.ft. — Capital Value

1984 1993

1984 1993

Chichester ■ (population 28,000)

Sunderland □ (population 196,000)

Source: Hillier Parker

2.10

cinemas and theatres; museums and libraries; educational, health and sports facilities; cafes, pubs, restaurants; and other venues. In combination these make a town centre different from a shopping centre and provide much of its character.

2.44 The most successful places, like historic towns, have created a synergy between their visitor appeal or their arts, culture and entertainment offer, and shopping, which has enabled them to support more facilities than their population on its own could afford (ETB, 1989). Thus towns such as Bath, Chester and York have become well known as successful retail centres (even though higher rents may have caused some shops to close or move). Their centres combine attractive independent specialist shops and services, with a wide range of nationally-known multiples. The impact can be seen by comparing property values in two dissimilar towns; despite its smaller population, property values in historic Chichester have now overtaken much larger Sunderland (Exhibit 2.10). Other towns such as Ipswich and Hull have enhanced their historic core and may have found it easier to attract new development on the fringes as a result.

2.45 The impact of tourism can be very considerable. Thus an Office of Population Census and Statistics survey of one-day leisure trips in 1989 found that some £2 billion was spent on catering and retail-related areas (OPCS 1989). A study of *Retailing in Historic Towns* for the English Historic Towns Forum found that visitors brought additional spending estimated at £27 per visit and that 75% of tourists to such towns combine tourism and shopping (Donaldsons 1992).

2.46 While most towns cannot expect to rely on tourists, the success of many historic towns and metropolitan cities offer lessons for others which are discussed in **Chapters 11**

related travel has risen from about 40 minutes per day in 1961 to 70 minutes in the mid-1980s, moving closer to US levels (Gershuny 1987). As PPG6 makes clear, while shopping tends to be the major function, the town centre is the focal point of a whole range of commercial and community activities. These help to keep the town alive at different times, and their buildings contribute to the town's sense of identity. While they vary from town to town, attractions which bring people to town include and **12**. There are also other potential attractions, such as colleges, that can bring spending to town centres. Thus a recent study on Sheffield estimated that the growing number of students at the two universities currently account for £85 million a year of expenditure in the city, while the universities also play a part in animating the city and using buildings and sites that would otherwise be vacant (Foley 1992). However, despite this potential, and the roles that real town centres play in transmitting culture and attracting visitors to Britain, there are some disturbing trends that are making many town centres seem dead 'out of hours'.

2.47   **Cultural losses:** First there has been a loss of space for cultural activities. Cinemas have closed down or been turned into bingo halls. Although cinema audiences have increased from a low point of 70 million visits a year five years ago, to around 100 million, the growth is tending to take place in multi-screen cinemas on edge-of-centre or out-of-town sites.

2.48   Many private theatres and dance halls have closed, though there has been a growth in art centres.   Perhaps 70 such venues have been set up over the last two decades, often making use of redundant buildings, such as town halls, though a number have subsequently closed. There has been an even greater increase in the number of museums, some 1,000 of which are independent. In some cases these have acted as major attractions, such as the Museum of Film, Photography and Television in Bradford, which attracts over a million visitors a year, but in most cases they depend on voluntary effort to keep going, and have struggled in the recession.

2.49   Libraries remain the most popular cultural facility and are used by over 50% of the population, particularly the elderly and students (Comedia 1993). However, they are having to rethink their role, which is now about creating opportunities and opening users' eyes to a wider world. They provide places to 'hang-out', and also act as open learning centres, where people can upgrade their skills, or obtain information, for example on training schemes or business services.

2.50   With their large footfall, often over 500,000 visitors yearly, libraries should be seen as town centre 'anchors'; good examples are Centrespace in Hounslow (which forms part of a large new covered shopping centre which also includes a multi-cultural events centre), and Cardiff Central Library. The new Croydon Library, forms the hub of a new town square, and uses new technology to provide visitors to the town centre with something they could not easily obtain elsewhere. However, the opening hours and service provided by libraries are under threat in many places as a result of local authority spending priorities.

2.51   **Entertainment dispersal:** Changes are also taking place in commercially provided entertainment. The closure of secondary shops has provided premises for a whole range of ethnic restaurants, which have widened choice in most towns. Although spending on physically-active pursuits is slowly increasing, town centres are losing out to more sophisticated facilities located next to plentiful car parking, such as the Oasis in Swindon.

2.52   There has been a shift away from pubs, many of which are now looking for a new role. This reflects a decline in the numbers of traditional heavy drinkers and concerns about 'drink and driving', as well as competition from home entertainment with, for example, the growth of video shops and takeaways. Many pubs are now emphasising food and appealing to the family. However, much of the new investment of companies like Whitbread is going away from town centres, and nearer to where customers live.

2.53   Some towns, such as Nottingham and Newcastle, have succeeded in attracting people to stay on after hours through concerted efforts to improve the environment and promote activity (although what is possible varies very much according to the type of town). However, many town centres feel dead out of hours, or appear dominated by young people, who, with little to do and little money to spend, are naturally going to hang around the centre. When these are pedestrianised and traffic is excluded at night, a few youngsters can seem like a gang, and there is a danger of a town getting a bad name. While there may be little new in their behaviour, despite what the media say, the fashion of 'circuit drinking' together with pedestrian streets that seem to offer no escape can deter other users. Worries about violence and crime are leading to major expenditure on surveillance by cameras, and shutters, and increasing insurance claims, all of which can discourage investment.

2.54   The main challenge for most town centres now is how to make themselves attractive enough to match the forces of dispersal and of individual vehicular mobility, and to maintain private investment in shopping and leisure facilities. There are enough successful towns in Britain to show that given the right attractions, high accessibility, and a good standard of amenity, people will stay on after work, or go out and use the facilities at night or weekend. What is not so clear, is whether the public and private policies that shape investment are able to overcome the natural 'institutional inertia' or tendency not to act until it is too late.

Private investment

2.55   The switch from independent shops to national multiples has been reflected in the decline of private landlords and the growth of ownership by national institutional investors. Ownership patterns in British high streets are complex, and it is hard to identify which organisations have most at stake, despite improving sources of information on investment performance (Investment Property Databank 1993). Many of the more desirable properties will have several layers of ownership between the freeholder and the occupying retailer (it was this problem, incidentally, that stopped a Private Member's Bill to enable owners of property in Oxford Street to contribute to improvements). The indications are, however, that a high proportion of **prime** shops, those in the best positions, contain investment by pension funds and insurance companies (Bernard Thorpe 1990). For example, in Woolwich 80% of the shopping centre is owned by one insurance company. However, prime properties are typically let on leases with upward-only rent review clauses, which insulate property owners from declines in demand until the lease ends (Guy 1994).

2.56   The expansion of multiple retailers and major leisure operators in town centres has been followed by the increase in investment by insurance companies and pension funds. As early as the 1930s, Montague Burton was collaborating with Clerical, Medical and General and the Eagle Star insurance companies to fund their rapid branch expansion. Burton managed to increase their branch network from 37 in 1919 to 641 in 1939 helped by the development of sale and lease-back techniques, whereby an insurance company financed the construction of a new store in return for receiving the free-hold with a long lease granted to Burton.

2.57   Many purpose-built shopping centres located within town centres have involved a partnership between the local authority, which has used its compulsory purchase powers to assemble the site, working in collaboration with a developer and an insurance company. Local authorities consequently have financial stakes in many town centre shopping schemes. The remaining interests are held by insurance companies and pension funds, but also property companies and, increasingly, overseas investors.

2.58   The ownership pattern of out-of-town shopping centres and business parks is similar, although the ownership and development role of the local authority is less than for the town centre schemes. Investing institutions have been cautious in investing in supermarkets and retail warehouses, but have recently shown an appetite for retail parks. Indeed, values of retail parks in the last year have risen more rapidly as a result of investor demand than any other type of commercial property.

2.59   Like the multiple retailer, the professional investor is heavily committed to the town centre, but is also seeking to spread his risk by investing out-of-town as well. Investment, from whatever source, ultimately depends on the return achieved and the prospect for a secure and growing income. Town centres contain by far the largest share of investment value, but a much smaller share of new investment. Like the multiple retailers, investors look for firm policy guidelines within which they could continue to support town centres. However, because they operate on a national basis and have limited management time, financial institutions do not usually get involved in the management of town centres, unlike the situation in the United States.

2.60   If town centre investment becomes less attractive relative to out-of-town, as the evidence suggests, town centres could find it difficult to attract sufficient funds to maintain and modernise their buildings. However, the substantial stake in town centres held by investors and traders may mean that, as American experience has suggested, the private sector could be persuaded to support declining town centres, if by doing so they reduce the fall in value of their long term investment which would otherwise occur. This has certainly become the experience in the US, though facilitated by somewhat different property ownership and taxation systems.

3 changing town centres

- British town and city centres have evolved over hundreds of years and are still changing.

- One possible scenario would be to follow the American model, with retailing shifting to the periphery along with other forms of employment.

- An attractive alternative model is provided by Continental towns and cities, which have retained livelier centres, where people live and work.

- If centres were to decline too far, the costs would be unacceptable in economic as well as environmental, social and cultural terms.

'It is by their centres that cities are recognised, judged and remembered. Most visitors to a city see nothing but the central area and one approach to it; and the only knowledge of a city that is shared by all who live in it is their knowledge of its centre. In the minds of residents and visitors alike, it is the image of a city's centre that is called up by the mention of its name; for all, in a real sense the centre is the city'

Quoted in Greater Peterborough Master Plan

3.01   This chapter considers in turn how British town centres have evolved, their alternative futures or options, and the possible cycle of decline if adverse trends are not kept under check.

The origins of British town centres

3.02   Although town centres are made up of buildings, which are supported by economic activity, they are much more complex entities. As we have seen, they are not just retail centres, to be measured simply in terms of the number or size of their shops. Nor should they be viewed in isolation or simply compared with their immediate neighbours. Each centre has a distinct history, which is bound up with the district and region of which it is part and with the variety of functions in which it has specialised (Exhibit 3.1). They are essentially organic and dynamic places that need to be cared for like a garden or a human being. Yet too often they are treated like objects that can be left to fend for themselves. With a growing concern for **sustainable development** our town and city centres have a value that far exceeds the cost of replacing their buildings.

3.03   A number of studies have explained the peculiar shape and nature of our present town and city centres, which are rooted in British history (eg. Burke 1976, Lloyd 1984). The origins of town centres lie in the social needs of human beings to gather together for company and protection. The earliest towns grew up in pleasant places that could be defended (the word 'town' derives from *zun* or *tun* which meant fence or hedge). They were often built at crossing points on rivers because of the importance of water, both for life and for transport. The first markets took place in churchyards, until

3.1

Town Centres are an important part of our heritage...

Shops in Sandwich

Market place in Norwich

Norwich City Council

they were ousted in 1285 by Edward I and took with them a market cross to help sanctify bargains. Towns then grew for the most part organically, though a few show the influence of an early plan, such as Bury St Edmunds, or Middlesbrough, a Victorian town with a similar grid to an American city. For the most part they were designed when the horse and cart was the main means of transport and nearly all the inhabitants lived close to the centre. Despite shopping centre developments, many still retain a tangle of central streets (Exhibit 3.2).

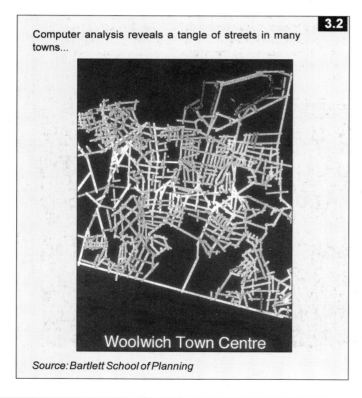

3.2

Computer analysis reveals a tangle of streets in many towns...

Woolwich Town Centre

Source: Bartlett School of Planning

3.04 A concentration of customers provided the conditions for the growth of trade and consequently manufacture. Traders lived on the premises and sold from the front of their workshops. Royal Charters ensured markets were spread out sufficiently to avoid excessive competition. Guilds controlled standards, and the Guildhall became the forerunner of our town halls and civic centres. Thus, Norwich, even in the early 13th century, had some 133 different trades in 63 guilds. Concentration encouraged innovation and capital accumulation, the basis for Britain leading the world in the exploitation of industry. British towns came to reflect a Protestant work ethic. Unlike continental towns, it has long been the practice of wealthier people to move as far out-of-town as transport allowed (Fishman 1993). Families could then live in picturesque places that were closer to nature, safer, and less polluted than the smoke-blackened industrialised cities. This was the origin of the suburban 'villa', a form which Britain exported to the American colonies. As early as 1579 a writer commented that:

> 'the manner of most Gentlemen and Noblemen also, is to house themselves, (if possibly they may) in the Suburbs of the Cities, because most commonly, the area there being somewhat at large, the place is healthy and through the distance from the body of the Town the noise is not so much.'

3.05 Shops as we know them are essentially a Victorian invention. A town like Abingdon, with a little over 4,000 inhabitants in 1790 had only four people described as shopkeepers plus six grocers. However, the industrial revolution led to rural emigration. Some towns grew large on the back of manufacturing, while the market towns began to import more of what they consumed. Thus in Sandwich in the mid 19th century there were 13 bakers, 10 grocers, and nine butchers, but by 1900 while the number of bakers was falling, there were two banks and two printers plus furniture retailers, hardware and variety stores. Today nearly all the shops in the High Street have been turned into houses and

there is one supermarket, which is itself likely to relocate away from the centre (URBED 1992).

3.06   In 1785 William Cowper commented that "God made the country and man made the town".

Peckham: a cycle of decline

Rye Lane, Peckham in South London once boasted of its 'Golden Mile'. However, for several decades it has been performing poorly. Rents are less than a third of those in Bromley, for example. This means that property is worth much less, and hence redevelopment is difficult to fund, leading to several potential schemes collapsing. The number of national multiples has declined and in 1989 only 15 of the centre's 300 shops were classified in the Multiple Ranking Index. Vacancy rates rose from 13% to 18% between 1986 and 1988 alone.

The initial causes of the decline lay in the redevelopment of the surrounding area in the 1970s and the loss of its traditional residents. A partial pedestrianisation scheme made it difficult for people from outside to park, but did not succeed in creating an attractive place to walk. A new shopping mall in the 1980s simply attracted existing multiples to relocate at one end of Rye Lane, and did not add enough to the attractions to overcome the drawbacks.

By the late 1980s the town centre faced increased competition from new centres, such as Surrey Quays, and improved centres, such as Lewisham and Bromley, as well as smaller centres that were more convenient but offered the same choice. As a consequence Peckham progressively lost its attractions, first its department stores, then comparison clothes shops like C & A and Marks and Spencer, and most recently Sainsburys.

At the present time most of the vacancy is in and around the shopping mall possibly because rentals are now too high. The Council has now set up a regeneration team for the area, and is investing £5 million in a health and fitness centre as part of a package of schemes which include a new Safeways, and a six screen cinema in the old Sainsbury's.

3.3

American versus Continental towns

US National Main Street Center

Out-of town mall: USA

Strip development: USA

Gottingen: Germany

Liege: Belgium

The influence of religion and cultural values on British urban development has been crucial as the Industrial Revolution caused society to polarise, and emphasised the perception of town centres as immoral and dirty places. The industrial revolution caused some market towns to fossilise, whilst others saw their character change permanently as they were overwhelmed by new industry and new people (Briggs 1963). The population of Bradford, for example, rose by 65% in the decade to 1831. Distinct `quarters' for production or distribution were created along with cheap housing for the new workforce. Some of these new industrial towns grew into great cities and they developed administrative and cultural functions, such as universities, theatres, libraries and cathedrals, to serve their growing populations.

3.07   Eventually some of the cities and towns grew into conurbations, with a multiplicity of centres, many of which lost much of their distinctive character in a vast suburban sprawl. In some cases, this has resulted in once traditional town centres, such as Peckham, losing many major shops, entertainment and other attractions and becoming little more than local shopping centres. The fortunes of the 19th century suburbs, created for the more affluent by the railway and tramways, have varied, some becoming 'gentrified', others going down-market.

3.08   Within this pattern of centres, which in many places appears more like a mosaic than a hierarchy, there is another distinct type of centre and that is the resort and its rival the 'historic town'. Over the last two centuries some towns developed as places to visit and stay, perhaps with a spa, or on the sea, so combining the functions of health and recreation in the full sense of the word. Such towns missed out on the Industrial Revolution and retain a planned form and historic character. They have risen and fallen in popularity with different social classes over the ages, and occasionally enjoyed a renaissance. Thus, Cobbett commented of Cheltenham in 1820. 'The whole town .... looked delightfully dull. I did not see more than four of five carriages. The place really appeared to be sinking very fast". Today it is a smart place to live and visit - which may provide some hope!

3.09   The history of towns and cities can be written in many terms - economic, physical and social or cultural. But above all, their history seems to be a product of the efforts of masses of people to better themselves and more occasionally to collaborate in regulating conditions for the good of the wider community. The European Commission's Green Paper on the Environment has this to say:

"The historical centres of our cities have been savaged by the intrusion of anonymous boxes in the international style. Re-creating harmony with the old, means more than mimicking superficial stylistic elements. It requires respect for fundamental traditions in the choice of materials, diversity of buildings and multiplicity of purposes. Mere zoning must be replaced by developing the city as a product which will assure a new quality of social and economic life" (CEC 1992).

Alternative futures

3.10   In looking to the future, the choice has to be faced in many places of whether we go down the American route, pursue what some call the Continental model, or find some British compromise (Exhibit 3.3). Of course most British towns and cities do not yet face the same crisis as American

cities and have far more planning controls over the way they develop. However, there are perhaps valuable lessons that can be learned from their experience.

Richmond, Virginia: the decline of Downtown USA

Richmond, the state capital, is typical of many North American cities that have gone through the cycle of downtown decline. The two department stores that were the hub of the town remain closed despite the new hotels, office blocks, and warehouse conversions. The office workers and residents of the converted warehouses continued to shop out of town, and the remaining residents are too poor to support more than a few shops. As trade has followed the residents out of town, cities have typically pursued three waves of action over the last two decades. The first was 'beautification', with traffic-free areas, wider pavements and tree planting. However, trees and seats did not compensate for lack of convenience and choice. Without cars the roads seemed deserted and more dangerous. The second wave was major redevelopment, with a host of publicly backed projects, such as convention centres and hotels, office towers, mixed-use waterfront schemes and festival market places. However, in most cases these failed to bring life back to the centres. The department stores are still empty.

3.11 **The North American model:** In the USA dispersal has been so extensive that is has given rise to a new kind of place, variously called 'Edge Cities', 'Technoburbs' and 'Slurb', where the focus is the home, with the result that most people have no need to go into the traditional downtown, except perhaps at Christmas (Garreau 1991). This led to American town centre retail sales between 1977 and 1984 falling by 50% compared with an overall retail sales increase of 120%, and in many cities less than 20% of retail is left in the centre. A study of downtown districts for the National Trust for Historic Preservation found that whereas in 1976 the Central Business District was the primary retail centre in 70% of the 169 towns analysed with a population of over 10,000 just ten years later this was the case in only 26% of the towns (NTHP 1988). Many US downtowns are now largely given over to other functions. While the circumstances are different, the fact that we import so many American business and cultural ideas is causing some experts to be alarmed (Chase 1993).

3.12 As most North American 'downtowns' no longer see retailing as their prime function, they concentrated at first on encouraging office development and tourism, often through grand redevelopment projects. However, some have learned the dangers of allowing 'holes' to develop, where so many buildings are torn down for re-development or to create parking that there are not enough attractions left to attract shoppers. Attempts at 'beautification' have generally failed to turn the tide, and many pedestrian streets have had to be reopened to traffic to make them feel safer, for example Eugene, Oregon and Jackson, Michigan. The resulting 'doughnut' may not be sustainable as an urban form. Rather than relying on a few grand projects, thinking has shifted to pursuing a more comprehensive and incremental approach. Thus the current wave of initiatives is concerned with

'community building' and techniques such as Business Improvement Districts and Main Street programmes. The focus is on making the city centre somewhere special, and on catering for the growth of 'knowledge-based' work, and the related need for informal contacts. Many cities are pinning their hopes on the expansion of universities and health centres, with spin-off products, exemplified by the 20 acre Medical Biology Research Park under development in downtown Richmond.

3.13 Rather than making the same mistakes, we can learn from US experience. The lessons have been distilled by organisations such as the National Main Street Center, which supports local initiatives to make the most of the resources of small towns. The International Downtown Association, brings together those involved in town centre revitalisation in the larger places. All the practitioners agree on the importance of the different interests working towards a 'shared vision'. They now use the same approach to management that an out-of-town store takes for granted in terms, for example, of co-ordinated promotion and concern for cleanliness and security which they call Centralised Retail Management (IDA 1993). But they also try to emphasise what makes 'real' town centres different in terms of character, with specialist shops and services, and places of entertainment (McNulty 1985). In Baltimore, the marketing slogan says "Discover the difference Downtown"; Denver emphasises the unique nature of the central area compared to the suburban centres; Portland, Oregon has reversed decline by promoting a high quality of life as a place to live. British shopping centres tend to copy American practice, even down to terms like 'food court'. But they can also learn from the dangers of letting dispersal go too far. The Policy Studies Institute pointed out in *Britain in 2010*:

'...it has taken less than three decades to destroy the heartbeat of many American cities. It will take a century to repair the damage and return those cities to a semblance of health. Not all cities will survive... Office, commercial, housing and cultural and entertainments development in the downtown core must occur before any new retail district can take root.'

Robert Carey, President of Urban Centre Development in Oakland California (quoted in Davies)

'Experience in North America, where the process has gone much further, suggests that these developments in retailing, if they go ahead, are likely to undermine existing city centres, to erode the financial basis of city governments, to extend traffic congestion to the suburbs and to times outside the commuting rush hours, and to increase dependence on private cars at a time when, as part of the response to global warming, it may be necessary to reduce motoring. It therefore seems likely that greater advantage will be seen in the course followed by most continental European cities (and an increasing number of North American ones) of curbing development at out-of-town and suburban locations and concentrating instead on improving existing city centres with new shopping and leisure complexes, weather-proof arcades over existing shopping streets, pedestrian precincts, and improved public transport facilities.' (PSI 1991).

3.14 **The Continental model:** Britain also has the model of Continental towns to draw on. British visitors are often enchanted by the possibilities of discovering towns which are a pleasure to walk round. Yet many of these towns suffered far more than ours in the last war. Their quality of life does not necessarily come from having more sun, but from conscious efforts in restoring old buildings and encouraging people to live close to the centre, and discouraging dispersal (TEST 1989). In many towns, cars have been excluded from central streets and service vehicles provided with limited access, whilst in others access is restricted to residents. Another feature is restrictive management of car-parking. It is widely accepted that commuter parking increases peak-hour congestion and that the main priority should be given to residents and shoppers.

Charleroi, Belgium: creating convivial cities

Southern Belgium has suffered from many of the same problems of industrial decline as Northern England, and with the loss of coal and steel, unemployment is over 25% in places. Yet the town centres feel much livelier than their British equivalents for a number of reasons. Far more people live close to the centre, typically in four to five storey blocks of flats, as in Charleroi, which has a population of 250,000. This means that there are many more people within walking distance of the centre, which also helps public transport to attract more custom. There are far more independent shops, and relatively few superstores, shopping malls and retail parks. There is typically a much higher level of pedestrianisation, particularly of secondary streets. These have been taken over by cafes and restaurants as well as boutiques, all of which make the streets feel safer and more colourful, and full of vitality.

As in Britain, many of the best parking spaces are occupied by traders, but more spaces are provided through echelon parking, and under-ground car parks rather than multi-storey structures. These allow more space to be given over to the public. The extension of the pedestrianised area in Charleroi, including putting some trams underground, is part of a major town project which has sought to involve the whole community in conquering the spirit of depression. Changing attitudes are being helped through an EC backed 'Urban Observatory'.

Few continental local authorities have increased the number of central car-parking spaces available in the last decade. If anything there has been a tendency, especially in the large cities, towards reducing them (Hass-Klau 1990). These policies have been paralleled by the powerful promotion of both public transport and cycling, often combined with marketing campaigns on sensible travel behaviour. Tremendous efforts have also been made in keeping town centres alive in the evening by promoting restaurants, bars, pubs, theatres and cinemas. As in Britain, this policy has been most successful in the larger towns (Parkinson 1992).

3.15 Even in the German Ruhr or industrial southern Belgium, in places that have many similarities with our northern towns, the town centres are fashionable places to meet people or look for clothes in the small boutiques that make the side streets so attractive. In Germany too, instead of losing all their trade to out-of-town centres, many towns have gone 'up market'; they draw middle-class shoppers because of the quality of their food and service and through their networks of attractive pedestrianised streets. The larger towns have invested heavily in light rail and underground systems.

3.16 Many British people too are concerned about the quality of life in towns. Their liking for 'urbanity', the qualities which make towns special, offers a ray of hope, occasionally celebrated in events like Urban Renaissance Year. Most of our towns still possess a considerable heritage. Despite the drastic surgery of the last 30 years in terms of road schemes and shopping centres, the choice for most towns is still open.

Cycle of decline

3.17 The possible consequences of letting dispersal go too far are well summed up in a powerful book by the American urban historian Robert Fishman entitled 'Bourgeois Utopias: The Rise and Fall of Suburbia' (Fishman 1993). He typifies the planners' criticisms as follows:

'First, decentralisation has been a social and economic disaster for the old city and for the poor, who have been increasingly relegated to its crowded, decayed zones. It has segregated American society into an affluent outer city and an indigent inner city, while erecting even higher barriers that prevent the poor from sharing in the jobs and housing of the technoburbs.

'Second, decentralisation has been seen as a cultural disaster. While the rich and diverse architectural heritage of the cities decays, the technoburb has been built up as a standardised and simplified sprawl, consuming time and space, destroying the natural landscape. The wealth that post-industrial America has generated has been used to create an ugly and wasteful pseudo-city, too spread out to be efficient, too superficial to create a true culture.'

3.18 US experience suggests that there are a number of steps in the process of decline. The first order effects come from peripheral centres attracting the most mobile and affluent consumers. This leaves the old centre dependent on a more local and poorer market, as it is they who live closest. The most obvious response is for the shops and services to go 'downmarket'. A recent report on the impact of the Merry

'Dudley has been severely affected. The centre has lost major multiple retailers. There has been an increase in vacancies; there has been a decline in retailing in the centre; there has been a decline in rentals and there has been a marked reduction in shopping flows for pure comparison shopping purposes since Phase 5 of Merry Hill opened.'

Merry Hill Impact Study Roger Tym & Partners, DoE

Hill regional shopping centre noted a similar effect in Dudley where "the retail composition of the town centre has deteriorated in quality due to the proliferation of discount/low-order retail operations" (DoE 1993). Similarly, a study on Sheffield found that the response of many city centre retailers to a drop in turnover, caused by the opening of Meadowhall, was to introduce low-cost merchandise, hold extended sales periods or generally reduce prices (Foley 1992). There is also an indication that the poor end up paying more, as they buy in smaller quantities in shops that often charge higher prices (Piauchaud 1974).

3.19   The second order effects occur as the loss of trade causes stores progressively to close down and, in many cases, move. This in turn reduces activity and attraction, and the effect can be to deter customers from using the centre, thus discouraging the private investment needed for the centre to find a new role. Buildings become neglected and decay, then fall empty and derelict and are eventually cleared and not replaced, creating what has been referred to as a doughnut with a hole in the middle. This danger was recognised in the 1988 NEDO report which saw the failure to redevelop vacant sites resulting from the impact of out-of-town stores as damaging to the vitality and viability of the centre as a whole. The Merry Hill impact study found pessimism amongst local property agents about the prospects of more retail properties becoming empty in Dudley, as leases came up for renewal. However, Landlord and Tenant law makes it difficult to shed interests and delays the process of adaptation.

3.20   Unfortunately by the time the threat to investment is recognised, confidence may have evaporated. Furthermore, whereas in the US there are mechanisms for directing public and private resources to the centre, for example, special tax

districts, in Britain the funds required are hard to come by. The consequence is that solutions, like pedestrianisation or shop front improvements can in effect be little more than 'putting cosmetics on a corpse'. Instead, as the research report on *Improving Inner City Shopping Centres* stressed, there is a need for a more comprehensive approach (DoE 1988).

3.21   The district centre that loses its trade because its main food store closes can also risk following this route. Even if it is replaced by a 'cut price' store, if the more affluent customers go elsewhere, the centre ends up serving a poorer market (Shearman 1993). In towns that lose their trade and become empty, the 'undesirables' or 'misfits' stand out more, creating a further source of conflict.

3.22   While we cannot predict the future, we can certainly recognise the options today. Town centres cannot stand still, nor can they readily recover a position or role once it has been lost. Many towns are already experiencing the power and impact of out-of-town centres, modelled on American lines. The obvious effects are in centres like Dudley and Sheffield that are close to regional shopping centres. However our survey of local authority planning officers established that 15% of market and 28% of suburban town centres also feel they are declining. As one firm of surveyors put it:

'...High Streets rarely show signs of rapid decay; it is a gradual process. There are nearly always tenants to be found in every shop unit although some of these may be the local charity shops. What is not so evident is the gradual reduction in the level of choice offered to the shopper with the departure of major names and important individual traders. The deterioration of a balanced trade mix and strong anchor tenants limits

There are two groups 'those who have money and no time, and those with time but no money. The 'have nots' have practically nothing except time. They are more concerned about surviving than finding new ways to express themselves and comparatively little retail energy is directed at helping them'

Royal Society of Arts Symposium Jean Carr

variety and the general attractiveness of the centre. Pedestrian flows decrease, precipitating a further run down in the quality of shopping that can be provided, again leading to a falling number of visitors. Such a downward cycle is difficult to break.'

The Changing Face of Retailing, Fuller Peiser

3.23   Overall, 36% of respondents said that competition from an out-of-town or edge-of-town development was a major problem for their centre and 49% that it was a minor problem. Though it may not be surprising that 56% of respondents from declining centres saw this competition as a major problem, it was also the view of 29% of respondents from vibrant centres. Of the market towns who answered the question, half thought that an out-of-town foodstore had had an adverse or possible negative impact and only 11% thought it had a beneficial impact.

3.24   The danger is that if the trends of dispersal and mobility are not checked or countered, the hub of some town and city centres could disintegrate. History shows how places can easily become redundant when they lose their economic base. But town centres also have enormous resources, provided they are mobilised. There are now enough success stories, such as York, Norwich, Nottingham and Wolverhampton, to show what can be achieved. But there are also some alarming warnings. Many of London's town centres, for example, illustrate the costs of decline. These include the loss of employment (for shops can account for 20% of local jobs according to the NEDO study in 1988), decay and eventual demolition of familiar buildings, and loss of pride and hope among those who end up living there. It is not perhaps surprising in such places that crime escalates with increased

shop-lifting, and insurance claims, as well as sporadic violence. The warning was given by the NEDO report:

'The crucial point seems to be that competition and market forces do not overcome problems associated with declining High Street shopping areas. There appear to be factors stopping market forces working in a positive and constructive way... The changing structure of retailing has made High Streets more homogeneous... Whether the loss of retailing in certain High Streets will, in fact, lead to dereliction and substantial loss of vitality cannot be established on the facts available; the necessary information is not to hand... Depressed shopping areas, while still offering investment opportunities and where retailers can act as a catalyst to rejuvenation, are likely to suffer from a shortfall in the investment needed to maintain a thriving High Street.'

Distributive Trades Economic Development Committee (1988), The Future of the High Street, London: HMSO.

4   the impact of public policies

- Despite the importance given to town centres, in practice many local authorities have taken a passive approach, spending much of their time processing applications and fighting appeals. However, town centre management is catching on, particularly among the large authorities, as are the ideas of sustainable development and compact centres.

- Although living-over-the-shop has received considerable publicity, the greatest housing gains are likely to come from sites on the edge of the town centre, sometimes as an alternative to retail expansion.

- Public transport has not yet been developed sufficiently to provide an attractive option to cars, particularly for getting to work or school; though more consideration is being given to pedestrians in most places, until recently, cyclists have been generally neglected.

- Increased interest in conservation and the role of the arts in urban regeneration is definitely having an impact on our larger cities, though smaller towns are often lagging behind.

- Health and education are the great untapped opportunities for town centres, but trends seem to be leading these uses away from central locations.

- Who should be involved in funding town centre improvements and how property can be made available for alternative uses are key unresolved issues.

'The Government will encourage attractive and convenient urban areas, in which people will want to live and work; new development in locations which minimise energy consumption over the lifetime of that development; initiatives that lead to the regeneration of urban land and buildings, and to the restoration of derelict and contaminated land for development or open space...'

Sustainable Development: the UK Strategy, HMSO

4.01   If our town centres are not attractive, accessible or pleasant enough to compete, who or what is to blame? While it is impossible to isolate particular policies, this chapter considers in turn six main areas of public policy, with particular regard to what planners can influence. It deals briefly with land use, housing, transport, culture, education and health, and finance.

Land-use planning

4.02   In Britain we take pride in the sophistication of our planning system. In recommending permission for a new out-of-town regional centre near Manchester, for example, the Inspector at the public inquiry argued that planning would stop our cities following the American model. Major inquiries, such as that for Bluewater Park in Dartford, bring together wide ranging evidence on qualitative as well as quantitative considerations, all of which are extensively proved and weighed (see Lee Donaldson 1991). However, the enquiry process is only as good as the evidence available to it.

4.03   The publication of the revised Planning Policy Guidance notes 6 and 13 reflects a shift in thinking towards promoting town centres as the preferred location for new retail investment. At the same time as evidence of the undesirable impact of some out-of-town retailing became available there was a fresh concern for sustainable development, reflected in the 1990 Environment White Paper. Local authorities are being encouraged to plan positively and to assess the capacity of their town centres for further development. Where development is not possible in the town centre, edge-of-town centre locations may be preferred where they are close enough to enable people to walk into town, thus enabling one journey

to serve several different purposes. Development proposals are now to be considered with regard to their impact on the vitality and viability of town centres, the accessibility by a choice of modes, including public transport, cycling and walking, and the impact on overall levels of traffic. Development on out-of-town sites is now being discouraged where they would result in an unacceptable impact on the town centre. These principles have been expressed in a number of ministerial statements and decisions, such as at Ludlow. Thus Tony Baldry, addressing the CORE Westminster Conference in October 1993 on behalf of the Department of Environment said:

> 'I see PPG6 as an evolution of policy, not a major shift, our basic stance remains the same. It is not the role of the planning system to preserve existing commercial interests. Nor is it the purpose of the planning system to inhibit competition between retailers or methods of retailing. But we need to make sure the effects of competition do not deny access to shopping opportunities to large parts of society... We are encouraging retailers to compete in the same marketplace, rather than locate all over the shop. Planning for choice must be our guiding principle'.

4.04   Planning is often criticised as being too negative, when in fact planners play a range of roles, from acting as advocates and facilitators, to managing improvement projects, and promoting various kinds of development. As both the role and the underlying values have shifted considerably over the last 20 years, we need to start by considering the impact of the various roles.

4.05   **Development plans:** Our research found that town centres have an ambiguous position within many authorities.

On the one hand, our survey found that most planners consider them to be among the two or three most important issues, and most Unitary Development Plans devote a chapter to town centres or shopping (Exhibit 4.1). However, as was said in one of our seminars, 'there are no votes in the town centre, and since the Business Rate no money either'. The fact that most authorities comprise a number of centres makes it hard to devote much time or money to any one of them. It is only with the recession, the obvious signs of vacancy, and publicity for a number of revitalisation projects, that many authorities have started to give their centres priority. This is in marked contrast to most continental towns.

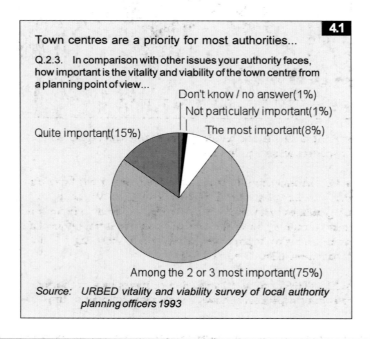

4.1

Town centres are a priority for most authorities...

Q.2.3. In comparison with other issues your authority faces, how important is the vitality and viability of the town centre from a planning point of view...

Don't know / no answer(1%)

Not particularly important(1%)

Quite important(15%)

The most important(8%)

Among the 2 or 3 most important(75%)

Source: URBED vitality and viability survey of local authority planning officers 1993

4.06   In the redevelopment of towns after the Second World War, little emphasis was placed on retaining the town's character. Town centres were often taken for granted. For example, there is little reference to them in Abercrombie's plan for London; instead the priority was on rehousing people at lower densities away from the centre, and disentangling conflicting uses.

4.07   Many authorities have only come to value the character of their town centres recently. This has largely been a result of pressure from conservation groups, often following fights such as the "Rape of Worcester", where land was cleared for development for new roads. Studies such as Lord Esher's pioneering plan for York, stopped large areas being cleared because they highlighted the importance of ordinary buildings that people had taken for granted. In the 1980s, attention shifted to **adaptive re-use** (Aldous 1990). Significantly, perhaps towns like Chesterfield, that have retained their character, have lost relatively little trade to nearby out-of-town regional centres such as Meadowhall.

4.08   Allied to the growing concern for heritage has been the realisation that in losing old buildings we have also lost some of the variety that comes from independent small businesses. While it is impossible to say how far redevelopment was responsible, rising rents and shortage of suitable premises were often blamed for businesses closing down in the past. The Use Classes Order is far broader than the situation in continental countries like Italy, for example. It is harder to maintain a diversity of shops in the high street than in a managed shopping mall.

4.09   Plans can contain policies to discourage changes of use which would result in the loss of valued facilities. But rules restricting a change of use are of little help when a town centre is really on the decline, and could simply lead to space being left vacant to decay. Furthermore, though the prime area may remain relatively strong, space in the secondary areas can readily go down-market without planners having any real control. Whereas it is possible to protect a group of buildings of architectural interest through designation of a conservation area, there is no such power to conserve particular uses or businesses that may be vital to the centre maintaining its position.

4.10 Some local authorities, particularly the larger cities such as Birmingham, have produced positive planning frameworks that go beyond the conventional land use plan (Exhibit 4.2). However, most local plans or Unitary Development Plans seem to lack vision or understanding of what is happening to the town centre and why. To the outsider, many read as a series of rules to try and keep things as they are rather than as guidance for making things better. Some may be seen in retrospect as little more than rearranging the deck-chairs on the Titanic.

4.11 Where a town centre is declining, it is often more important to enable new uses to take over and diversify the centre than to keep space vacant in the hopes of attracting the right user. Yet our survey found that many local authorities are not in touch with the main business occupiers in drawing up their plans. Though it is often important, for example, to define the primary frontages and to set policies for maintaining shop windows, it is likely that of greater importance will be devising and promoting improvement programmes and drawing up planning briefs for sites with development potential. In centres with very high levels of vacancy and that are declining, a much more relaxed planning regime in

A symposium helped set the basis for Birmingham's planning framework...

specific areas may be required if only to encourage private businesses to take an interest.

4.12 **Improvement programmes:** An important function that planners play is in helping to devise improvement programmes. However, there is still a tendency to focus on 'beautification', for example new street furniture, rather than on measures to improve the quality of the shopping mix and broaden the centre's attractions.

4.13 PPG6 in paras 18 and 19 encourages local authorities to adopt the process of **town centre management** to improve co-ordination. A growing number of authorities are now going beyond the 'janitorial' role, as research for the Association of Town Centre Management is bringing out (ATCM 1994).

4.14 Outside a few comprehensive schemes, however, such as Horsham town centre (see **8.19**), efforts are often fragmented (DoE 1989). While many local authorities have provided incentives for improving shop-fronts, the results often lack impact because they are on too small a scale. One of the benefits of town centre management should be the commitment this implies to co-ordinating the work of different departments and agencies, and there are now over 75 full time managers. The area where most has been achieved is probably Kent, where the county council has taken the lead in commissioning strategies. Similarly the Welsh Development Agency has funded the preparation of studies for a number of towns and assisted implementation. In both places it is recognised that environmental improvements need to be linked to wider economic development programmes.

4.15 **Town Centre Schemes:** Local authorities have often participated as partners in development schemes. However, with the collapse of the property boom, finance for major speculative developments has become increasingly hard to attract outside a relatively few places. For many places the challenge is how to manage decline. A key concern for most local authorities is resourcing town centre improvements and their subsequent maintenance and management. As efforts shift from promoting retail expansion and town centre redevelopment to making the most of what exists and town centre refurbishment, so the question needs to be resolved of where the resources will come from.

4.16 Since the last war most local authorities have played a key role in town centre development through a variety of partnership schemes. This has left many of them owning freeholds which could reduce in value if the town centre declines. There are pressures on them to dispose of remaining land holdings, which could lead to the loss of land which is needed for parking or open space. Authorities have often sought to finance projects through 'planning gain', which is not only restricted in scope, but also much less available since the collapse of the property boom. Undoubtedly in some cases there are competing objectives, which may lead to the good of the town centre being sacrificed.

4.17 There is still a need for planners to identify in development plans appropriate sites for new retail development that will reinforce rather than reduce the town centres appeal. In the absence of planners identifying appropriate sites for superstores and laying down planning conditions, it is not surprising that store groups compete for sites elsewhere. Too much time is then spent dealing with unwanted planning applications in the wrong place that could better have been put into improving the existing centre. Too little time is spent on producing a good brief.

Housing

4.18 When town centres were still blackened by soot and smog, the priorities in many British towns were to tackle slums, reduce densities and move people out. Conditions have now changed and with a general growth in the number of childless households, for many people the town centre should be an ideal place to live. It can offer social opportunities and 'fast food' for the young, libraries, health clinics and much more for the elderly. In all cases it saves time and money on transport. That is one of the reasons why the Government has encouraged "Flats over the shop" with financial incentives. *Living Over the Shop* with grants of up to 50% is being promoted by many authorities, through leaflets that emphasise the benefits both in terms of regular income and improved security, and links with housing associations (Petherick 1992). Though there are some excellent examples, the impact is thought by some housing associations to be not worth the effort, and longer-term schemes may provide better returns. For example, private builders are being drawn into Estate Action schemes on the edge of many centres that widen the tenure as well as improving the stock. Our survey found that only 43% of towns had undertaken housing initiatives, including most major cities but also some smaller towns, but many more were considering them.

4.19 **Opportunities for infill/re-use:** There is little doubt that towns with people living near their centres feel livelier and safer. Though extra housing may not revive shopping centres that have lost their market, it is an excellent way of bringing the secondary and fringe areas back to life. Major

cities, such as Glasgow, Manchester, and to some extent Leeds, have led the way in attracting people back to live, sometimes by converting redundant warehouses or buildings on waterside sites, helped by Government grants such as City Grant and in some instances the Business Expansion Scheme. In Birmingham, for example, new housing in the Jewellery Quarter has helped to create a 'smart' area on the edge of the town centre with wine bars and restaurants, and significantly increased the population.

4.20 Progress in industrial and commercial towns is far more mixed. Some, such as Luton, have built houses for the elderly, while in Preston and Swansea the old docks have been turned into 'urban villages'. However in most places uncertainty about demand and low prevailing values have caused private developers to build elsewhere. Market and historic towns, such as Lewes, Chichester or Kendal, have attracted specialist developers building sheltered housing for the elderly, often in small clusters on infill sites. In smaller towns the lead has sometimes come from local people

Housing in Towns...

4.3

1: Granby Village: Manchester

2: Infill housing: Kendal

3: Living over the bank: Leicester

seeking to conserve old buildings; good examples are Stroud and Gravesend, where such schemes have acted as a catalyst for further improvements (Exhibit 4.3). But Britain still lags far behind continental towns and cities, for example in Belgium and Germany. On the continent, many local authorities closely monitor the numbers of people living in the town centre, and promote housing as they know this helps to keep the town centre alive by night as well as day.

4.21 **Development schemes:** There are many places where re-using large vacant sites for housing could be the key to the future vitality and viability of the town centre. An example is Woolwich, where the closure of the Arsenal has created a 'hole' on the edge of the centre, with initial proposals coming forward for retail use, rather than for housing. Many market towns are also having to contend with vacant agricultural and commercial premises, such as a former cattle market or vacant shops and banks. With industry and offices often preferring out-of-town locations because of ease of access, and with very little finance available for new offices because of the overhang of empty property, an obvious alternative use is housing, even though it pays less for the land than retail.

4.22 House builders, including housing associations, go where it is easiest and most profitable to build. The Housing Corporation tends now to favour new build over refurbishment. Refurbishment is also seen as more complex, while central sites are often over-valued by owners and their advisors who wait for 'something to turn up'. Without a change in the financial equation, progress will not keep pace with decline. More housing in and near town centres could save historic buildings, improve security through natural surveillance, and create living communities.

Transport

4.23 One of the legacies of the past has been the image of the ideal modern city where transport was regarded as the link connecting detached areas of living, working and recreation. By the turn of the century, the widely-accepted transport concept which developed from this thinking was that cities had to be rebuilt to acquire a 'rational' road network in order to cater for the new demands of motor vehicle traffic. Modern road networks were superimposed on traditional cities and there was little realisation of the consequences this had for the traditional socio-economic urban structure.

4.24 **Road building**: The low suburban density which developed rapidly throughout the 20th century could in many places increasingly be achieved without rail links after the successful operation of motor buses. The importance of trams was largely underestimated; they were seen as old fashioned by many local authorities. Some cities, such as London and Manchester, had already started to scrap their trams during the 1920s and '30s (unlike on the Continent). This process was completed by the beginning of the 1960s. Road building and the rise in car ownership had far-reaching effects on the urban structure in terms of relocation of growth industries and middle class-housing to places which were no longer easily accessible by railway or any other rail-related transport mode. The more decentralised housing and jobs became, the more difficult it was to sustain a good public transport network.

4.25 Among a few others, it was the Buchanan Report, 30 years ago, which pointed out the whole spectrum of adverse effects motorisation had and would continue to have on the urban environment (MoT 1963). Although the content of the Buchanan Report was accepted in Britain, its full implications were either not seen or not believed. It was interpreted by some cities such as Leeds and Birmingham as a justification for massive urban road building.

4.26   It was not only public transport which was neglected; by-passes have taken time to build which has made it virtually impossible to protect town centre environments from car traffic. Clearly there were exceptions, and some local authorities tried to promote public transport vigorously, for instance South Yorkshire. By the end of the 1970s co-ordination between land-use and transport planning had in effect been abandoned. It is in particular here where some of our European neighbours have done better than Britain (TEST 1987, FoE 1992).

4.27   Until recently there was also a lack of recognition that land-use planning could have any kind of importance in determining the number and length of car trips. For most British local authorities creating alternatives to the car by promoting public transport and cycling, and in addition developing policies on traffic restraint, road pricing, traffic calming and pedestrianisation on a larger scale have remained unexplored and ambitious objectives (Hass-Klau 1992).

4.28   The 1989 National Road Traffic Forecasts envisaged overall traffic levels that would be between 83% and 142% higher by the year 2025 than in 1988 (NRTF 1989). Yet there is no possibility of increasing the road capacity at the rate to match this and on present trends, vehicle miles per road mile can only increase. Therefore congestion will get worse in intensity, spread and duration. If we are not physically and financially able to build sufficient roads in towns to match the demand of car use the logic has to be that 'demand must be matched to supply'.

4.29   The new direction has already been expressed by both the Department of the Environment and Department of Transport in a number of publications (DoT 1991, DoE 1994). Furthermore people are becoming increasingly dependent on the car so that the quality of public transport needs to be improved if it is to compete. The new package approach in England for local transport funding, with capital provision including both road and public transport proposals, certainly will introduce a greater flexibility to local authorities. The Government requires that these bids are supported by a comprehensive transport strategy, which can incorporate options other than road building, and this is clearly going in the right direction.

4.30   **Traffic management:** Some towns are already reversing earlier policies and 'putting people first'. Birmingham, York, Edinburgh, Oxford and Brighton, for instance have developed comprehensive programmes of environmentally-friendly transport policies. However, many others, especially market towns, have not yet been able to change their transport policy. One of the reasons is that with two tiers of authority, transport issues are dealt with by the Highways Departments of the county council, and districts have little influence in such matters. Even pedestrianisation, although a local matter, depends to a large extent on approval from the county as they deal with the traffic implications. As transport, apart from parking, is not their responsibility, towns are very often not particularly well informed about alternative policy options, or simply about the different types of transport guidelines available. This lack of knowledge is used by some county councils to veto anything which is not in the traditional engineering textbooks. One can therefore still find a large number of towns in which the main objective appears to be to keep motor vehicle traffic moving

1: Mini buses in Exeter

2: Park & ride: Exeter

3: Cycle parking: Nottingham

4: Car parking: Cardiff

Transport in towns...   4.4

1

2

3

4

quickly, mostly in the form of one-way street systems even when a bypass may have relieved the need for them. Instead of making car drivers welcome to the town centre, one-way systems can have the opposite effect, particularly for people who are unfamiliar with the town.

4.31 **Public transport:** Since deregulation in 1985, towns which want to influence public transport have to work with private operators. Many bus operators sold their bus stations and are now frequently setting down, picking up and laying over in traditional high streets. Whilst this may be more acceptable to passengers in some instances, it can add to

congestion, noise and smell. As a result of deregulation, passengers have the potential for more choice in the use of bus services. However in some town centre streets, this has led to serious congestion, with several operators competing with each other and fighting for passengers. Bus operators have sometimes become unpopular because their buses are driven at unreasonably high speeds and many models are old, noisy and dilapidated compared with what is possible. As there seems to be a reduced need for buses because of both growth in car ownership and the negative image of them, local authorities are now increasingly excluding buses from their main pedestrianised shopping streets, whereas some out-of-town superstores are attracting customers by offering free buses. However only 13% of local authorities in our survey had undertaken initiatives involving networks of mini-buses or rapid transit (Exhibit 4.4). Yet the experience of introducing quality public transport, as with the Manchester Metro or Nottingham's Shuttle bus, suggests that public transport could be made fashionable again.

4.32 Divisions and conflicts between county highway authorities and town vested interests, private bus companies, and a general shortage of finance, stop many town centres taking action early enough to prevent people taking to their cars and shopping where it is more convenient. When they do act, many are not able to reconcile access and amenity considerations. The challenge is to avoid the noose of the one-way inner ring road, the desert caused by a simplified version of pedestrianisation, and the trap of relying on a single multi-storey car park.

Culture - heritage, arts and tourism

4.33   Real town centres transmit our culture in a way that out-of-town centres never can. At their best they provide a major reason why tourists come to Britain (ETB 1991a). Our analysis shows that historic towns have proved to be among the most successful from an investment point of view. Most of these have received encouragement and financial support from English Heritage and the English Tourist Board or their Welsh equivalents, which have helped make new initiatives possible. However, until the present recession there was a tendency to go for big projects, and to compartmentalise recreation into a series of isolated centres. Only a third of local authorities reported taking initiatives to broaden the appeal of town centres by encouraging cultural activities or libraries and museums. Yet regular users of the library can also, for example, be customers for the book shops or bric-a-brac shops that may help to give many a town its special character.

4.34   There is a growing appreciation that people spend time and money in 'walkable places' where the public realm, that is the spaces between buildings, feels attractive and safe (Whyte 1988). Here town centres should have a real edge over their out-of-town competitors. Policies for community arts and the use of festivals and public art, are making many of our towns much more exciting. With investment being much harder to attract, the 'winners' in future are likely to be those that make the most of the town centre's existing resources. This is putting a fresh emphasis on what is sometimes called 'cultural planning' (Bianchini 1988).

4.35   In the larger cities, such as Sheffield, new sports facilities have acted as a catalyst for run-down areas, and created buildings of lasting quality, even though the cost has been criticised. In the smaller towns, such as Bury St Edmunds and Worcester, programmes for restoring historic areas, helped by Town Schemes supported by English Heritage, or by the Rural Development Commission have given old towns a new appeal. There have also been a spate

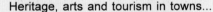

Heritage, arts and tourism in towns...   **4.5**

Brewery Arts Centre: Kendal   Piece Hall: Halifax   Chubb Media Centre: Wolverhampton   Stroud Day: Stroud

of imaginative museums, encouraged by a popular interest in heritage and the interpretation of local history, often run by volunteers. But while there have been plenty of arts, cultural and tourism studies, there have been disappointingly few examples of combining these different policies to bring town centres to life. Yet where towns have taken the initiative, as in the case of Kendal, Halifax or Wolverhampton, the results are plain to see (Exhibit 4.5).

4.36   The problems lie not just in cut-backs in the funding available to each of the agencies concerned, but also in a lack of resolve, a passive attitude or complacency. In particular there is an opportunity to use the restoration and adaptive re-use of redundant buildings to achieve a number of objectives simultaneously and this deserves more encouragement (DoE 1987).

Education and health

4.37   While many sectors are declining, demographic and other trends are causing health and education to expand, with more school leavers going on to higher education and an ageing population making more use of health facilities. Many US towns see social and educational services as the main future for their town centres as they generate activity and need to be near good public transport (International Downtown Association 1993). Yet in many places in Britain, there is a movement out-of-town in the belief that it will be cheaper and that the move can be paid for by selling off existing sites. Thus, the University of Greenwich plans to expand on a hospital site on the edge of Dartford, and had difficulty finding suitable premises in Woolwich, while the University of Huddersfield is also planning a new campus on

an old hospital, this time in a small village. In contrast in Lincoln a new university is being established on former railway land near the town centre.

4.38   While an institutional use may be ideal for an old hospital site, a concern for sustainable development argues for keeping such uses in traditional centres as proposed in PPG13. Just as importantly students, and perhaps patients and their visitors prefer it too. One of the reasons for moving out is that land is seen as cheaper away from town centres, and institutions tend over time to expand or merge. However, some countries, such as Sweden, encourage institutions to make use of existing buildings before they build anew, and so influence land values. Local authorities can assist the process by drawing up briefs for key sites, and should involve health authorities and colleges in their town centre strategies as they are such key players, as is happening in Sheffield, for example. PPG13 specifically mentions education and health facilities as examples of uses that need to be retained in town centres and not decentralised, yet only 13% of local authorities said they had undertaken initiatives involving education and training facilities, with examples including Luton, Islington and Southwark (Exhibit 4.6).

Finance

4.39   While public expenditure only accounts for a small part of the total investment in most town centres, it can play an important role is influencing private sector attitudes. Underlying all the current problems facing town centres is a concern over where the resources are to come from. While it is possible to change their roles and attractions, money is needed both for extensive improvements and their subsequent management and maintenance. Britain's system of public finance is unusual as commercial property taxes are collected by local authorities but then go to the Government for re-distribution. Yet some of the senior managers of our largest retailers still believe that the Business Rates they pay go directly to local authorities and should be spent on the town. They therefore see no reason for making any further financial contribution. There is also a lack of accountability or sense of responsibility for the condition of our town centres.

4.40 In the past, towns in areas of decline have been able to use the Urban Programme, sometimes supplemented with other public sources of capital funding, such as the European Commission, to support improvement programmes. Some-times these have helped the centre's diversification as for example with the Bradford Design Exchange or Nottingham's Lace Market area. More often they have been used for environmental improvement, such as the renovation of shop fronts and facades.

4.41 With competing demands and limited resources, local authorities have little capacity to invest effort and money in the town centres. Furthermore, as most districts comprise a number of centres, and there are few voters in the town centres, it is often hard to give the main centres the attention they deserve. Reliance is increasingly placed on donations from large retailers and several, such as Boots and Marks and Spencers, are providing practical as well as financial help. But most multiple retailers are not involved in town centre initiatives, and their local managers have little discretion. Land owners, who have a bigger stake do not pay taxes on their property and are insulated from the town centre's performance by the leasehold system. In a few cases financial institutions are supporting town centre management, but

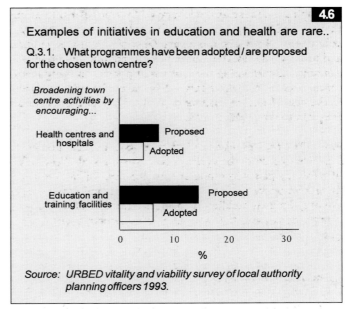

4.6

Examples of initiatives in education and health are rare..

Q.3.1. What programmes have been adopted / are proposed for the chosen town centre?

Source: URBED vitality and viability survey of local authority planning officers 1993.

most institutions have no further involvement in a town once an investment has been made.

4.42 Where town centre managers exist, they can easily find themselves having to spend all their time raising finance, rather than co-ordinating improvements. Furthermore, the process of revitalisation requires a long-term approach and so needs long-term sources of funding. One possible source is to use a mechanism like City Challenge to provide supplementary funding for strategies that have been drawn up with the involvement of the business community. Certainly City Challenge winners, such as Batley, Tipton, Harlesden and Lewisham, have all been able to do more for their town centres in ways that are encouraging local partnerships.

PART TWO • RESPONSES

5   assessing vitality and viability

- Assessing vitality and viability is of increasing importance in the preparation of local plans

- Performance can be monitored through the key indicators of pedestrian flow or footfall, which indicates how busy the centre is at different times, and yield on prime commercial property, which indicates how attractive the centre is to investors.

- It is also important to look at the underlying components of a healthy town centre, and these can be analysed through a health check that considers the attractions in terms of diversity and critical mass, accessibility in terms of mobility and linkages, amenity in terms of security and identity, and action in terms of organisational capacity and resourcing.

- The indicators can be applied in drawing up profiles and also in undertaking performance reviews.They can be assessed in terms of a simple SWOT analysis (strengths, weaknesses,opportunities and threats) to judge whether the town is at risk.

Marco Polo describes a bridge, stone by stone. 'But which is the stone that supports the bridge?' Kublai Khan asks. ' The bridge is not supported by one stone or another,' Marco Polo answers, 'but by the line of the arch that they form'. Kublai Khan remains silent, reflecting. Then he adds, 'Why do you speak of the stones? It is only the arch that matters to me.' Polo answers: 'Without stones there is no arch'.

Italo Calvino
Invisible Cities.

5.01   Increasing pressures on town centres and limited public resources require a reliable means of assessing their health or relative success so that positive and appropriate action can be taken before a crisis develops. This chapter looks at what is meant by vitality and viability and the problems of measuring the performance of town centres. It proposes a range of indicators that can provide both quantitative assessment and an understanding of the underlying components of health.

The concepts

5.02   The revised version of PPG6 places an increased importance on the assessment of the vitality and viability of town centres. It encourages assessment as part of development plan preparation and as an important element in deciding whether proposals for new retail development are acceptable. One of the reasons for this research was to help in the definition and measurement of these concepts.

5.03   Since being referred to in July 1986 by the Secretary of State for the Environment in a House of Commons Ministerial reply, the concepts of vitality and viability have become firmly associated with town centres and have been incorporated into many local authority strategies and development plans. However, there has been much debate as to the meaning of the terms, both by local authorities and professional experts. As the literature review on Out-of-Town Retailing put it, "For experienced traders and surveyors, the existence of vitality and viability is easy to recognise, but difficult to define" (DoE 1992a).

5.04   Vitality and viability are both concerned with and derive from words meaning life - vitality coming to English in the sixteenth century from the Latin *vitalitas* (*vita*) and viability in the nineteenth century from the French *viable* (*vie*). The use of both terms highlights the need to consider whether a centre feels lively ('animation' being one definition of vitality) and whether it has a capacity for living (to use an accepted definition of viability). Thus **vitality** is reflected in how busy a centre is at different times and in different parts whilst **viability** refers to the ability of the centre to attract continuing investment, not only to maintain the fabric, but also to allow for improvement and adaption to changing needs.

5.05   Vitality contributes to achieving viability, through a series of processes, initiatives and actions with economic, environmental, and cultural aspects. One illustration of this is the experience of major railway termini and airports. Where once thousands of passengers passed rapidly through the terminal or station (vitality), new shops, restaurants, bars, and a greatly enhanced environment have turned many into viable trading areas, generating substantial investment by both retailers and operators. At Gatwick Airport a considerable amount of shopping is done by people who go specifically for that purpose rather than to fly or meet someone. Another classic example is Union Station, Washington DC, where the many commuters provided a ready market for the specialist shops and restaurants following the refurbishment of the station buildings and these have now become an attraction in themselves (Cantacuzino 1989). Victoria and Liverpool Street Stations in London perhaps provide the best British examples. Such places have exploited their vitality to attract investment in retailing and other services that is generally of a specialist or 'upmarket' nature. This contrasts with the experience of those traditional centres, considered earlier, where a reduction in vitality has led to the retail offer moving downmarket,

'...Towns depend for much of their custom on other needs and attractions that bring customers to a town centre in the first place, and the reverse applies too. It is this complex interaction between the different town centre functions that creates much of the 'vitality and viability' that may sometime need protecting from too much out-of-town development'.

Rt Hon Michael Howard MP, Britain in 2010: Future Patterns of Shopping, Royal Society of Arts Symposium providing a cheaper and more limited range of goods and services.

5.06   A survey of almost 100 county and metropolitan authorities, as part of the study *The Effects of Major Out-of-Town Retail Development*, found that "Few authorities knew how or what to assess as a measure of vitality and viability". None of the authorities knew of reports that specifically addressed the issue, though thirteen possible indicators were suggested to be of some importance, including poor environment, retail investment levels, and insufficient car parking.

5.07   Two principal factors appear to have contributed to the absence of agreed measures. One is the fairly commonly-held view amongst professionals, retailers and some local authorities that "you only have to walk down the street" to understand the health of a town centre. While it is true that the quality of maintenances of the shops, buildings and streets gives a good impression of how well a centre is doing, few people know enough centres for long enough for their opinion to be relied upon. Public inquiries show that interpretations vary greatly. The second factor is the absence of standardised and available information on what is happening to individual town centres. Without generally understood measures, too much time is being spent in fruitless arguments at public inquiries. The question of whether to allow a new retail development has continued to be focussed on aspects of economic impact, such as trade diversion, and some aspects of social and environmental impact, such as transport and land-use issues. However, reliable information on turnover is not generally available in the absence of a Census of Distribution. Calculating catchment areas and consumer expenditure is also fraught with problems, particularly because in Britain most people live

close to a number of centres, which form more of a network than a hierarchy.

5.08   To overcome some of the problems, the focus is shifting onto two questions. The first is whether town centres have sufficient vitality and viability to cope with change. The second is, whether new development would upset major agreed plans or improvement strategies, and lead to reduced choice and possibly increased travel. The revised PPG6, issued in July 1993, whilst accepting that in practice "most aspects of vitality and viability will be difficult to assess with confidence" has attempted to further their use by including two indicators that "can usually provide the main criteria for the purposes of a planning application or appeal" together with five "other factors which may be relevant". Each has a short explanation and most have been widely discussed in articles in the property press since publication. However, as they at least in part arose from the early work on this study, we here set out some of the reasoning behind them and propose a fuller framework of measures as foreshadowed in a footnote to PPG6.

5.09   It should first be emphasised that we have found no single indicator that can effectively measure the health of a town centre. Thus we accept that in isolation each of the indicators or measures proposed can be criticised as not providing a true picture. However, we believe that together they can provide an effective insight into the performance of a town centre and so offer a framework for assessing vitality and viability. In particular, like a doctor taking someone's temperature or pulse, they can be used to tell whether a town is vulnerable or at risk in comparison with others. We should also emphasise that they can be most effectively used as indicators of change over time. Hence the assessment should

'This human congress is the genius of the place, its reason for being, its great marginal edge. This is the engine, the city's true export. Whatever makes this congress easier, more spontaneous, more enjoyable is not at all a frill. It is the heart of the centre of the city.'

*William Whyte,
Rediscovering the Center City.*

not be a 'one-off' but something that is done on a regular, possibly annual, basis in each centre.

Pedestrian flow

5.10   One of the two key indicators is **pedestrian flow** or footfall. This provides the most basic measure of usage, counting the number of people passing a particular point at a particular time. The more people on the streets, the livelier the centre will feel. A paper produced by the Oxford Institute of Retail Management referred to footfall as "a direct indicator of the vitality of shopping streets" (OXIRM 1986). Many shopping centres regularly monitor footfall in order to attract and retain retail tenants. In Meadowhall, for instance, visitors are constantly counted and tabulated, allowing immediate comparison with the previous day, week or year, and the setting of targets for some years ahead. The shopping mall above Birmingham New Street station for example, enjoys a footfall of over 750,000 a week, an important factor in attracting private investment.

5.11   It is important to stress that pedestrian flow is about measuring vitality rather than viability. To be useful as an indicator, it is essential that a number of counts are taken at different locations, not just in the prime shopping area, and at different times of the day and evening. Some information is already gathered both by researchers and by local authorities, though there are differences in method. It is perhaps worth noting that many schools organise pedestrian flow counts as part of the Geography GCSE course. 50% of respondents to our survey (including 89% of those from major cities) said that they regarded pedestrian flow as a key indicator of vitality and 43% thought it useful.

5.12   Property Market Research Services have undertaken counts in approximately 100 centres and these are available through Goad. These counts are conducted at 30 locations in the main shopping streets on a Friday and Saturday. However, many were conducted some years ago and where they have been updated there is often little comparison that can be made with earlier surveys as they were conducted at different times of the year. Goad are looking at how this service could be

---

Newcastle: analysing pedestrian flow

Pedestrian flow counts have been used to assess the impact of out-of-town centres, as well as measures to improve existing centres. Since 1976, a series of counts have been undertaken by the Oxford Institute of Retail Management in the same week in February each year in Newcastle. In 1987, the year following the opening of the Metro Centre in neighbouring Gateshead, 80 fifteen minute counts were undertaken together with a cordon count at the entrances to Eldon Square. These figures were then grossed up to provide one hour counts. The figures were then compared with previous years, both overall and individually. Though the 1987 count showed a slight decrease from the previous year (4% down), the researchers did not consider this significant, merely reflecting factors such as weather and other issues.

However, there were significant variations within the centre when compared with previous years. The trend appeared to be an increase in flows in Eldon Square and a drop in the rest of the city centre. There was a considerable drop in flow in a number of streets in the southern part of the city. These streets were dominated by discount stores, an amusement arcade and high levels of vacancy. The changes were "associated first with the opening of the Eldon Square centre in 1976, and secondly with the reinforcement of the Eldon Square area as the core of the shopping centre by the opening of new metro stations in the vicinity, a bus station beneath the Eldon Square shops and the declining use of bus stations in the southern part of the city."

improved, drawing on experience of continental surveys. Specifically commissioned surveys are also available through URPI who use a regular team of fieldworkers. If comparisons are to be made between different places (as happens in Germany, for example), there will need to be a code of practice so that pedestrian flow is measured on a standard basis. We would recommend producing rounded off estimates for weekly flows, for both the prime locations, the main gateways, and for areas that are in transition. This can be achieved by sample counts on Saturdays and a weekday, undertaken at the same time of year, and groups of local authorities may want to collaborate. Comparative figures should also help in planning pedestrianisation and other schemes.

5.13   What can be learned from monitoring footfall can perhaps best be illustrated by a number of existing surveys. In Manchester surveys are used at Christmas time to assess the impact of city centre promotional activity (Centre for Employment Research, 1990). In Worcester, consistent counts were undertaken by the City Council in 1990 and 1992, before and after the opening of the Crowngate Shopping Centre (Worcester City Council 1993). Based on samples of 10 minute periods over three hours in 32 central locations the results showed a clear variation in usage of streets as a result of the new centre, and a significant increase in total flow in the town centre. In Ipswich a comprehensive study has helped to focus improvements where they are most needed .

5.14   Pedestrian flow can be used to assess initiatives to improve the town centre. A number of surveys have been undertaken in Germany and Austria before and after pedestrianisation (Hass-Klau 1993). Pedestrian counts were regularly taken over many years, and revealed significant increases in streets that were pedestrianised compared with

those that were not. We believe that the evidence of change revealed in surveys such as these provides a valuable indicator of how vital a centre is and argues strongly for regular counts in all town centres.

Yield

5.15   **Yield** is the second, and more complex indicator, in PPG6 and is a measure which enables values of properties of different size, location, and other characteristics to be compared. It is the ratio of rental income to capital value and is expressed in terms of the open market rents of a property as a percentage of the capital value. Thus, the higher the yield the lower the rental income is valued, and vice versa. A high yield is an indication of concern by investors that rental income might grow less rapidly and be less secure than in a property with a low yield. Yields are based on the evidence of transactions where individual properties are bought and sold. Because the circumstances of individual properties vary, transactional evidence needs to be interpreted to allow comparison on a like for like basis between different towns and over time. The volume of transactions is small relative to the number of properties, so the interpretation of evidence by the valuer necessarily involves an element of judgment.

5.16   The shop investment market uses the yield of a modern standard sized shop unit in the highest rented position in the town centre (the **prime** yield) as its standard. **Yields** are commonly expressed in terms of this standard and transactions are interpreted in terms of it. Transactions may show discounts from the prime yield to reflect location, physical characteristics, lease length and tenant covenant. The standard yield represents the most expensive or prime location.

The degree to which values decline with distance from this point vary from town to town. It may be useful to measure yields in a secondary location as well as those of the prime area.

5.17 The level of yield broadly represents the market's evaluation of the risk and return attached to the income stream of shop rents. The market is made up of purchasers of freehold and long leasehold property. These include small companies and private individuals but, particularly in the larger town centres, also include major property companies and financial institutions (eg. insurance companies and pension funds) which tend to set the tone of the market.

5.18 The market's assessment of return, and the rental growth which would drive this, is influenced by factors such as population and economic growth and level of affluence in the catchment area, together with attractiveness to visitors. The assessment of risk takes into account whether the demand by retailers to occupy the property might fall. This can happen not only if the spending power in the catchment area experiences relative decline but also if there is competition from alternative premises, both within the town centre and outside it. Thus the increase of new shop property in an expanding town may be considered to limit the opportunity for rental growth. The yield in a fast growing town where new shops keep pace with demand (eg. a New Town) might be higher than a more slowly growing town where development is constrained (eg. an historic town). Similarly, yields may rise in the short term following a major town centre shopping development.

5.19 Factors which affect yield are therefore complex, and need to be interpreted with reference to the circumstances in each individual town. Broadly speaking, however, low yields indicate that a town is considered to be attractive and as a result should be more likely to attract investment than a town with high yields. As a measure of retail viability, yields are a valuable indictor, but one which needs to be used with care. The level of yield of its own is of less value than in comparison with other yields at different points in time and in different locations. Yields measured consistently over time can give an indication of the direction in which a particular town centre is moving. This trend can be compared with national levels of yield and with those of towns of similar size and type, or with neighbouring and competing towns. A comparative analysis of this type, conducted on a regular basis, can give an indication of how the viability of retailing in a town centre is changing.

Sheffield: using yields

Sheffield is the fourth largest city in the country, and the decline of the steel industry left a large area of vacant land, part of which has been developed for Meadowhall, which is a regional shopping centre. The impact of Meadowhall has been estimated to have taken 15-20% of the city's trade. However, the impact can also be seen in terms of the yield indicator, and its relation to rentals.

In 1988, before Meadowhall opened, Sheffield and Nottingham were both rated relatively highly by investors with yields of 4.75% and 4.5% respectively. However, after Meadowhall opened in 1991 Sheffield's yield rose to 7.5% in 1992 compared to 5.75% in Nottingham. This reflected the downward assessment of the rental growth prospects. The practical implications have been that a number of retail-based development schemes have failed to attract funding, and this has made it harder to diversify the city centre. When the yield is related to the rentals, Sheffield comes in the bottom quartile of the residual table, (see appendix A) and thus may be regarded as 'at risk' if further development were to take place out of town.

5.20   Experience has shown that yields tend to be heavily influenced by town size. Towns with large shopping areas in their centres tend to have lower yields than smaller towns. As part of this research the effect of town size was standardised by means of regression so that the level of yield was measured relative to the level of shop rent (see **Appendix A**). The analysis derived a 'residual yield index' and this methodology may be useful to local authorities and others when judging changes in the viability within a particular area.   Analysis of

this type provides a more sensitive indicator of yields and yield movements (Exhibit 5.1).

5.21   The yield of shop property in individual towns can be obtained from valuers specialising in shop investment property. The Inland Revenue (Valuation Office) is able to provide valuations of shop yields for town centres within their areas. There are a number of large national firms of Chartered Surveyors who provide a national coverage of shop property. These firms are able to supply yields for most towns on a consistent national basis. Some have databases of shop yields going back a number of years. There are also a number of published sources of national figures showing the average yield of all shop property transactions. Hillier Parker publishes Average Yields on a quarterly basis which give the open market average of prime yields based on a weighted basket of 400 rent points across the country representing a notional investment portfolio. Investment Property Databank publish a monthly average yield based on a sample of monthly valued institutional property, as well as profiles on individual town to their subscribers. Other indices are published by Richard Ellis (monthly), and Healey and Baker (quarterly covering prime property - ie the lowest yield in the country). The Valuation Office will be publishing yields on 550 town centres in its Six Monthly Property Market report, starting with the Spring '94 edition.

				5.1
Different types of towns vary widely in how they are seen by investors...				
Rank	**Town**	**Rent/sq.ft.**	**Yield**	**Residual**
1	Newbury	77.50	5.75	-1.53
2	Weybridge	40.00	7.00	-1.26
=	Bridgewater	40.00	7.00	-1.26
=	Chippenham	40.00	7.00	-1.26
5	Inverness	59.00	6.50	-1.23
6	Durham	80.00	6.00	-1.22
=	Ashford, Kent	50.00	6.75	-1.22
8	Worcester	95.00	5.75	-1.15
9	Sevenoaks	45.00	7.00	-1.11
=	Lichfield	45.00	7.00	-1.11
389	Holloway	55.00	9.50	1.66
=	East Ham	55.00	9.50	1.66
391	Cwmbran	65.00		
392	Grimsby, Freeman St.	15.00	11.00	1.93
393	Gateshead	20.00	11.00	2.11
394	North Shields	37.50	10.75	2.42
395	Ashington	30.00	11.00	2.44
396	Workington	35.00	11.00	2.59
=	Wallsend	35.00	11.00	2.59
398	Barrow	52.50	11.00	3.10

Source: Hillier Parker Residual Yield Index : May 1992 figures.

Other indicators

5.22   In addition to these two key variables, there are a number of other ways of monitoring whether a town is losing its basic appeal. Trends in **demand** for shop units from national multiples are recorded by and published by organisations such as Focus, and partially signalled to local authorities by changes in planning applications. These provide a guide to the town's changing appeal compared with it competitors. So too can the change in the number of multiples and the town's position in terms of its **multiple ranking** (Hillier Parker 1991a).

5.23   By analysing **space in use** in a centre a picture can also be developed of how various functions inter-relate (Exhibit 5.2). At present there is a somewhat confused variety of information sources, but this should be largely resolved following the computerisation of the Valuation Office's records. Information is available through Goad on retail usage, which is broken down into convenience, comparison, service and vacant. Each of the first three categories is further broken down to provide more information on different types of shop and service. For most town centres this information is regularly updated, annually for 400 centres, and earlier records are available that can give an indication of change. Whilst this refers to the centre as a whole, other sources can provide information on actual unit use. For example, shop-by-shop listings, with sketch maps, are provided for over 450 centres in the British Isles in the annually updated Retail Directory (Newman Books). The Yellow Pages can also be used as a source of information on the number of shops in different categories. They provide statistical services, which include information on employment.

5.24   Information on non-retail space in town centres is less easy to find at present. Some local authorities, such as Manchester, produce annual reports on office development that monitor schemes from outline planning to completion and usually attempt to assess the general performance of existing space. Monitoring the development pipeline (as for example

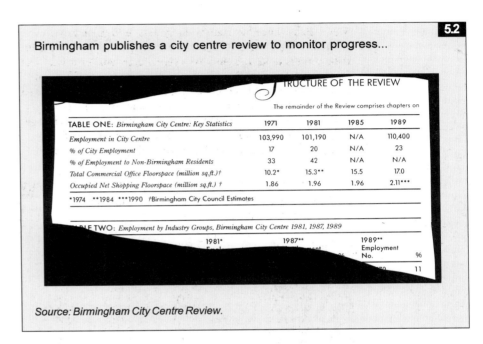

Birmingham publishes a city centre review to monitor progress...

STRUCTURE OF THE REVIEW

The remainder of the Review comprises chapters on

TABLE ONE: *Birmingham City Centre: Key Statistics*	1971	1981	1985	1989
Employment in City Centre	103,990	101,190	N/A	110,400
% of City Employment	17	20	N/A	23
% of Employment to Non-Birmingham Residents	33	42	N/A	N/A
Total Commercial Office Floorspace (million sq.ft.)†	10.2*	15.3**	15.5	17.0
Occupied Net Shopping Floorspace (million sq.ft.) †	1.86	1.96	1.96	2.11***

*1974   **1984   ***1990   †Birmingham City Council Estimates

TABLE TWO: *Employment by Industry Groups, Birmingham City Centre 1981, 1987, 1989*

	1981*	1987**	1989** Employment No.	%
			70	11

Source: Birmingham City Centre Review.

undertaken for London Boroughs by the London Research Centre) can provide a useful indicator of the viability of the market in a particular sector, though in many cases this will be merely reflecting national trends. In other instances, a consultants' study can provide an initial insight into uses in a centre which can then be updated over time. Though not specific in terms of sites, the study on Sheffield central area looked at the extent of activity and the likely changes in them in eight categories in the city centre: retailing, commercial uses, transport, housing, education, manufacturing, arts and leisure and tourism (Foley 1992). It is particularly important to look at population trends for the centre of town compared with the district as a whole, and this could be monitored between census years by using information on the housing stock, for example the numbers of Council Tax payers.

5.25 One difficulty is taking account of qualitative differences, for example where shops close to be replaced by ones that draw fewer customers to the centre. When assessing health, particular attention needs to be given to whether the **quality** of the town's attractions may be changing fundamentally through changes in the retailer representation or **profile**. It is important to identify the 'anchor store' or magnet which gives the centre its particular appeal and whose loss could change the centre's role. This will depend on the type of town; in a historic town the key attractions may be a number of specialist shops, while a good Marks and Spencer is often seen as the test of whether a suburban town is retaining its pull. Comparison can be made with national averages, but it would be better to compare the town with both its immediate competitors and similar types of town, that is those playing in the same division or league.

5.26 **Vacancy rates** are much used in assessing town centre health, and in 1993 some 12% of all units in town centres were vacant according to Goad. 71% of the respondents to our survey said they thought vacancy was a key indicator and 24% that it was useful. PPG6 suggests that street level vacancy in the primary retail area should be taken into account when measuring vitality and viability, though with the caveat that it should be used with care as "vacancies can arise even in the strongest towns". Our research shows there is good reason for caution over vacancy figures.

5.27 The most readily obtainable figures for retail vacancy, published by Goad, include both property that is awaiting redevelopment and that which is under construction. In other instances, vacancy levels do not adequately reflect a decline that has occurred, as the leasehold structure of commercial property holding in most town centres often means businesses continue to trade until the end of their lease, even if turnover has fallen substantially. In many other instances, shops have been replaced by a charity shop or discount store that would not be reflected in vacancy figures, but has had a major effect on the range and quality of retail offer. In other cases retail closures in fringe areas have led to change of use rather than vacancy. Vacancy needs to be analysed in different parts of the town centre. There is no substitute for closer inspection and probing to understand why the situation is the way it is and how it is changing, for better or worse. Vacancy needs to be related to the physical **structure** of the town, for example distinguishing between areas that are pedestrianised or traffic calmed, and different levels of accessibility (see **5.31**).

5.28 Regular monitoring of pedestrian flow and retail property yields should be undertaken in all significant town centres, together with checks on how the **quality** of the centre may be changing through discussions with key retailers and the Chamber of Commerce and analysis of who is opening and who is closing. By monitoring these over time, local authorities and other interested parties will be able to see how the performance of the centre is changing, both in itself and in relation to neighbouring or similar centres.

Elements of a healthy town centre

5.29 Whilst the indicators should enable a centre to assess its general state of health, they do not explain where the strengths or weaknesses lie. To continue the medical analogy, once the first signs of ill-health are detected, further tests are required to attempt to diagnose the problem before an appropriate remedy can be applied. Unfortunately, with town centres there is an added complication in that there are many different views on what constitutes a successful centre and no simple definition. Also, like any organism, health is multi-dimensional. It involves economic and socio-cultural as well as physical dimensions. In order to develop some appropriate and practical tests, we looked at nearly 200 possible measures of health. For example, some research companies analyse the census data to produce demographic profiles of the population of a town which can then be related to what they consume and therefore what shops or services would do best (CACI 1993). Though many of these could provide useful insights into particular issues, for the most part we ruled them out as being either not readily available, not sufficiently distinguishable between health and decline, or requiring too great a subjective input to be meaningful, unless the same person was involved each time. After testing ideas in the local authority survey, regional seminars, our case studies and through consultation with a wide variety of informed opinion, we concluded that a practical assessment framework was needed. This should focus on four basic qualities that underlie the health of a town centre: attractions, accessibility, amenity and action - the 4 'A's (Exhibit 5.3). These essentially subjective concepts are developed further in the guidelines for good practice in **Part Three**, and in the check-list in **Appendix B** and are briefly described below.

5.30 **Attractions:** These are the foundation of healthy town centres, and refer to what draws in the customers (Exhibit 5.4). The range or **diversity** of shops/services was seen as a principal factor for town centre health by 96% of the respondents to our survey. Whilst the diversity of attractions undoubtedly relates

to the nature and composition of retailing in a centre, measured for example by the number of multiples, specialist shops or markets in the centre, it also should consider other functions. These include arts, cultural or entertainment facilities, educational, health and other services, and even the availability of space for people living or working in the centre, all of which help to keep a centre feeling alive. It is useful to monitor businesses and activities closing, and the number and type of new businesses that open up or move in and whether they survive. It is also desirable to analyse a plan of the town to see the extent of the prime area and where the main attractions are located, as this can explain why pedestrian flow falls off in some areas. The Goad sketch plan of the layout of the shops provides a good starting point as this is backed up by a statistical analysis of retailer representation. Some of the potential sources of information are referred to in **Appendix B**.

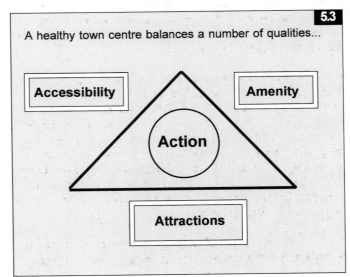

5.3

A healthy town centre balances a number of qualities...

Accessibility

Amenity

Action

Attractions

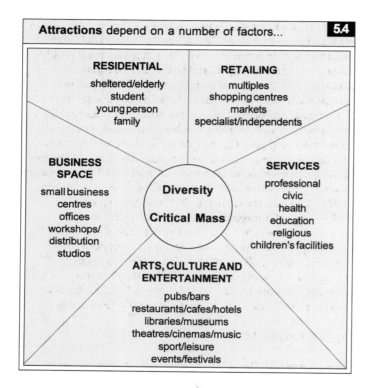

Attractions depend on a number of factors... **5.4**

RESIDENTIAL

sheltered/elderly
student
young person
family

RETAILING

multiples
shopping centres
markets
specialist/independents

BUSINESS SPACE

small business
centres
offices
workshops/
distribution
studios

Diversity

Critical Mass

SERVICES

professional
civic
health
education
religious
children's facilities

ARTS, CULTURE AND ENTERTAINMENT

pubs/bars
restaurants/cafes/hotels
libraries/museums
theatres/cinemas/music
sport/leisure
events/festivals

5.31   Diversity must be balanced by **critical mass**, that is the concentration of enough activity to give customers visible choice. For example, there may need to be three or four places to eat in a street before it becomes a destination for an evening out. At times attractions fail because they are not readily visible. There may also be thresholds to decline, where the loss of one attraction can lead to the loss of others who were dependent to some extent on its drawing power. In smaller towns, the tipping point may be reached through the

loss of an in town centre supermarket or basic food shops, whilst in the larger centres it may be the loss of variety or a department store that has a significant effect, such as Marks and Spencer. A problem can also arise when too many shop windows in the heart of the town are either vacant or replaced by non-retail and static shop fronts such as banks and building societies.

5.32   **Accessibility:** This refers to *how easy it is to reach the centre*, and is far broader than most people think (Exhibit 5.5). It has two main aspects. The first, **mobility**, refers to the time and cost of getting to the centre from where people live. It is important to promote passenger-friendly public transport (51% of respondents to our survey, including 88% of major city respondents, rating this as one of five key factors for town centre health) and ease of access for those arriving on foot or by bike. However, there is no escaping that the majority of people spending money in major stores (outside city centres) increasingly arrive by car (as retailers like Marks and Spencers know well from their research). 39% of all respondents, but only 25% of those in suburban centres, thought good traffic management and signage was one of the top five factors for health. Striking a balance between the needs of car-borne travellers and a high standard of amenity is extremely difficult and depends on the situation. Research for the London Planning Advisory Committee suggests that the relative success of competing centres is influenced by the ease of parking, even though more people may arrive by bus and foot (LPAC 1994). Large cities and historic towns can do far more to promote the use of park and ride or rapid transit than smaller towns for example, and also need to plan routes where cyclists can ride safely. In contrast, in market towns free short-stay parking may be needed to compete with out-of-town centres. Suburban centres also need to provide readily accessible short stay surface parking if they are to retain a good choice of shops.

5.33   However, access is about more than providing ample and convenient car parking, though 85% of respondents to our survey, but only 66% of those in major cities, thought this one of the top five factors. It also depends upon local accessibility or **linkages**. Parking, bus and rail stations need to

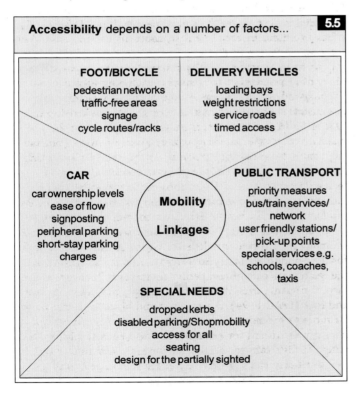

Accessibility depends on a number of factors...   **5.5**

FOOT/BICYCLE
pedestrian networks
traffic-free areas
signage
cycle routes/racks

DELIVERY VEHICLES
loading bays
weight restrictions
service roads
timed access

CAR
car ownership levels
ease of flow
signposting
peripheral parking
short-stay parking
charges

Mobility

Linkages

PUBLIC TRANSPORT
priority measures
bus/train services/
network
user friendly stations/
pick-up points
special services e.g.
schools, coaches,
taxis

SPECIAL NEEDS
dropped kerbs
disabled parking/Shopmobility
access for all
seating
design for the partially sighted

be easily found and well integrated with the core of the town centre. Linkages relate not just to ease of passage without barriers, steps or subways - a crucial factor for many people using town centres with disabilities, heavy shopping or young children - but also ease of navigation, as in the sense of knowing where to go for particular attractions or facilities. Good signage or being able to cross roads easily and safely is one aspect. A useful series of leaflets from the Pedestrians Association point out that people ask for 'a central area that will be a pleasure to visit, a journey that compares in ease and cost with those to other places out-of-town, and a convenient stopping place when they get there' (Pedestrians Association, 1993). Our case study of Woolwich found that a major problem was the quality of what has been termed 'spatial integration', essentially the linkages between the pedestrianised shopping centre and the surrounding catchment area (Hillier 1984). Though the amount of research is very limited compared with say Germany, there is evidence from places such as Leicester and Chichester that exclusion of the car is associated with retail success when there is a network of pedestrian streets.
(Edward Erdman 1990).

5.34   **Amenity:** The third component of a healthy centre refers to *how pleasant a centre is as a place to be* (Exhibit 5.6). Many studies have shown the importance of a clean and attractive environment, (one of the five key factors for a healthy centre according to 92% of respondents to our survey), but what precisely does it mean? Simply restoring shop fronts or improving fascias have little impact if the town as a whole seems unwelcoming. They may not even be noticed if the centre is busy enough, though they add to the visitors' experience. However, poorly maintained places generally are a deterrent. In some American cities, cleanliness has been linked with **security** through 'crime and grime' initiatives (security was considered one of the top five factors by only 28% of our respondents but 37% of those in industrial towns). A centre that is perceived as dirty or dangerous acts as a deterrent, even if it perhaps scores well in other features. Sometimes total exclusion of cars, particularly at night, makes places seem more threatening.

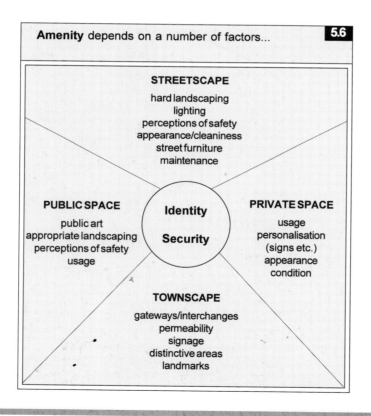

5.35 Amenity is also about image and **identity**. A common complaint is that 'all shopping centres look the same'. A town centre has the opportunity to overcome this by emphasising factors such as heritage and making the most of what have been termed `quality streets',(TEST 1987). This can range from refurbishing old buildings to ensuring that new buildings and open spaces are designed to be memorable and to respect their context. It can also include promotional or other events, which use the centre as a stage or backdrop. The experience most people have of a town is largely based on the smaller things; these range from interesting looking shops and streets, and a friendly attitude, to high standards in public facilities such as toilets and bus shelters. Attention to quality at every level may have a far greater impact than conspicuous expenditure on a few large scale projects, such as repaving; in urban design terms it is usually the case that 'less is more.'

5.36 **Action:** The fourth component of health is concerned with *making things happen*. Fundamentally, success in improving a town centre depends on **organisational capacity** and reflects the ability of the local authority and all the other 'actors', such as major retailers, small businesses, and voluntary associations, to work together to promote the good of the town - applying what is often termed community spirit or civic pride. In all of the successful towns that we looked at in our case studies, what stood out was the existence of a local authority who gave priority to its town centre. There was not always a town centre manager, but in every case there was a dedicated team who had the well-being of the centre at heart. Action also depends on **resourcing**. Experience generally suggests that if the will is there, the funding will follow. If the public sector takes a lead, the businesses are more likely to play their part.

6 devising town centre strategies

- With increased competition, all towns need to be paying more attention to the health of their centres, which can be at least as challenging as developing a new shopping centre.

- Success depends on resolving strategic issues, first tackling the basic complaints and then tackling the economic and social as well as the physical problems by pursuing an incremental approach.

- Profiles are needed to monitor how the town centre is doing and to identify where improvements may be needed, making full use of comparisons with other towns.

- Well-structured events can be used to draw different interests together and build consensus, around a 'shared vision'.

- Strategies and action programmes should be used to co-ordinate different council departments and outside interests, and to focus resources where they will have most effect.

- Dedicated management, including town centre teams and development trusts, as well as town centre managers, can enable all the interests to work together.

'In partnership with the private sector, property owners, infrastructure agencies and the community, the local planning authority should assess the role of the town centre and the scope for change, renewal and diversification. They should identify and build on the essential qualities of the centre and seek to ensure that it meets the needs of the community it serves'.

Planning Policy Guidance

6.01   Faced with the strong challenges of private sector investment out-of-town and limited public sector funding, town centres large and small are having to pay much more attention to making the most of their particular resources. This chapter deals with the strategic choices facing many centres, then reviews how to devise profiles, vision statements, strategies and action programmes, and finally assesses what kind of management structure is needed.

Strategic choices

6.02   Almost every town is now facing stronger competition, and this requires the public and private sectors to work together over time. This is not easy, as the functions of a town centre cross most organisational boundaries, while the private sector is diffuse and may also be apathetic, or even hostile. The task of improving or revitalising town centres can, therefore, be as demanding as building a new shopping centre, with the extra complications of mixed ownership and funding.

6.03   There is a 'menu' of possible initiatives or programmes that can be used to revitalise a town centre, but what is possible and appropriate will depend on the situation, and it is important not to be driven by fashion or simply copying what the next town is doing. The local authority survey sought to find out the state of the art in terms of what local authorities had adopted or were proposing. There were great differences between the types of town, as might be expected, with the larger places tending to adopt a much broader programme than the smaller centres (Exhibit 6.1).

6.04   What stands out is that the most popular initiatives, which had been adopted by over two-thirds, were what might

---

6.1

There are over 30 different types of programmes that can be used to revitalise a town centre...

ATTRACTIONS
- a variety of multiple retailers
- good, friendly specialist shops
- town centre restaurants and cafes
- distinctive markets
- regular events
- education and health facilities
- cinemas, theatres, art centres or cultural zones
- libraries and museums
- town centre housing
- offices and business centres
- public service facilities

ACCESSIBILITY
- a comprehensive signing programme
- safe, convenient car parks
- pedestrian priority areas/traffic calming
- mini-bus/rapid transit systems
- public transport interchanges
- access for all
- distinctive gateways
- bus priority measures

AMENITY
- frequent cleaning
- effective lighting
- hard landscaping improvements
- greening/soft landscaping
- shop-front/building refurbishment
- temporary use of empty shops
- crime prevention initiatives
- removal of clutter

ACTION
- a strategic action programme
- development partnerships
- town centre management
- regular monitoring

be called the 'hygiene factors' - safe, convenient car parks, environmental improvements, frequent cleansing and pedestrian priority areas. In contrast measures to improve and create attractions, such as improving the range of shops or promoting regular events, had only been adopted by a little over a third, though these were more likely to have been adopted by vibrant centres than by declining ones. There were a whole range of initiatives, such as making use of education and training facilities and health centres, to broaden activities where there were very few examples. There were also a number of measures, such as traffic calming and crime prevention, where pro-grammes have been proposed, but not yet adopted in many cases. As many people are unaware of the full range of possibilities it is likely that a check-list will spark off ideas.

6.05   Discussions with town centre managers established that there are a number of common problems which arise when efforts are launched to improve a town centre. Some are to do with how to produce demonstrable success in order to maintain support, and also with 'what to do after the honeymoon is over'. Others are to do with improving the town's image, and, for example, securing positive publicity in the media. But above all there is the problem of securing collaboration and support from people who work for different departments and agencies and have different agendas, when budgets are very limited.

6.06   The health check technique outlined in **Appendix B** can provide a way through the maze. It also offers opportunities for bringing people together, so that they appreciate the problems and end up with a 'shared vision.' It is essential both to appreci-ate the range of options and also to relate these to local concerns. Methods can range from voluntary effort or in-house studies to the use of specialist consultants to provide an outside or expert view sometimes supplemented by surveys.

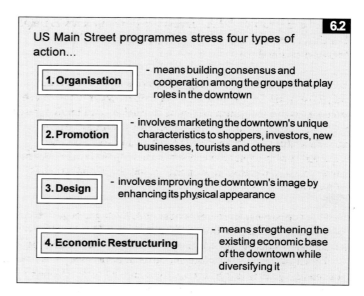

US Main Street programmes stress four types of action...

1. **Organisation** - means building consensus and cooperation among the groups that play roles in the downtown

2. **Promotion** - involves marketing the downtown's unique characteristics to shoppers, investors, new businesses, tourists and others

3. **Design** - involves improving the downtown's image by enhancing its physical appearance

4. **Economic Restructuring** - means strengthening the existing economic base of the downtown while diversifying it

6.07   Our research found that many of the most successful town centres are those where a clearly-defined strategy has been developed that considers not only land use, but also how the centre can best serve the needs of its communities. However initiated, the most successful strategies and 'visions' are those that are **realistic**, that is matched to available opportunities and resources, **positive** in the sense of providing a lead, and **shared** in the sense that people and organisations with different interests are willing to support them.

6.08   The organic nature of centres and their multiplicity of roles means that centres often have a choice of futures over time, albeit within national economic restrictions. Should retailing be expanded or should other functions be introduced or developed in the centre? Should the quality of parts of the centre be improved? What impact are developments in neighbouring centres or out-of-town likely to have and how can these be planned for?

6.09 In many centres strategic decisions need to be taken, recognising the trends that are irreversible. Market towns are unlikely to see the return of livestock markets and English resorts will not restore the mass two-week family holiday. Having appraised the performance of the centre and looked at the experience of comparable centres, local authorities and others involved must develop appropriate plans and management initiatives.

6.10 Success very much depends on reversing a negative image, and creating a climate of confidence. This involves both some 'early wins' or pilot projects, as well as more fundamental or flagship schemes. Nothing succeeds like success. However, it also means getting to grips with the elements or components of a healthy town centre. The starting point should be removing grievances, or tackling the hygiene factors before moving on to higher level concerns. In the course of the research we looked through countless plans and reports on town centres, and were struck by how many seemed to be ineffectual because they either tackled one aspect only, such as environmental improvements, or alternatively tried to cover too much.

6.11 Experience in the USA has shown the need to consider the economic and cultural or social as well as the physical aspects of a town centre. Thus, the US National Main Street Center's manuals and training programmes have been devised to deal with the four aspects of promotion, design, economic restructuring and organisation, as these tend to require different kinds of expertise and involve different groups of people (Exhibit 6.2).

Examples of strategic approaches

- In Birmingham, there has been a concerted effort to improve the city's image as an international city, including downgrading the Inner Ring Road so that pedestrians can cross at grade (or on the level), and promoting a series of distinct quarters linked by a network of traffic free streets.

- In Maidstone, the county town and one of a number of town centre management initiatives supported by Kent County Council, a strategy has been put together by a partnership with major companies to make the town somewhere special, instead of 'any town'.

- In Nottingham, a long-term strategy has made the City Centre feel quite continental, with cafes opening on to a network of pedestrian streets, which has been part funded by the European Commission. Town centre management is ensuring that the bus and car park operators all play their part in making the centre attractive and safe to visit.

- In smaller towns, such as Petersfield in Hampshire, concerted improvements linked to new by-passes have added to the amenity of the town, and have helped retain trade in town. In other towns, such as Beverley in Yorkshire or Abingdon in Oxfordshire, efforts have concentrated on providing housing in town rather than going for retail expansion.

- In Worcester, along with a number of centres that are now regarded as 'historic towns', the character has been enhanced with specialist shops and places to eat. New developments have been carefully integrated to reinforce the town's appeal, for example, combining a new bus station with a splendid covered shopping centre.

- In Bexleyhealth, the local authority succeeded in creating a major town centre out of a small town in part by making parking very easy. They not only attracted major retailers to expand, but also secured the relocation of a building society's headquarters plus a four star hotel, a ten-pin bowling centre and a new police headquarters.

6.12 An extensive research project on *Revitalizing Downtown* contrasted the 'incremental' with the 'catalyst' approach, where reliance is placed on a single large-scale project. It found frequent failure of the catalyst approach when applied to a sharply declining downtown in a region of poor economic performance.

'The selection of an appropriate strategy for the economic condition of the downtown and its region proved to be a fundamental reason - as important as the questions of who was running the programme, the appropriateness of the financial incentives and the Government regulations associated with the strategy, for the success or failure of the revitalisation strategy'.

National Trust for Historic Preservation (1988),
Revitalizing Downtown.

In Britain too, whatever the structure, and there is no one right answer, successful town centres or those that have reversed decline seem to follow a process which focuses attention and resources on the strategic issues.

Profile and positioning

6.13 What successful places seem to have in common is that they have gone through a process, often painful, out of which an agreed town centre strategy has emerged, and this typically involves a number of stages. Assessing the current performance of the centre is essential to devising an informed and appropriate strategy. One of the principal aims of the new planning guidance on town centres is to encourage planning authorities to provide "positive policies in plans to encourage

6.3

Key issues for profiles are...

- what kind of town centre is it and what are the main functions it performs?

- where do the customers come from and how have they been changing in terms, for examples, of socio-economic group, spending power, race, age and sex?

- how do customers get to the town centre?

- which are the main competitors?

- how well does it compare with its competition and also with similar towns elsewhere?

- what are the town centre's main strengths and weaknesses?

- how is the town perceived by different groups?

uses that will contribute to town centre vitality and viability". Having assessed the various functions of the town centre and their relative strengths, the opportunities for "change, renewal and diversification" should be clearer. In determining the needs of the centre and the community, and the options for the future, planning authorities must address the interests of existing and potential investors in the centre. PPG6 draws attention to the "dynamic nature of the retail industry". A positive town centre strategy will recognise these changes and future trends and by working with the private sector will seek to balance the developments in retailing, for instance, with the needs of the town centre and the community it serves.

6.14 The first stage is to understand what kind of town one is dealing with, and where it is currently positioned. There is a wealth of published information to be tapped, and there is no need for local authorities to be at a disadvantage compared

Key issues for health checks...

- has the town been losing customers significantly, and if so where and why?

  - footfall
  - (or turnover indices from a major multiple)
  - yield
  - multiple ranking
  - views of anchor retailer
  - traders surveys
  - shoppers surveys

- how does the town compare with its main competitors and is action underway in areas where there are weaknesses?

  - strengths
  - weaknesses
  - opportunities
  - threats

with private businesses. The indicators proposed in PPG6 and discussed in Chapter 5 should provide more objective means of making such assessments, and of comparing the performance of a particular centre with similar centres. The experience of similar towns can also provide ideas and lessons for action and help identify alternative futures. Thus Leicester and Bradford are two centres where decisions need to be taken as to what their future roles should be. Should they seek to reverse the decline in their ranking in the *Shopping Centres of Great Britain* classification (Hillier Parker 1991a) and, if so, how can they plan and effectively manage a retail recruitment strategy? Or should they seek to promote other functions, for example by attracting more people, such as students, to live near the city centre? (Exhibit 6.3).

6.15   The second stage is to review the statistical and other factual information that can provide a **profile** of the town and

its centre, and how they are changing. The profile should include factors such as the population size nature and change, main economic functions, the town's location in relation to competing centres, and major initiatives just completed, underway or planned that could have a significant effect on the town centre. Many local authorities will already have this information available, perhaps published by their economic development department. For others, much is available through Goad, (particularly Statistical Summary and Town Focus reports), the Unit for Retail Planning Information (URPI) or from OPCS publications. These then need to be analysed and conclusions drawn on each of the key issues.

6.16   The analysis of performance should then be taken a step further by considering each of the elements of a healthy town centre set out above. This could be done in a number of ways, and in the regional seminars and case studies undertaken as part of the research we tried a variety of assessment and scoring systems. However, we believe that the most practical approach is to adopt a system already much used by consultants and with which many local authorities and town centre managers are familiar. This makes use of a **SWOT analysis**, that is Strengths, Weaknesses, Opportunities and Threats, for each of the four elements of attractions, accessibility, amenity and action, and their underlying components.

6.17   The process of assessing performance provides a good opportunity for bringing different interests together. The SWOT analysis allows for identification of good and poor aspects of a centre, both current and potential. Though it is to an extent subjective, our research suggests it is easier and more meaningful to determine whether a particular feature can be regarded as a strength or weakness in comparison with other towns than to decide where on a scoring or ranking

Worcester: monitoring space in use

The City of Worcester, which has a population of 75,000, produces a variety of pieces of information on its centre. An *Annual Retail Monitor* produced by the Technical Services Department seeks "to aid potential investors, researchers and retailers who are considering Worcester as a possible location". It provides details on local planning policy, on the regional context of the city's retailing, on the retail structure in the centre, on recent developments and the historic heritage of the city, as well as details on access and servicing. The City Council policy on development is summarised. The monitor also provides regular information reviewed on the usage and amount of retail floorspace and details on pedestrian flow in the centre.

The Retail Monitor is one of a number of publications on the city centre that include maps of ground floor occupiers, policy on conservation and on living over the shop. The monitor includes a series of contact names and numbers, as well as relevant maps, tables and a brief profile of the population of the area. It offers a source for more detailed information and the opportunity for users to request the inclusion of other information in future editions.

scale it should be placed. We believe this is best undertaken by a number of people together, at the very least including the different departments in a local authority, perhaps co-ordinated by the town centre manager or the local planning officer.

6.18   The management arrangement should depend on the size and type of town. However, the process would typically include a number of representatives of the private and voluntary sectors in the town, such as major shop managers, town centre employers, transport operators, the Chamber of Commerce or Trade and local community, religious or educational

representatives, and perhaps local experts such as the Crime Prevention Design Advisor. This is called in some places a **town forum**. Those attending the session should have previously been provided with a copy of the town profile with sufficient comparative data, either with other centres or over time, to make use of the figures. Where there are strong disagreements, further research may be needed, for example drawing on comparisons with similar or competing places. While the forum may only meet occasionally, some process for feedback and ongoing communication, such as a newsletter, is essential once the process has begun.

6.19   The process may also involve further research, such as an environmental **audit** or **surveys** of important groups. An excellent source of information is to undertake a traders survey which can both find out how well the independent businesses are doing and also establish their views on priorities. Similarly, a survey of shoppers, can find out where they come from, how they get there, what they like and dislike and what improvements are needed. Where resources are limited, community organisations may be able to help, and surveys can also be undertaken in association with local schools. Appendix B provides a list of the factors that could be assessed in a health check, many of which could also be quantified if resources allow. (Exhibit 6.4)

6.20   Health checks are particularly important when a major new development has been proposed. Whilst we would recommend that the key indicators are monitored on an annual basis, with perhaps Summer and Winter pedestrian counts, the SWOT analysis would normally happen every two years as part of the overall management of the town centre. However, when a new development is proposed that could potentially harm the vitality and viability of the town centre,

6.5

Key issues for visions are...

- what league can the centre play in?

- what makes a town or city centre of this type successful?

- what is special about this centre in terms of attractions, accessibility and amenity?

- how is the town centre made up?

- how well are the different areas performing, economic, physical and socio/cultural

- what are the main opportunities and threats in terms of making the centre a more vital and viable place?

a special analysis should be undertaken. Further analysis may then be called for to assess the **capacity** of the centre against the changing market, and the likely impact of the new development, taking account of likely travel patterns and modal splits.

6.21   Profiles and health checks should be updated annually in centres that are at risk so that the centre's performance is kept under review. They can form a valuable input into the process of drawing up a new strategy for the town centre. They can also be used in preparing a handbook or prospectus for the town to help in attracting and retaining investment, as in Worcester, for example.

Visions and priorities

6.22   Having determined what kind of place the town centre is, the next part of the process is to look at what it could become or 'what league it should be playing in'. This means developing a

shared vision for the centre that at the same time needs to be practical to be convincing, readily comprehensible to encourage people to contribute, and robust enough to survive in an uncertain world (Exhibit 6.5).

6.23   To be a shared vision, it is essential that various parties with an interest in the centre have an input into its formulation, and this is an evolving process. One proven way of doing this is through questionnaires or other consultative processes. Thus through the Summer of 1992, Marks and Spencer sponsored an exhibition called Going to Town is Coming to Town that toured over 30 towns and cities. In each case general exhibits on the benefits of town centres were accompanied by specific exhibits relating to the town centre in question. Comment sheets were provided for local people to make known their views on the centre. In some cases such as Margate, this was linked to the development of a new strategy and a series of consultative workshops.

6.24   As part of the process of mobilising investment, more and more towns are not only publishing strategies or commissioning consultants' reports, but are also organising events to bring different interests together around a shared vision. Before successful change can take place key people have to 'see in their mind's eye' what is proposed, and feel involved. Reports, however well-written or illustrated, are not enough. Yet public meetings are often counter-productive as they can reinforce a sense of conflict and division.

6.25   Various types of events have been organised which may be referred to **'action planning'**, and which are derived from experience in the USA. These have three features in common. First, they bring leading representatives of the main interests together, both public and private.

Birmingham: creating a vision through action planning

Birmingham City Centre suffered from a declining industrial base and an image of being dominated by the car. The Council decided to promote a new role for the centre as an international city with flagship projects of an International Convention Centre and the Arena, and these secured major grants from the EC. However, a related problem was how to improve the quality of the city centre. A symposium was organised by consultants in 1988. Key people running the city were joined for two days by experts from all over the world to brainstorm the problems and opportunities. This symposium took place at Highbury Hall, and the report was adopted as the strategy for the city centre under the name of the Highbury Initiative.

The resulting strategy was implemented soon after through the promotion of a series of quarters with distinctive identities, linked on foot. The 'concrete collar' of the inner ring road was broken, and is being turned into a 'boulevard'. The first stage was the creation of Centenary Square, linked through to the Central Library and beyond by sinking the road. The next step was the exclusion of traffic from a large part of New Street, and another new open space, Victoria Square, was created around a grand fountain. One distinctive feature is a succession of commissioned sculptures, paid for through a 'Percent for Art' policy.

A follow-up symposium was held a year and a half later to involve the business community further and build a sense of partnership and confidence. This led to support for local improvement associations and city centre management, together with a design study to produce planning briefs for major sites. Evidence of success can be seen from a survey by DTZ of property managers throughout the country which showed Corporation Street as now the third most profitable location for retailing, only beaten by two out-of-town centres. Also New Street is much busier since it was pedestrianised.

However, there are divided views over whether the concentration of effort on the city centre has adversely affected Council investment in the city as a whole.

Second they involve both 'key note' presentations to raise people's sights and small group workshops to share views. Third, they result in the publication of a report or broadsheet that aims to secure wide-spread support and a high profile. The format of these events can vary widely from the use of small teams of professionals, as in Urban Design Action Teams, to two-day symposia (Urban Design Group Quarterly 1994). The end product may include a visualisation of the possibilities or it may be sufficient to draw on examples from elsewhere (and here study tours can be a great help). Action planning events help to set 'agendas' and may lead on to more detailed work on the problems and opportunities that were highlighted as critical to the centre's future. To be effective the vision should be as brief as possible and it helps if it can be expressed as a slogan like *'Glasgow 's/Miles Better* ☺'. The key is finding the common interests on which consensus can be built.

Strategies and action programmes

6.26 Visions are of no real use if they cannot be turned into results. It is vital that there is the will and capacity to follow events up, to avoid raising expectations that are not fulfilled. Revitalising a centre that is in decline is not a rapid process; in many cases it may take continuous effort over a decade or more. Hence, it is essential that there are some 'early wins' that can enthuse consumers, businesses and investors whilst longer term projects are implemented. A strategy should, therefore, include a range of projects covering the economic, environmental, social and cultural needs of the centre. They may draw on audits of areas where there are particular problems or opportunities (Exhibit 6.6).

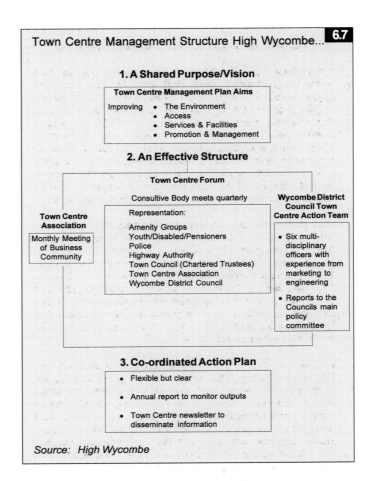

6.6

Key issues for strategies are...

- what are the strengths, weaknesses, opportunities and threats?

- why is the town centre important and what pressures is it facing?

- what are the main problems that affect the town's vitality and viability?

- what can be done in the short, medium (1-2 years), and longer term to improve the centre?

- who needs to do what in order that the opportunities are realised?

6.7

Town Centre Management Structure High Wycombe...

1. A Shared Purpose/Vision

Town Centre Management Plan Aims

Improving
- The Environment
- Access
- Services & Facilities
- Promotion & Management

2. An Effective Structure

Town Centre Forum

Consultive Body meets quarterly

Representation:

Amenity Groups
Youth/Disabled/Pensioners
Police
Highway Authority
Town Council (Chartered Trustees)
Town Centre Association
Wycombe District Council

Town Centre Association

Monthly Meeting of Business Community

Wycombe District Council Town Centre Action Team

- Six multi-disciplinary officers with experience from marketing to engineering

- Reports to the Councils main policy committee

3. Co-ordinated Action Plan

- Flexible but clear

- Annual report to monitor outputs

- Town Centre newsletter to disseminate information

Source: High Wycombe

6.27   Strategies and action programmes need to be produced and published periodically to attract resources and co-ordinate efforts. While 'vision' events can be excellent ways of involving people, strategies and action programmes need careful research and negotiation. However, a strategy that is commissioned by a group that brings together the key interests has a much greater chance of being implemented than a document emanating from within a single department or authority. Some places have a formal 'Forum', and a growing number are experimenting with different forms of public/private partnership (Michell, 1986). Thus, in Nottingham a dozen organisations and companies are represented on the city centre steering group, and in Tunbridge Wells over twice that number.

6.28   Town centre strategies are an important adjunct to the local Development Plan, as they deal with more complex issues than can be dealt with through land use plans alone. The end product may be quite short, but is best illustrated with maps, diagrams and tables. Appendices can provide details, such as costings. The strategy needs to cover not just physical improvements and measures to improve access, but also promotion and events, economic development and training, including retailer retention and recruitment. It should identify pilot projects for immediate action, such as holding a special event or improving cleansing, as well as flagship schemes, that is those that will turn the centre around. It is essential to set a timescale and identify the agency or people responsible.

Dedicated management

6.29   The final ingredient of the process for ensuring vital and viable centres is to have effective and dedicated management which is encouraged in PPG6, (paras 18, 19). There are now over 75 towns with town centre managers in place and many more with some form of town centre management. The choice of approach needs to reflect local circumstances. In some instances town centre management is an early result of the development of a vision and strategy for the centre, whilst in others it is the means by which the vision and strategy are developed. Whichever way around, it is important that any new initiative should from part of a clear strategy and this is best prepared before someone is employed to carry it out. If there is already a town centre manager in place he or she should make sure a strategy is drawn up in ways that bring different interests together.

6.30   Town centre management is important not only in that it helps to keep a strategy on course, but also because it can present a real face to local residents and businesses who might otherwise become disenchanted with progress. There is someone or some organisation responsible for fostering communications and co-ordinating improvements, just as there is in a large shopping centre. Town centre management can also have a positive impact on how a centre is perceived.

A number of leading retailers, Marks and Spencer, Boots, and WH Smith amongst them, have recognised this and have played an active role in promoting town centre management.

6.31   Most town centre managers are employed by the local authority, as in Nottingham and Newport; some by a partnership between the local authority and the Chamber of Commerce, as in Bath; and, in a few cases, by a private company. Nearly always there is a steering group or committee that brings together various interests in the centre. Successful towns do not always need a town centre manager and both Preston and High Wycombe, for example, decided not to follow that route. However, both have developed alternative systems of management that allow for continued monitoring of the centre, for consultation with key interest groups in the centre, and for bringing forward development proposals and other initiatives that would in other places be done by the town centre manager (Exhibit 6.7).

6.32   Town centre management is beginning to draw both on the experience of US towns and cities, particularly through the National Main Street Center, and on shopping centre management. The functions of a town centre manager can be summarised as being janitorial, managerial, and promotional (ATCM, 1992). **Janitorial** functions include attending to many of the priorities that are often overlooked in town centres: the general appearance and maintenance of the centre. Thus in Nottingham, as well as "litter free zones" and graffiti squads, a city centre ranger has been seconded who checks daily on maintenance requirements, putting right immediately what is within his ability and notifying larger jobs for priority action.

6.33   The **managerial** role involves co-ordinating the efforts of different department and agencies, and liaising with private

Maidstone: building and working in partnership

Maidstone is Kent's county town, but was regarded by many people as 'Any Town' following piecemeal development in the 1960s and traffic congestion. The initiative followed awareness of the town centre management concept, and a seminar on the future of the town centre in September 1990, organised by the Borough Council which drew 200 targeted guests. Discussions were held with key players about providing sponsorship. Consultants then worked on the leisure component and a key site, and this evolved into 'A Vision for Maidstone'. The town centre manager was appointed in December 1991 and a Charter of Partnership published in March 1992 at the formal launch of the initiative.

Maidstone Town Centre Management Initiative has now adopted some 17 different programmes that are improving the centre despite competition from out of town. Co-ordination is provided by a *Strategy for Action* that has been supported by a number of organisations. These include the Borough and County Councils, the Chamber of Commerce and six prominent local employers, including three retailers and a major insurance company. The strategy starts by putting Maidstone in context, then presents a basic vision based on the results of a SWOT analysis. The strategy contains five elements each of which involves a number of actions under the headings of improvements to the quality of life, access, communications and choices. An action plan sets out responsibilities and time scales.

The quality of the strategy and the commitment of the local partners was one of the reasons Maidstone became one of the few British winners of funding from the European Commission under the LIFE programme for an initiative to encourage public transport and reduce dependency on cars whilst maintaining the commercial viability of the town centre. This is worth £120,000 for three years, supplemented by part of the County's edge-of-town road programme which is being redirected as a result.

Maidstone's *Strategy for Action* includes a 42 point Action Programme

THE ACTION PLAN

Improvements in Quality of Life

PROJECT	AGENCY	TIMESCALE
Urban Design Framework (Earl St./Market Buildings. 1st stage works).	MBC KCC SA TCMI	February 1993
Urban Design Framework (High St./King Street, primary studies).	TCMI MBC KCC PS	Spring 1993
Planting improvement of entrance points to the town	MBC KCC	Spring 1993

Improvement in Access

PROJECT	AGENCY	TIMESCALE
Action on further pedestrianisation	MBC KCC TCMI	1993 onwards
Car park improvements	MBC	1992/1994
T.C. Traffic Management Action Plan	MBC KCC	1993/2003

Improvement in Communication

PROJECT	AGENCY	TIMESCALE
Continuing dialogue	TCM MBC KCC PS	ongoing
Action Plan Reviews	TCMI	monthly
T.C.M. to act as consultee	TCMI MBC KCC	ongoing

Improvement in Choices

PROJECT	AGENCY	TIMESCALE
Disabled Facilities	MBC	1993
Shopping Guide	TCMI	1993
Discouraging cheap letting	TCMI MBC PS	ongoing

Source: Maidstone Town Centre Management Initiative,

sector interests. As direct employees and budgets are always restricted, the skills are those essentially of a project manager. It is significant perhaps that in the USA, initiatives in small towns seem to involve much more voluntary effort, and are typically co-ordinated by someone with a background in the voluntary sector. In Britain many towns are designating a planner as town centre manager, but some are recruiting people from the private sector and a few are creating teams.

6.34 **Promotional** aspects are also an important element. It is essential to market the centre through staging events, special promotions and through co-ordinating existing initiatives, whilst at the same time keeping local businesses and communities informed on latest initiatives. In Preston and Chippenham, for example, new traffic management schemes have been explained through colourful and helpful leaflets containing clear maps or visualisations of the new schemes and details on the restrictions introduced. In Nottingham this has been taken further with regular meetings between the city centre manager and both retailers and contractors in order to keep disruption to a minimum. In Herne Bay, as in many places, a successful festival enabled local people to see the centre in a new way and was seen as the most distinctive part of the role of town centre management. Some towns have seen the value of setting up a company for this purpose. Not-for-profit bodies, such as development trusts or building preservation trusts, can also be useful, particularly in smaller towns, in bringing different interests together around a major project, as for example in Stroud, (AHF 1993, DTA 1994).

Brigg: employing a project officer

Many small towns lack the capacity to turn themselves around and use consultants or project teams to provide the necessary boost. Brigg, near Scunthorpe, with a population of 5,500, established a project team in 1989, following an environmental audit by the Civic Trust at the request of Glanford Borough Council. The strategy for revival was based on upgrading the environment following the development of a new road system. Different grant regimes were mobilised by the project team and small scale investment was stimulated. This promoted substantial positive publicity (some 1,500 column inches) and attracted over 3,000 visitors to the project shop in a year. As a result, co-operation improved between existing organisations, such as the Chamber of Trade, and a Civic Society was established.

With a project budget of £50,000 per annum, it has been estimated that the private sector invested some £3 million in property refurbishment in the first three years of the project. The public investment was about £9 million, largely due to the cost of a new link road to open up a business park and remove traffic from the town centre, as well as the refurbishment of several public buildings. However, lasting success is not easy. The project officer comments on "the desperate nature of short term core funding" and notes that "the ultimate test of a project's success is the way the community feels about itself."

Ilford: introducing town centre management

Ilford was one of the first town centres to have a Town Centre Manager, a post which is combined with commercial liaison. The appointment was made in 1986, after work had started on a major scheme to upgrade the town centre with a new relief road, a pedestrianised precinct, (including a new town clock) and a 300,000 sq ft new shopping centre. The management functions were seen as involving promotion, management and development. Specific town developments undertaken have included the establishment of a Park and Ride Scheme at Christmas, a shopmobility scheme for the disabled, programmes of entertainment in the pedestrian precinct, and economic monitoring of the centre's health. There is a Town Centre Working Group that meets monthly bringing together officers whose remit covered the town centre, which reports to a Town Centre Executive of Chief Officers. There are close links with the traders associations.

7   types of town centre

- Though centres are often classified through a retail hierarchy, this gives only a partial picture of the type of centre, and the terms are often mis-applied.

- A number of quantitatively-based methods are available, but all have their limitations.

- A system of five main types of town centre has been used, which is practical and enables useful comparisons to be made. They are market towns, industrial towns, suburban centres, metropolitan cities, and resorts and historic towns.

'Cities are amalgams of buildings and people. They are inhabited settings from which daily rituals - the mundane and the extraordinary, the random and the stage - derive their validity. In the urban artifact and its mutations are condensed continuities of time and place. The city is the ultimate memorial of our struggles and glories: it is where the pride of the past is set on display.'

Spiro Kostof :
The City Shaped.

7.01   The remaining chapters of this report are concerned with Good Practice. The aim is to highlight examples of initiatives, actions and processes identified through the local authority questionnaire, the case studies and the team's knowledge of other centres to provide some examples that could be applied more generally. However, we are extremely aware of the dangers of simply seeking to replicate what has been done in one town in another when this may be in-appropriate. This chapter, therefore, considers the possible roles of a town centre, examines some existing classifications of towns, then proposes a revised classification based on five archetypes that describe most town centres. Finally, the results of our local authority survey are described in more detail. The following chapters then look at issues and good practice for the main types of centre (though a number of these have wider applications).

The functions of town centres

7.02   Town centres are complex entities with a variety of functions that have developed over time, which distinguishes them from out-of-town developments that tend to be mono or possibly bi-functional. Though retailing is still the domi-nant function of nearly all UK centres, evidence from the US suggests that it should not be assumed this will always be the case. Whilst it is by no means certain that UK centres will follow the American pattern, it is important when thinking about the future of centres that all the various functions are taken into account, including their roles as transport inter-changes, centres for arts, culture and entertainment, places to live or visit.

7.03   The variety of functions identified in Chapter 2 makes classifying town centres difficult. However, because retailing underpins the viability and vitality of most towns, and the fact that in some towns it is the function most at risk, it is a good place to start. It is also the easiest function to obtain information on. The conventional ways of classifying town centres are in terms of their retail function and also where they draw their customers from, which some call the retail hierarchy (Davies 1989). Retail location is dominated by two conflicting forces: the desire to minimise travel time, which leads to a dispersal of shops amongst the population versus the desire to minimise search time, which leads to the clustering of shops selling comparison goods in centres. This has led to a division of shopping centres into **convenience** shopping such as food and newspapers, where ease of access is paramount, and **comparison** shopping such as fashion and furnishings, where the desire for choice takes precedence over the desire to minimise journey time.

7.04   The number of comparison multiple retailers in a centre has been used to develop a ranking of over 800 town centres, and to classify them into a number of categories that essentially distinguish between **regional** and **district centres** (Reynolds 1992). The ranking provides an indication of the main type of retail function in a particular town centre. It also provides an insight into how a town centre is perceived by some of the key investors - the multiple retailers.

7.05   Smaller centres, such as market towns and suburban centres, that do not provide a specialist function tend to be classified as district centres, and depend on convenience shopping for their main business. Convenience shopping accounts for roughly half of consumer expenditure and has remained relatively static overall. However, superstores (usually with 25,000 sq. ft gross floor area plus parking) are changing the picture; smaller supermarkets, butchers and bakers are closing down and food is bought outside town centres or on the edge of towns, along with other products such as toiletries. Convenience is increasingly confined to small neighbourhood shops or petrol stations that stay open all hours.

7.06   Regional centres are distinguished by serving a catchment population of at least 100,000, more usually 250,000 and above. They contain stores with sales areas of over 10,000 square feet compared to the standard shop unit of barely 2,000 square feet. Regional centres rely on shoppers from a wide catchment who might individually only visit once a month or less, and these centres are, therefore, more **externally dependent**. In the 1989 *Shopping Centres of Great Britain*, listing 160 centres were classified as regional and 660 as district. However the terms have come to be used somewhat loosely and often inappropriately. The terms national, major, district and local may be helpful in describing centres that form part of a network in a conurbation(LPAC 1994).

7.07   Over the past decade a third type of shopping has emerged which has been called **specialist** or leisure shopping, and which is found particularly in historic towns. Here a trip to shop is combined with enjoying the town and its visitor attractions and perhaps a meal or a drink. This desire to combine shopping with tourism or a fun day out has produced a significant growth in multiple retailer representation in many historic towns, which often already had a broad range of independent and specialist shops, Chester being a classic example. Some coastal resorts, such as Brighton and Southport, have benefited from this phenomenon and have become fashionable shopping centres.

7.08   However, the type and size of retailing function alone cannot describe a town centre. Bath and Sheffield, Oldham and Bury St Edmunds, Hackney and Northallerton are pairs of centres with similar rankings in terms of number of multiples, but great differences in other respects, and on the whole the

experience of one is unlikely to be relevant to the other. A further drawback to the retail hierarchy as a means of classifying town centres as a whole is that it appears not to be well understood by local authority planning officers. Nearly half the respondents to our survey placed their centre in a different classification from that identified in the latest multiple ranking, and this is not surprising as most centres perform different roles for different groups of people.

Existing classifications

7.09   As a town centre's potential is greatly influenced by the nature of its catchment area, we explored a number of ways of classifying by catchment area before coming up with the system we have used in this report. The Bartlett School considered the various existing classifications of towns in terms of their main characteristics. The most thorough work on classifying catchment areas has been undertaken by the Centre for Urban and Regional Development Studies (CURDS) at the University of Newcastle (Champion 1990). This used Census and employment data to come up with a 19-fold classification of the 280 Local Labour Market Areas in the UK, which distinguishes between northern and southern centres. However, whilst it is extremely helpful in differentiating between types of town, we concluded that it is less so in identifying similar town centres. It is limiting in that there are obviously significantly more town centres than Local Labour Market Areas, and this leads to many smaller towns being classified in terms of their dominant neighbour. Also it has too many categories to be readily used. We therefore looked further.

7.10   Other classifications considered included work by John Craig, which again draws on Census and socio-economic data to produce some 28 clusters that boil down to ten groups within six families and these are usefully brought together in an edition of Built Environment on *Rating Places* (Breheny 1989). The Office of Population Census and Statistics uses an eight-fold classification, which is perfectly manageable, but which does not distinguish between scale of town centre (Leeds and Halifax are in the same category for example) (OPCS, 1990). There are also a host of studies into various aspects of the quality of life, which rate towns basically in terms of their attractiveness as places to live. However, they cover too broad an area to be of much use in assessing town centres.

7.11 Many other sources of data are complex. For example the report for the DoE on *Developing Indicators to Assess the Potential for Urban Regeneration* puts forward 47 different indicators in six categories, many of which are revealing, but not easy to weigh up (DoE 1992d). A few composite indices have been prepared, like the Local Enterprise Activity Potential (LEAP), which enable an assessment to be made about how well a centre is doing against a yardstick based on its basic character-istics or profile, but they provide only limited insight into town centre types.

7.12 Research revealed the wealth of data that was held by commercial information sources, and which is regularly used by major retailers in making location and expansion decisions. This includes data on purchasing practices, which can also be clustered into 'life-style' patterns, which indicate the kinds of shops and services that are likely to be in demand. For example, one classification groups urban areas into 25 different categories, made up of ten different lifestyles, from the 'affluent minority' to 'under privileged Britain', while another has no less than 56 different consumer group profiles (CACI 1993). Much of the information is collected and analysed by market research organisations, such as Property Intelligence, Credit and Data Marketing Services, CACI, MOSAIC, Credit and Property Market Research, and is also obtainable through bodies such as URPI and CCN. Though

fascinating, the information available is in most cases too detailed, and sometimes too expensive for general application by local authorities.

7.13 The easiest way of classifying town centres would be in terms of population size, but this is not really practical within Britain. Though many retailers still judge potential market in terms of 'chimney pots', the population of local authority districts does not correspond to their catchment area. Further-more, unlike the USA or many Continental towns, our towns are generally clustered so closely together that their catchment areas overlap. While the major multiples, such as Marks and Spencers and Boots use sophisticated computer-based pro-grammes that show their catchment areas, based on store surveys and travel information as well as census data, the market varies according to the type of shop or centre, and so there is no single answer. Given the complexity and in many cases the limitations of applying town classifications to town centres, we have developed a simpler classification that seeks to group centres that share a number of characteristics and thus can learn most from each other.

The main types of town centre

7.14 To a large extent the problems and opportunities of town centres depend on three main variables. These are:

- **location**: where is the centre situated in relation to competing centres and to what extent is it restrained or assisted by geographical features?

- **history**: how did the town originate, develop and what have been its major economic roles over time?

- **population**: how many and what kind of people live in the town and its catchment area and how is this changing or expected to change?

7.15 Based on the these criteria and deliberately keeping to the fewest classifications possible that still illustrate distinct differences between the functions of centres and allow for the development of comparisons, we have identified five archetypes. Each of these could possibly be further broken down on the basis of size, affluence or specialisation, but we believe, that on the whole, sufficient similarities exist between the centres to make the distinctions chosen meaningful. We have chosen a system which approximates to the categories used in both the Census and the kind of approach developed by CURDS, reflecting differences in social class or life style.

7.16 There is a view that a distinction needs to be drawn between Northern and Southern towns and cities, as their population characteristics are so different. However, with most of the investors, developers and multiples operating nationally, and with national media, the differences are now much less marked within each type of town, though of course different regions may have a preponderance of a particular type of town.

7.17 The main types of town centres we identified (and which formed case studies) are (Exhibit 7.1):

- **Market Towns**: such as Horsham and Bury St.Edmunds;

- **Industrial Towns**: such as Newport and Preston;

- **Suburban Centres**: such as Woolwich and Bexleyheath;

- **Metropolitan Cities**: such as Sheffield and Nottingham; and

- **Resorts and Historic Towns:** such as Margate and Worcester.

7.18 A typical **Market Town** like Newmarket, Sleaford, Maidstone or Witney is relatively remote from other urban areas and has traditionally served the needs of a substantial rural community. Its character and functions reflect a development over centuries rather than a specific period. Its buildings are largely domestic in scale and its central street pattern has often been the same for several hundred years. The town is typically small; some have a population of 10,000, but this can rise to 50,000 and in some cases 75,000. However, it also serves a rural hinterland that may double or treble the population of those potentially dependent on the town. The population is likely to have grown substantially in the last decades, particularly if it is in Eastern or Southern England. Its residents have above average levels of car ownership and are on average more homogeneous, affluent and educated than the nation as a whole. It is likely to be a district shopping centre.

7.19 An **Industrial Town** like Newport, Bury or Wolverhampton is usually located close to other towns or to a Metropolitan City, which often may overshadow it. It grew rapidly in response to the needs of industry and most of the town centre buildings are nineteenth and twentieth century, often with a substantial amount of post-war redevelopment. Some of the buildings are on a substantial scale, reflecting both the functions and periods of prosperous development. The town has a population of between 25,000 and 200,000, though it may be smaller if it is a mining community. The proximity of other towns limits the extent of additional catchment population, and many residents have ready access to neighbouring and distant centres through the proximity of motorways. On the whole the population has fewer cars than the national average and is less affluent. The smaller towns are usually district shopping centres and the larger ones are regional.

7.20 The typical **Suburban Centre** like Peckham, Woolwich or the Belgrave Road area in Leicester is in close proximity both to similar centres and to the Metropolitan City centre. It has good public transport access to the city centre, which was probably the reason it was developed. It is on a major route out of the city and has to cope with substantial amounts of through traffic. Though retaining some evidence of an earlier identity, for the most part the built environment reflects development in the nineteenth and twentieth centuries. As a centre serving a city it has substantial amounts of housing rather than workspace immediately adjacent to the core retail area. Its catchment population overlaps others and ranges from extremely poor to very wealthy. This used to be dictated by distance from the centre, but the 1980s saw considerable development of housing for the more affluent in relatively central locations. If an inner city centre it is likely to have a high ethnic minority population, which may long have been a distinct feature. It has about a 50% chance of being a district or a regional shopping centre, though the terms do not really apply.

7.21 **Metropolitan Cities** like Manchester and Nottingham are few in number but have great impact as they dominate regions. They grew rapidly from the end of the eighteenth century as industry and associated services were developed. Only exceeded by what have been termed World Cities, which include London, the Metropolitan Cities provide a wide range of functions for large populations. Long dependent on access to labour and markets, they have the best road and rail links both regionally and nationally. The city centre buildings are large in scale, often with substantial nineteenth century developments, such as civic halls, exchanges, stations and theatres. Because of the size of the city centre many have a series of distinct quarters fulfilling different roles. Their district populations range from between 250,000 and one million, and have generally declined over the last decades. The centre provides a resource for a far larger catchment area in the surrounding region. All are either Metropolitan or Major Regional shopping centres.

7.22 **Resorts and Historic Towns** like Margate, Exeter and Norwich are classified together as to an extent not found in other towns they have attractions that depend on tourists. Thus they face a number of common problems and opportunities. The main draw in Historic Towns is heritage, on the back of which many have developed other attractions. In most resorts it was traditionally other attractions that drew people to the town, though as tastes and holiday habits change many are now seeking to emphasise their heritage, such as piers, theatres, and former grand hotels. Access in both kinds of town is difficult, with the sea imposing restrictions in resorts, and the nature of the built environment and street pattern providing difficulties in Historic Towns. Typically with populations from 20,000 upwards, the services offered in the centre provide in most cases for a national and in some an international catchment. It may be useful to think of towns in this category deriving 20% of their shoppers from outside their immediate catchment area. The resident population, whilst relatively affluent, may include substantial numbers of retired people, students, those in receipt of benefit or working in catering and related industries, all of whom have limited incomes. Many resorts and historic towns are regional shopping centres, often with stores that depend on the extended nature of the catchment population.

7.23 These categories illustrate types of centres with similar features which call for similar approaches. The organic nature of town centres means that some centres will always be changing and may have characteristics of more than one type. For instance, the centres of both Bradford and Leicester have many of the functions and populations of metropolitan cities and yet have become largely overshadowed by the growth of Leeds and Nottingham and may be better considered as industrial towns. Others, such as Halifax, may be shifting from being seen as industrial towns to having the attraction of historic towns, with a critical mass of visitor attractions.

Local authority survey results

7.24   Of the 336 usable replies obtained from local authority planning officers, we classified 130 as being from Market Towns, 116 from Industrial Towns, 36 from Suburban Centres, 46 from Resorts and Historic Towns and 8 from Metropolitan Cities, (representing 80% of all such centres in England and Wales) (Exhibit 7.2). 6% of all respondents said their centre was vibrant, including three of the Metropolitan Cities (38%). Overall, 29% thought they were improving, including 37% of Resorts and Historic Towns, but only 25% of Market Towns; 19% were declining, including 28% of Suburban Centres, but no Metropolitan Cities. Over half of the respondents would have described their centre differently five years ago.

7.25   **Problems:** 61% of all respondents said that the recession was a major problem, including 74% of the more tourist dependent Resorts and Historic Towns, but only 54% of Market Towns. Only four respondents thought it no problem. 81% of Suburban Centres said that lack of powers to initiate development was a major problem, compared to 64% overall. 53% of all centres, but 75% of Metropolitan Cities, thought that lack of resources was a major problem.

7.26   35% of all respondents, interestingly including 75% of Metropolitan Cities, saw out-of-town centre or edge-of-town competition as or becoming a major problem.(Exhibit 7.3) 49% thought it a minor problem and 13%, including 21% of Market Towns, thought it no problem. All types of centre were broadly similar in their view of competition from other towns, with 37% regarding it as a major problem, 49% as a minor problem and 12% (including 25% of Metropolitan Cities) as no problem.

7.27   34% of respondents thought that the opening of an out-of-town foodstore had had a negative or major adverse affect on their centre compared to 6% who thought it had been beneficial. The responses from all types of towns were broadly similar. No answer was given by 42% of Market Towns and Suburban Centres, presumably because in most cases no store has yet opened.

7.28   Chapter 5 summarised the broad findings in respect of indicators and measures for assessing vitality and viability. However, there were a number of instances where differences were apparent between types of town. Whilst overall half saw pedestrian flow as a key indicator, 88% of Metropolitan Cities did so. 67% of Suburban Centres thought the number of multiple retailers to be a key indicator, a view shared by only 43% of Market Towns and 38% of Metropolitan Cities. On the other hand, 75% of the Metropolitan Cities thought rent levels/commercial yields were a key indicator as against 38% of Market Towns and 31% of Suburban Centres.

7.29   **Key factors:** The range and diversity of shops and services was regarded as the most important factor that determines town centre health by 94% of Suburban Centres, 76% of all respondents and 61% of Resorts and Historic Towns. 13% of the Historic Towns thought a clean and attractive environment and large catchment area were the most important factors. 37% of Industrial Towns thought that a sense of security was one of the top five factors, compared with only 21% of Market Towns. Whilst 92% of Industrial Towns and 87% of Market Towns thought ample and convenient parking one of the top five factors, only 73% of Resorts and Historic Towns and 62% of Metropolitan Cities regarded it as so important. Instead cities thought frequent and affordable public transport was one of the five key factors, a view shared by less than half of the Market Towns and Resorts and Historic Towns.

7.30 Half of Metropolitan Cities and 48% of Market Towns said that good traffic management and signage was one of the five most important factors, but only a quarter of Suburban Centres agreed. Three times as many Market Towns and Metropolitan Cities thought town centre housing was one of the five factors as did Industrial Towns. 38% of Metropolitan Cities classed business accommodation in their top five compared with only 12% of all centres and just 8% of Suburban Centres. Overall 84% said that the town centre was either the most important or one of the two or three most important issues facing the authority from a planning viewpoint. All Metropolitan Cities thought so, but only 72% of Suburban Centres agreed. Only two respondents, both from Market Towns, said that the centre was not particularly important.

7.31 Whereas local businesses have had a major involvement in developing plans to improve the town centre in 63% of Metropolitan Cities, this was only so in 10% of Market Towns and 17% of all centres. In 16% of Market Towns and 11% of Industrial Towns there has been little or no involvement.

7.32 The differences between these types of town reinforce our view that, though general lessons can be learned, it is best to consider good practice as well as performance in relationship to the type of town concerned. However, as many towns fall under several types, the lessons that follow will often have a wider application. For example, we have referred to security under industrial and commercial towns whereas it is of course a much wider concern. **Appendix C** identifies some of the places where good practice can be found.

Some appropriate initiatives for different types of town.

Market towns

Bury St Edmunds: securing the right retail mix

Petersfield: creating an environment to be proud of

Horsham: introducing effective traffic management

Beverley: ensuring a balance of uses

Metropolitan cities

Nottingham: creating a positive image

Manchester: developing superior public transport

Leeds: ensuring mixed uses (Corn Exchange)

Birmingham: establishing distinctive quarters

Suburban centres

Industrial towns

Camden Lock: creating cultural actitivty zones

Harrow: co-ordinating local transport

Ilford: making friendlier streets

Swansea: undertaking imaginative refurbishment

Bradford: creating welcoming gateways

ndustrial towns

Wolverhampton: maintaining safer cities

Middlesbrough: creating quality public spaces

Brighton: developing a multiplicity of attractions

Resorts and historic towns

York: promoting visitor management

Worcester: enhancing heritage

PART THREE • GOOD PRACTICE

8 market towns

- Market towns typically have a distinctive character, changing roles, traffic and parking problems, a growing population, and some vacant space.

- The right retail mix should be promoted by encouraging missing shops or services to fill gaps, and by locating new developments, such as food superstores, where they will reinforce the centre.

- Planning briefs should be published for key sites on the edge-of-the-town centre.

- Once the town has been by-passed, traffic in the centre should be calmed by widening pavements, where appropriate, allowing on-street short-term parking or two-way streets.

- Environmental audits should be encouraged that make use of voluntary effort, where possible, followed up by actions to remove eyesores and promote a sense of civic pride, using design specialists.

'The market town is a traditional and familiar part of the English scene; so much so that it tends to be taken for granted.'

The English Market Town, Jonathan Brown

8.01   In this and succeeding chapters, we first review the typical characteristics of each type of town arising from their development and the impact of recent trends. An example is provided of a centre that highlights the common issues. The second part of each chapter proposes a series of approaches that have been adopted to enhance vitality and viability with an example that provides an illustration of good practice from a town of similar type, but which may well also offer lessons for other types of town. In each case the approaches need to form part of a coherent strategy if significant results are to be obtained.

8.02   Of the 131 responses from market towns, 3% said that the town centre was vibrant, 26% improving, 56% stable and 15% declining. A surprising finding of the study has been the number of market town centres that are declining, and this is reflected in the significant proportion that also score poorly in terms of the yield indicator. Market towns have limited catchment areas, even though the population is often rising. Part of the problem lies in the dependency of most market towns on convenience shopping, particularly food. They have, therefore, been particularly vulnerable to the aggressive competition between grocery chains to secure sites. These have often been facilitated by the availability of sites off by-passes, and relaxed planning regimes. Smaller towns often lack the resources to match the sophisticated developer.

Common features

8.03   **Distinctive character:** Market towns have long been places to trade, and though in many cases the old agricultural markets have closed, most still retain regular outdoor general markets, with a strong emphasis on food. Almost four fifths of respondents said they were district centres. Most of the buildings in the town centre are domestic in scale, but are interspersed by public buildings, such as the parish church and some of the many pubs, and perhaps a town or guild-hall, cornmarket, sessions house, maltings, endowed grammar school or theatre.

8.04   Much of their character comes from the use of local materials and their long history of development. Many buildings were constructed on traditional long, narrow 'burgage' plots with a limited street presence, and are now listed as being of special interest or form part of a conservation area. The towns have largely retained their historic central street pattern, often on a river and with a single street that broadens to form the market place, or a cross or "Y" shaped plan with the market traditionally held at the road junction.

8.05   **Changing roles:** Though affected by industrial development, the surviving market towns were not overwhelmed by it. Instead they evolved as technology and society changed. However, the pace of change in recent decades has produced greater challenges. Agricultural developments and increased personal and corporate mobility are having a significant effect on the traditional roles of many towns. Merchants, processors and other agricultural services have been consolidated and many livestock markets have gone. Many other services, such as hospitals, social services and even local authority offices, once essential in a relatively remote centre are now often situated in larger centres.

8.06   As traditional markets, services and jobs have been lost, the dependence on the town centre of many residents in surrounding rural communities has been broken. Increased car ownership has largely replaced the market bus, and so

Sleaford: a small Lincolnshire market town

Located at a river crossing on the London to Hull road, Sleaford has had a regular market since the 11th century. Held between the crossroads of two major routes and the Norman-fronted church, today it is a thriving general market, Monday being the most popular day. The town's cattle and poultry markets closed in the 1980s and many other agricultural activities withdrew from the centre at about the same time, leaving redundant sites and buildings. Some of these were used to extend the retail floorspace in the late 1980s with the opening of a series of yards and courts off the main shopping street. The early 1990s saw the development of an edge-of-town supermarket. However, the effects of recession and increasing competition from improving neighbouring towns such as Lincoln and Newark has since resulted in the closure of a number of small retailers and the withdrawal of the Co-op store.

The town's population increased by 17% in the decade to 1991, with a considerable number of new houses built. The housing boom attracted many national and local builders, contributing to the wide variety of new houses available from small affordable units to large executive style houses. The use of some central sites has allowed the provision of retirement accommodation close to the shops. The three secondary schools offer high quality education to 2,000 students and are a major attraction. The opening of the western by-pass now complements the long-established northern by-pass and between them they have succeeded in removing most of the heavy goods and all of the through traffic from the town. The change led to a major reappraisal of the role of the town centre through a commissioned study. The consultants, appointed by the District Council, developed a vision and strategy for the town which has won the support of the Town and County Councils and the Chamber of Commerce and is now receiving widespread publicity.

neighbouring centres or out-of-town locations have become attractive and practical places to shop, work, learn or seek recreation.

8.07   Growing populations: many of the towns have been some of the principal beneficiaries of the counter-urbanisation movement. In some cases towns were designated to take overspill from major cities and saw a relatively sudden population increase, whilst in others county structure plans identified major housing development programmes that have produced a more incremental rise. Growth has been particularly apparent in towns in the east and south east of England. In many cases this has been sustained over a considerable period and in some areas is planned to continue. A comparison of population change in the various census classifications shows that in both the early 1970s and the mid 1980s, the 'Remote mainly rural' category showed the second highest level of population growth of all OPCS categories (Simmie 1993). However, in some cases a rising population has not automatically benefited the town centre, with many new residents being more willing to travel for services to neighbouring centres.

8.08   Traffic and parking problems: growing populations, visitors and increased mobility have all created additional traffic. Often with narrow streets, but on important routes, the town centres have in many cases been experiencing problems for many years. By-passes have largely relieved the congestion caused by through traffic in most towns, but cannot deal with problems caused by large vehicles unloading in narrow streets or traffic generated by attractions within the town itself, such as the market. A new by-pass has a significant effect on a town centre. By providing a fast route for through traffic if offers an opportunity for making the centre more pedestrian friendly, but may also leave the centre isolated, while new stores set up out-of-town.

8.09   The dispersed nature of surrounding settlements and high incidence of car ownership in most rural areas, means that frequent public transport services are usually not a commercially viable option. This in turn means that ample short and long-term car parking must be provided in or close to the centre for those who work in or visit the town whether for shopping or other activities. The historic street pattern and the narrowness of many streets, the conservation area status of many centres, and in some cases the proximity of residential areas to the town centre, restrict opportunities for developing car parks in many centres. Often the market area is not available for parking on the days of peak demand.

8.10   Vacant space: Many market towns have a considerable number of vacant or underused sites and buildings. Some are former agricultural buildings, such as warehouses or maltings, that have high conversion costs, limited opportunity for new uses and reluctant owners. In some instances former corn exchanges, court buildings, town halls and other public sector buildings are also vacant. There are often substantial areas of unused backlands, perhaps with restricted access through a combination of traditional land ownership and current conservation restrictions.

8.11   Vacant retail space is increasingly a problem as shops in historic buildings close under the combined assaults of out-of-town or edge-of-town supermarkets, the increasing accessibility of larger centres, reduced passing trade caused by a decline in other functions or perhaps a new by-pass and the recession. Some of the many pubs in the centre are also closing or under threat as the brewing industry is re-structured and drinking habits change. Banks and building societies are also rationalising their branch networks, with potential closures in smaller towns.

Witney: strengthening the town centre through positive planning

Witney is a small market town of almost 20,000 people in Oxfordshire. The local authority recognised that the centre faced a series of challenges, including traffic, servicing, lack of parking and modern retail units, as the well as threats from out of town. At the same time there were a number of major sites on the edge of the town centre including a former gasworks, the old cattle market and several under-used burgage plots. The Council produced a master plan in 1982, which went out to consultation, followed by a detailed development brief which set out key objectives for the site. Because the 15 hectares was in 26 ownerships, the Council entered into an agreement with a developer and Waitrose who already had a small store in the town. The Council secured a Compulsory Purchase Order and the developer acquired the land and transferred it to the Council. The developer then drew up the scheme and secured funding on the basis of a 125 year lease.

The scheme included an 18,000 sq ft net Waitrose foodstore, plus 25 small unit shops around a pedestrian street. There is a 750 space free car park, which also serves the town centre. Planning gains included the pedestrianisation of the market square, new public toilets, a riverside walk and a new relief road. At the same time, a major private housing scheme was promoted, with 200 units, of which 130 were sheltered, on land partly owned by the Council. The scheme is terraced and fits in well.

The development has been commercially successful and also won the 1989 RTPI Planning Achievement Award. It has helped Witney to attract a wider range of shops and eating places, and more customers as a result. The Council was also able to overcome an out-of-town appeal through demonstrating that its scheme would meet local needs.

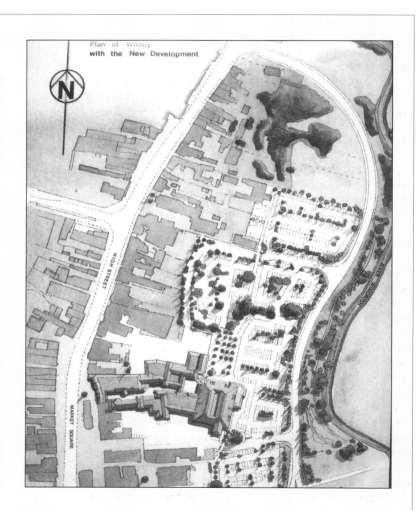

Plan of Witney with the New Development

The right retail mix

8.12   As district centres, market towns are particularly susceptible to the development of new food retailing out-of-town. In
many centres, specialist food shops, such as fishmongers, have
closed and there has been a considerable growth in what are
perceived as 'non-shops', such as building society branches, on
the High Street. The pressure for development of new food stores
outside these towns is increasing. Whilst in the 1980s nearly all
foodstores over 20,000 square feet were developed in towns with
populations above 30,000, since 1990 a quarter of new stores
have been developed in smaller towns (Hillier Parker 1991b).
Half of the market towns who answered the question on the
effects of an out-of-town food superstore said it had a possible
negative or major adverse impact, compared with 13% who
thought it had been beneficial.

8.13   Given the pressure for development out-of-town, what
can be done to retain an attractive and viable retail mix? A key
element is for local authorities to undertake an appraisal of the
mix of shops and demand (perhaps combining information from
Goad with a survey of town centre retailers and market stall
holders). They can then identify how the retail offer in the
centre can be made attractive to local residents and visitors. For
most market towns this is not about attracting national multiples,
but building a distinct identity for the centre, based on independent and specialist shops and the character of the market.
Efforts may be needed to encourage small shops to improve their
window displays or signs and change their opening hours, for
example with late-night opening, or in some of the smaller
towns, no longer closing for lunch. Here management and staff
training directed particularly at new retailers could help
encourage improvements possibly supported by Training and
Enterprise Councils. Retailer recruitment strategies can be a

Petersfield: benefitting from a by-pass

This Hampshire town is one of six that have been part of the Department of Transport By-pass Demonstration Project which is looking at
how towns can best benefit from a by-pass. This is a joint initiative
between the County and District Councils, with advice and support
from the Department of Transport and specialist consultants, as well
as a town forum that has local business representation. The removal
of A3 traffic, which used to cause major town centre congestion, has
been followed by a series of initiatives to narrow carriageways, improve
the environment and to slow remaining traffic. The old A3 carriageway
was over 13 metres wide in some places, but by introducing wider
pavements and on-street parking, distinguished by different surface
finishes, this has been reduced to 6.75 metres with a 600mm border
on each side, again in a different surface finish. By using other
surfaces at a number of key junctions, the road is further interrupted
to create a more enclosed feeling that slows traffic.

The wider pavements have been used to introduce new lamp-posts,
bus shelters, cycle racks, seating, planters and litter bins. A range of
different trees, each chosen for its particular location, are being
planted. Further phases of work will see the removal of a one-way
system and the creation of a new public space and a 20 mph zone.

Beverley: Regenerating a market town

Twenty years ago Beverley showed many signs of physical and economic decline with vacant properties, numerous cleared sites and buildings in need of repair. Some of these were affected by planning blight through land assembled in the 1960s for major redevelopment that was not implemented. Road improvement schemes had not occurred and traffic congestion was a significant problem in the town centre.

The Council undertook a number of initiatives that radically changed this decline. The existing road improvement and redevelopment proposals were abandoned. The Council reassessed its own property portfolio to free sites for development. A Town Scheme was set-up to grant-aid listed building repairs. The local authority established the philosophy of integrating residential development into the town centre and identified areas of priority for action. Redevelopment briefs aimed at stimulating development were drawn up for key sites. A detailed assessment of the potential for pedestrianisation resulted in a pedestrian priority area that used natural materials to emphasise the quality of the town centre.

A number of schemes have been completed on key sites. A development pioneered by a residents' co-operative with support from a Housing Association subsequently won design awards. The redevelopment of a former heavy engineering site close to the 13th century minster for a mixed housing development includes private housing and local authority and Housing Association sheltered housing. This site was developed by a consortium who agreed to the nature of the mixed use scheme and submitted detailed design proposals. Disposal of the site was through a building agreement with the land conveyed direct to the ultimate purchaser and the developer paying a fee to the Council for each plot. A shopping development which reflects historic plot width has also replaced an unsightly disused garage in the heart of the shopping centre.

means of reviving vacant shops and increasing the town's attractiveness. They involve identifying gaps in what a town centre offers, and then going out to attract appropriate traders to set up. The experience in British town centres is still limited, but in Falkirk some 38 new retailers were attracted over a five year period including 12 specialist shops. In the USA it is an important ingredient in town centre management, and there are specialist consultants.

8.14 The next stage is to identify development sites that are both attractive to retail investors and that will benefit the existing traders. Often this will involve upgrading a secondary area. Many market towns have extensive underused backlands or other redundant sites that can be linked to existing shopping streets through the creation of arcades to provide space for retail expansion and adjacent car parking. However, to succeed these must generate sufficient footfall. This can best be achieved by positioning an anchor or 'magnet' store, such as a supermarket, at the far end or by ensuring that the arcade links a car park and the main shopping street, as in the recent Rams Walk development in Petersfield, Hampshire. Given a substantial footfall, smaller specialist shops can be incorporated in the scheme as in Craven Court in Skipton, Yorkshire, or perhaps a new market hall, as in Market Harborough, Leicestershire. By identifying suitable central or edge-of-town centre sites for retail expansion, the town may be able to offer opportunities for development that are as attractive to potential investors as an out-of-town site. Approximately one third of market town respondents had adopted programmes to encourage new retailers, or distinctive markets, and slightly fewer included encouraging places to eat. Between 10% and 18% were proposing to adopt such programmes at the time of our survey.

Balance of uses

8.15   Though new retailing may be the spur for development in many towns, there are usually many other opportunities on vacant sites. There is often demand for better accommodation for small businesses than that available above a shop or in an unrefurbished building. Typically the space sought is in a variety of unit sizes up to about 750 square feet. 38% of market town respondents had adopted programmes for encouraging town centre offices and business space and they were proposed by a further 12%. Such development is rarely initiated by the private sector, but might be undertaken through a partnership that could involve agencies such as English Estates, the Rural Development Commission, or the Development Board for Rural Wales or perhaps a local Enterprise Agency. In some instances workspace could be combined with flats or retail units.

8.16   From the earliest days, people have lived in the centre of market towns, often with part of the house as the shop or workshop. In a number of towns, space above shops that was vacant, used as storage or perhaps let as basic offices has been converted to housing. Redundant buildings and vacant sites have provided space for in-fill housing developments, sometimes of sheltered or retirement housing. 48% of market town respondents have adopted programmes for town centre housing, and 34% are proposing doing so.

8.17   Once again the key to success is to assess the market and to look at both existing provision and demand. The planning authority should be innovative and flexible when assessing proposals, whilst seeking to maintain quality in areas of distinctive character. In some instances it may be that development partnerships involving both the local authority

---

Kendal: maintaining a living community

Kendal is a market and industrial town with a population of 24,000 on the edge of the Lake District with a number of specialist industries. Though its traditional narrow yards were largely unoccupied in the 1960s and some were cleared, by 1976 the District Council's Draft Town Centre Plan drew attention to the importance of those remaining. A Conservation Area Town Scheme was established and grants were used to encourage the first projects which "brought about the return of fashionable living and working areas in the heart of the town and created a new design consciousness among developers and architects which is unique to Kendal". Both housing refurbishment and infill, typically three storey terraces, sometimes with balconies, have been encouraged in the centre. Earlier, an old brewery had become an arts centre, with a theatre, galleries, restaurant and creche, as well as space for classes. A variety of charitable and other organisations provided the funding, with a substantial donation from the president of one of the large local employers.

The historic character of the town centre has been enhanced through facelifts of key shopping streets, pedestrianisation, planting and signing, as well as specially-designed lighting. Open spaces are well linked and regular events bring people into the town. The local planning authority took a very positive attitude to the refurbishment of the centre and as well as pulling together sources of grant aid and providing design advice, it took into account the special quality of the centre when determining permissions. The District Council has also established an interdisciplinary Town Centre Management Group, assisted by a (part-time) Town Centre Officer, to further the attractiveness of the centre.

Horsham: Providing a traffic free environment

Horsham in East Sussex has undertaken particularly extensive traffic calming and pedestrianisation schemes for a town of its size. A relatively prosperous medium sized town, with a population of 40,000 in its built up area, it was a sleepy market town until the railway turned it into a commuter town for London.

The centre today is the result of collaboration between the District and County Councils who set up a multi-disciplinary team to create improved access and an attractive traffic-free shopping environment under a strategy of 'People First'. This combines new roads, a new open air speciality shopping centre, a refurbished and extended shopping mall, new offices for a major insurance company based in the town, and the refurbishment of the Carfax involving partial pedestrianisation and the introduction of a 20 mile per hour zone as the basis for a traffic calming scheme. The Council, which owned most of the land, was able to use CPO and planning powers to construct the public realm works, release development sites and market them to development partners including an insurance company and the joint lessee (with the Council) of the shopping mall. There is now a town centre manager, who was the project manager, and who is funded by Horsham District Council.

The Horsham scheme succeeds because the parking is well linked to the town centre. The ring road does not act as a barrier, as it does not enclose the town completely and there is a well-designed bridge over it. The 20mph zone and traffic calming measures extend into adjoining streets. The square was liked for its relaxed and pleasant traffic-free atmosphere and for being a good meeting place. The new mall was under cover, but could still benefit from an improved variety of shops.

Despite the general praise and the scheme winning a number of awards, trade has not been as good as expected. Horsham has suffered from the impact of a new sub-regional shopping centre in neighbouring Crawley, which offers a much larger choice of shops under one roof, with integral parking, which is free.

and a private developer can be established. Some of the best results have been secured when the council has used planning briefs and land ownership to secure an 'edge-of-centre' scheme that strengthens the town centre as a whole.

Effective traffic management

8.18   By-passes have not been the whole answer to the problems of traffic in towns and sometimes create additional problems as well as opportunities. The Department of Transport is currently undertaking a research project, *The By-pass Demonstration Project*, that is examining appropriate initiatives to follow the opening of a by-pass (DoT 1992). These have included the creation of pedestrian priority zones, the introduction of one-way systems, allowing on-street limited waiting, and various traffic-calming measures. Sometimes a by-pass will enable a one-way system to be replaced by two-way traffic, which often reduces speeds and so feels less dominating. A third of market towns responding to our survey had adopted programmes for traffic-calming and a further 43% proposed doing so.

8.19   The aim of many market town traffic management systems probably echoes that proposed for Leominster, Herefordshire: "to achieve a town centre traffic circulation system which satisfies the safety and comfort requirements of shoppers while enabling efficient servicing of premises." This may involve limiting access by large or heavy vehicles through weight restrictions, introducing co-ordinated signing strategies (a policy adopted by 36% of market towns and proposed in 31%), widening existing narrow pavements and introducing traffic-calming on a one-way system or perhaps, pedestrianising the core shopping streets (Hass-Klau 1992).

The concern should be to secure the mobility for all; if mothers with prams and disabled people in wheel chairs can get around easily, others will also benefit. Over half of local authorities in market towns have adopted programmes for pedestrian priority areas and 38% are proposing to do so. There is also scope for making buses more attractive, through publicising their routes and timetables and perhaps investigating new services that complement the trains.

8.20 Restricting traffic requires careful design in market towns, where many trips into the town centre are of relatively short duration, or involve carrying substantial amounts of bulky foods. A number of systems exist to facilitate short-stay parking in town centres. These range from free on-street limited period disc parking in Northallerton, North Yorkshire, through short-stay free central car parks in Ringwood, Hampshire, to a parking refund system when purchasing goods in town centre shops in Petersfield. Some smaller towns, such as Daventry near Northampton, have made free parking their main attraction. Even where parking charges are made, there is a clear benefit in promoting short-term, easily accessible parking near to the centre, with longer-term sites further out. 69% of market town respondents had adopted programmes for establishing safe, convenient car parks and 29% were proposing to do so.

High Wycombe: creating a welcoming environment

High Wycombe in Buckinghamshire has a population of 80,000 and a retail catchment area of 200,000. Landscape consultants helped produce a comprehensive strategy for the town centre in 1987 that resulted in pedestrian priority in three of the main shopping streets and the refurbishment of two squares. The District Council notes that "these works have been fundamental in developing economic confidence in the retail area".

This action has been accompanied by other initiatives, such as the reuse of a redundant site to provide a community centre with space for charitable and craft organisations in a new-build development around a central courtyard, and the creation of a new Tourist Information Centre through a prominent corner in-fill development. The latter acted as a catalyst for the private sector refurbishment of neighbouring properties. At the same time the central 1970s shopping mall, the Octagon, was given a complete overhaul, including providing new roof lights, new floor and ceiling finishes and a new entrance and cafe.

A new theatre was opened in 1993. Since 1991, town centre developments have been overseen by a small team of officers within the local authority who are implementing a management plan with a £50,000 annual budget in partnership with the business community and local interest groups.

Ann Priest / WDC

An environment to be proud of

8.21 Attracting people to the town centre has many aspects, but the historic nature of the centres of many market towns provides an obvious way of promoting a distinctive and cared-for environment. Programmes to improve amenity are the most popular approach in market towns according to our survey. Nearly two-thirds of respondents have adopted programmes for environmental improvements and a similar proportion for frequent cleansing. Historic buildings can be repaired and preserved, in some cases with funding from English Heritage or CADW through the over 350 Town Schemes, and here building preservation trusts can have an important role to play in promoting mixed use projects. Shop fronts can be improved and restored, through a combination of local authority grants and contributions from retailers. Almost half of the centres have adopted programmes for shop front enhancement and 30% propose doing so, though only one in eight have adopted programmes for alternative use of empty shops and 14% propose so doing.

8.22 The removal of through traffic from a town centre presents opportunities to create a more pedestrian friendly environment and to upgrade the public realm. Our research shows it to be important that this is done as part of a wider stategy rather than being an end in itself. The emphasis of any investment must be on creating a high quality environment that is attractive to both users of the centre and investors. There are now some excellent guides to what quality involves produced by bodies such as the Institution of Civil Engineers, the Civic Trust, and the Pedestrians Association (Civic Trust 1993, ICE 1993, Pedestrians Asociation 1993)and these could be used as a basis for environmental audits. A first step is to systematically record what creates their identity and what

detracts from it. Here there is scope for volunteers, for example from amenity groups or colleges, to make an important contribution perhaps backing up landscape or urban design specialists.

8.23 Building restoration and major environmental works are long-term projects. Often there is a need for more immediate results. Planting and greening as part of "Britain in Bloom" has been undertaken in many towns. By involving local businesses and residents as sponsors and using their properties for display, 'greening' provides an opportunity to focus the energy of diverse interests. The experience of continental schemes suggest that it should also be an opportunity for innovation and expression to create distinctive displays, rather than simply reproducing the hanging baskets seen in other towns. The same applies to lighting, which can be used to make the centre feel safer at night as well as adding to the town's sense of identity.

Bury St Edmunds: a medieval masterpiece

Having held a regular market for centuries and with a legacy of historic buildings and street pattern reflecting this evolutionary development, Bury St Edmunds is today a viable and largely vital centre. Most of the town centre is a Conservation Area and it contains many listed buildings. Much of the town's retailing is contained within old buildings, though there has been some in-fill development over time. A number of schemes have been proposed to expand the shopping area in response to identified demand. The largest of these, in the late 1980s, would have used the 11 acre cattle market site to almost double the retailing space available in the centre. A combination of reasons meant that the scheme had not proceeded by the time the economic downturn made development less viable.

The continued success of the secondary and local shops is considered to be of critical importance to the vitality and viability of the town centre. In this respect the Council has put substantial efforts into enhancing the historic quality of the town centre and following a series of studies, a new traffic management scheme was introduced that has allowed the pedestrianisation of some of the main shopping streets and traffic restrictions in others. As many of these were extremely narrow for the traffic-flow they previously supported, this has improved the experience of those visiting the centre.

Traffic measures have been supported by a range of amenity initiatives that have included high quality hard landscaping, a comprehensive signage programme and a sponsored greening initiative that emphasises the character of the centre. The Council has commissioned a series of studies that have looked at the performance of the town and related issues, such as forecasts for car park usage into the next century. These are used to guide policies for development, whilst ensuring that the distinctive character of the historic centre is not lost. The new local plan lays great emphasis on maintaining the vitality and viability of the centre.

9 industrial towns

- Industrial town centres typically have redundant people and buildings, falling populations and spending power, substantial ethnic minority communities, obsolescent facilities, and fears for safety.

- Where investment prospects are limited, the focus should be on retaining existing retailers and diversifying the town's attractions, and making the most of resources, such as landmark buildings and water, through imaginative refurbishment.

- Confidence should be boosted by creating and maintaining welcoming gateways for people coming by either car or public transport with well-designed interchanges, and clear direct pedestrian routes to the centre.

- Spaces should be designed to feel safe and distinctive, so that people want to linger or even live close to town, for example using greening and lighting schemes as well as measures to counter crime. Events can also be used to promote a better image and a sense of community spirit.

- Towns would feel safer if more people lived in the centre.

'..the areas where different industries had developed in the early years of industrial change continued to expand through the Victorian period. Large towns grew into great cities; smaller towns into large ones; a few new towns were established. Many adjoining towns consolidated, thickly or loosely, into what we now call conurbations..'

The Making of English Towns, David Lloyd.

9.01 Of the 115 respondents that completed a questionnaire for industrial towns, 5% said their centre was vibrant 29% that it was improving, 43% stable, and 23% declining.

Common features

9.02 **Redundant people and buildings:** These towns typically grew to prominence on the back of a limited range of products or processes, such as textiles, coal, steel, engineering, or docks; the basic activities often complemented those elsewhere in the region. Though the industry provided the wealth for investment in civic buildings and other necessities of urban life, its narrow base made the centres particularly susceptible to a down-turn. As first traditional and then more high-tech industries, such as defence and aerospace, declined, not only has unemployment risen, but also towns have lost a substantial part of their economic base and in extreme cases the reason for their existence. However, the original industry continues to give many towns their distinctive character and affects the lifestyle of the region.

9.03 Though Government or European funding has helped to attract new industries and activities to some of these towns, inward investors generally prefer to locate in sites with good motorway access and in 'green field' or waterfront surroundings, rather than in old industrial buildings or in central sites where access is difficult or substantial investment in reclamation is required. There is some evidence that the traditional large firm culture and skills base of many industrial towns also has restricted the growth of new enterprises and local demand for space.

9.04 **Falling population and spending power:** The traditional industrial areas have had several decades of population decline, with generally the greatest decline in the largest towns. Even the New Towns have slowed down. The general trend has been for those who can afford it to move out of the inner areas, most of which were developed in Victorian times.

9.05 For most industrial towns, the combination of rising unemployment, falling population and loss of more affluent residents has reduced the spending power of the local community on which many of the functions of the town centre depend. Research on Local Labour Market Areas has shown that industrial towns perform poorly on a wide range of economic criteria (Breheny 1989). Many of them are ranked in the lowest quartile in Local Labour Market statistics and are also in the lower reaches of other economic assessments (such as the Credit and Data Marketing Services (CDMS) 26 level prosperity index).

9.06 **Ethnic Minorities:** The growth of industry drew in labour. Initially this was from rural areas and through natural growth. But many industries, particularly textiles and metal processing, provided employment for immigrant communities, who then settled in the town. The main exceptions were mining and shipbuilding which depended on skilled workforces with an apprenticeship period. However, in a textile town like Bradford, for example, there are now some forty different communities represented on the local Community Forum. In the smaller towns there is a tendency for a particular ethnic group to make up a major proportion of the ethnic minority population. Ethnic minorities often take over shops in fringe areas, sometimes opening them as restaurants. Many of the shops and restaurants are open long hours, providing both a service and an attraction after most others have closed.

Whilst this has benefitted the town as a whole, the centre is in many cases not providing the goods and services required by the ethnic communities and is thus losing a significant percentage of its catchment area's spending power.

Preston: diversifying the centre

Preston was an ancient market town which became dominated by cotton, suffered a decline and was in the doldrums before enjoying a renaissance since the mid 1980s. The average annual retail investment property performance recorded by the Investment Property Databank over the 1980s was higher than in any other British town, and the town centre is once again lively.

The town has succeeded in diversifying its economy and has developed the former docklands area for housing, offices and warehousing, plus a multiplex cinema and other leisure facilities. The town itself benefited from the 300,000 square feet Fishergate shopping centre opened in 1987. It also continues to have a daily indoor market, an outside market four times a week and a twice weekly 'car boot' market using the otherwise vacant stalls.

More recently extensive investment has been made in pedestrianisation and improving the amenity of the centre. Great effort has been made to provide a distinctive environment, for example, through pavement motifs that include the Borough and County crests and the recreation of the Gilbert Scott designed lamp standards in the market square.

Although there is not a town centre manager, the centre has been given priority since the early 1980s, when the Council and Chamber of Trade developed a strategy with a five-year timetable. They also produced design guidance, and succeeded in getting a 1960s shopping centre upgraded, thus overcoming a common problem. All work in the town centre has been accompanied by extensive consultation and well-produced information.

9.07 **Obsolescent town centre facilities:** Many industrial towns experienced the redevelopment of their centres in the 1960s and 70s. Concrete shopping malls, multi-storey car parks, office blocks and bus stations replaced brick and stone buildings. Today many of these developments are economically and functionally obsolescent. The shopping malls have often aged badly and are in many cases inefficient, with little natural light and high energy demands. When these are shut they create an evening void in the town centre, particularly where they have drawn many of the multiples away from the High Street, leaving mainly financial services and shops with poor window displays. Often the multi-storey car parks and bus stations present significant security problems as well as looking unattractive.

9.08 **Fears for safety:** Though rising crime rates are a national phenomenon, many industrial town centres have promoted particular fears. As well as the poor design of twenty or thirty year old multi-storey car parks and bus stations, there are the added problems of shuttered and nearly deserted pedestrianised streets after dark, frequented only by young people. Comedia's *Out of Hours* surveys in Middlesbrough and Preston, for example, found that fear of crime was a major reason why more use was not made of the town centre in an evening. In addition, there is often little in the form of entertainment other than pubs and clubs. Public transport is limited and car parks or street parking are poorly lit. In some centres there is regular public disorder in evenings and occasional violence. Graffiti and broken or dilapidated street furniture further reinforce a poor image, encouraging others to go elsewhere.

9.09 The response by industrial towns to the challenges they face has varied in intensity and results. To an extent this may be related to when in the economic cycle their primary industry most suffered and what legacy it left. While there is no easy answer, progress depends on making the most of existing resources, including imaginative refurbishment, improving the gateways and creating quality public spaces and safer cities. The relatively high position of Preston on the residual yield index and its good performance on a number of other indicators provides a positive example of what can be achieved.

Halifax: capitalising on inheritance

Halifax has become known as an urban regeneration success story, in part due to the involvement of the Civic Trust and Business in the Community, and the support of the Prince of Wales. A report in 1984 *A Strategy for Prosperity* provided a vision that built on the town's considerable heritage.

The Council set up the Calderdale Inheritance Project with its own identity and staffed by secondees from the Council, local companies and the Department of the Environment. It pioneered a holistic approach to urban regeneration creating processes which harness latent resources within the local community as the engine of regeneration. It made a virtue out of the scarcity of public funds and used commercial and environmental arguments to obtain the support of the local and national business community. The programme promotes high quality enhancement of town centres as a means of attracting trade and improving the investment climate of the area in general. The centre now contains a number of major visitor attractions, from the 18th century Piece Hall market place to a new children's museum.

One important element has been Dean Clough Mills, comprising 1¼ million square feet of multi-storey buildings originally the home of Crossley Carpets who employed 6,000 people at the turn of the century. Closed by Carpet International in 1982, the site was purchased by a local entrepreneur who subdivided it for business, education and arts activities. By 1993 Dean Clough was home to 200 companies employing 3,000 people.

Imaginative refurbishment

9.10   In many industrial towns a key factor in maintaining vitality and viability has been to reuse vacant factories, mills, and waterside sites on the edge of the town centre, particularly those that form landmarks as with Dean Clough Mills in Halifax (DoE 1987). Reuse brings both psychological and economic benefits. The redundant buildings can provide space for new and expanding activities, such as workspace for small firms. Larger sites can be used to attract inward investment, as in the case of Newport, which has attracted a host of new employers to the edge-of-town. A number of projects have now been successfully undertaken which combine a mix of uses, with workspace above and cultural or entertainment facilities such as exhibition or performance space, restaurants and bars, or other publicly welcoming spaces on the ground floor. In some cases, as in Bradford's Little Germany or a number of former docklands, this has helped to create a new 'quarter' that adds to the centre's diversity (Falk 1993). In other instances, buildings such as banks have been turned into wine bars or housing. There are also a few examples of refurbishment for health uses, including a former church in Newport that has become a health and sports club, or for education in the town centre, for example in Luton or in Stoke where a university occupies part of the railway station, but these are all too rare at the moment.

9.11   In most instances refurbishment schemes have been undertaken by the local authority, often using European or Government grants, or through a partnership between the public and private sectors; for example, the Upper George Yard scheme in Halifax involved a cocktail of grants, including a training scheme, and support from five different private companies. In several instances, it has been the

---

Bury: refurbishing a '60s shopping centre

Originally developed in three phases in 1969/70 as Bury Precinct, the Millgate Centre was showing increasing vacancy levels by the late-1980s and rental levels were suffering. The town also had an under-representation of major multiples and few large retail units and was beginning to lose trade to surrounding centres such as Bolton. The shopping centre owners, MEPC and Norwich Union, together with the local authority who owned the land therefore decided to refurbish the precinct and to create a shopping arcade for the 1990s. The £6.5 million scheme involved extending the retail units to provide a narrower central arcade, which was then covered, providing rear extensions and fire sprinkler systems, and creating a more attractive shopping environment through planting and signage.

The centre remained open throughout the refurbishment, with an information office to keep traders and the public informed of progress. The scheme was completed in August 1992 and the larger store units proved attractive, so in early 1994 the centre was fully occupied. A key target for the centre management, was to increase pedestrian flow. The first year marketing was aimed at local people and the second year took advantage of the large numbers of people entering the town through the adjacent metro and bus interchange. The covering of the central arcade resulted in a substantial saving in energy bills for stores in the centre and the refurbishment allowed rents to rise. The security guards, who were seen as hostile by some users, were replaced by "mall-ladies" who provide friendly and helpful information. This is partially to emphasise the secure nature of the centre, which is further promoted by crime prevention initiatives and "women's weeks".

The centre won the British Council of Shopping Centres refurbishment award in 1992 and is seen as the first step in the wider renaissance of the town centre that will include a summer festival in 1994. The centre management company is actively involved in Bury's town centre management strategy.

availability of grants that has determined the nature of the refurbishment. However, the key to a successful scheme is understanding demand and matching the space and the level of service provided to that. 40% of industrial town respondents said that their local authority had adopted programmes for encouraging town centre offices and business centres and 12% were proposing to do so.

9.12   Post-war buildings also often need refurbishing. Many 1960s covered shopping centres and their car parks fall below the standards expected by both retailers and customers. In some instances shopping centres, such as St Georges in Preston which was built in 1964, were refurbished in the 1980s, often in response to retail development elsewhere in the centre. However, in many other cases the planned redevelopment/refurbishment of other buildings, has not

Neath: creating a welcome in the hilltops

Neath, like many South Wales valley towns, suffered from the loss of traditional industry and the impact of a by-pass that took trade away. However, the local authority recognised the value of making the most of the town's character. A regeneration plan was drawn up in the late 1980s. The first step was to build a new road link, improving access from the surrounding catchment area. The opportunity was also taken to move the inner ring road outwards to create development space in the town centre. Environmental improvements included extensive pedestrianisation but only during the busiest shopping periods. The bus and railway stations became part of an integrated scheme.

The next stage was to develop land on the edge of the town centre for a mixed use scheme. This included a new Safeways superstore, and DIY superstore and individual shop and office units and some 135 housing units overlooking water. The scheme was completed in 1993 and included the restoration of a section of the Neath canal and Neath Castle. The pedestrianised streets are used for events, such as a huge annual fair and market which attracts people from some distance and the town now looks busy most of the time. The scheme has transformed the make-up and attractiveness of the town centre, and a number of national multiples and local speciality shops have located within the centre since the scheme began.

The scheme was undertaken by the borough council in partnership with private developers, and with grant assistance from the Welsh Office and the Welsh Development Agency.

Neath District Council

Wolverhampton: attracting people to town

Faced with strong competition from other towns, Wolverhampton Council has put a great deal of effort into improving the town's image through extensive 'greening' and other improvements to the built environment. Today the town presents a good quality environment and a positive image to people arriving on foot, by public transport or by private car. A recently refurbished bus station, better directional signs and town maps guide pedestrians and motorists in and around the centre. The pedestrianised shopping core, accessible car parks, ring-and-ride and free town centre bus services as well as a shopmobility unit for disabled shoppers, all contribute towards making Wolverhampton an attractive place to shop in. New public and private developments skirt the main transport routes and so maximise their visibility and accessibility - including the Combined Courts, Police Station, offices and a 130 bed hotel. To further enhance the health and vitality of the town centre, especially outside shopping hours, the Council introduced a 'Living Over The Shop' Scheme which assists property owners to convert their empty upper floors into useful housing accommodation for rent.

Alongside retail and residential uses, the Council has promoted an 'entertainment quarter' to encourage new leisure and entertainment business to set up and expand in the town. A major success has been the refurbishment and extension of the former Chubb Lock Works to create the Light House Media and Conference Centre. The Media Centre comprises a two screen cinema, exhibition space, a cafe and wine bar complex, as well as several floors of office and studio workspace for small business. A number of grants have been given to convert historic buildings to restaurants and other leisure uses.

A funding package from the European Community, Central Government, and English Heritage has assisted these initiatives. The Council employs a Town Centre Manager to ensure a co-ordinated approach with the private sector. The council has recently commissioned a town centre 'audit' in preparation for the next stage of improving the town centre.

happened, possibly because the scheme was planned as a far larger private sector initiated scheme that depended on economic growth being maintained. About a third of local authorities in industrial towns have adopted programmes to encourage a broader representation by retailers in their centres, and nearly half have adopted programmes for encouraging distinctive markets. Where the prospects of attracting major investment are low, the priority is to retain existing retailers, for example by ensuring that there is not excessive out-of-town competition.

Welcoming gateways

9.13   In the last few years many industrial towns have invested substantially, often with the help of grants or through planning gain, to make the experience of going to town more pleasurable. In some cases, such as Bradford and Neath, high quality ring or distributor roads have been constructed taking advantage of Derelict Land and European regional grants which have improved access, enhanced the experience of arriving in the town and reduced traffic in the centre. 74% of industrial towns have adopted programmes to encourage pedestrian priority areas and 46% have undertaken traffic calming. The results are often very attractive, particularly where the design is distinctive, as for example in Wakefield. In other instances bus and rail stations have been improved or redeveloped and in some cases, such as Wolverhampton and Huddersfield, linked to each other to create interchanges. These can be memorable buildings, as for example in Halifax. 24% of industrial town respondents have adopted programmes for interchanges, but only 12% have programmes for mini-buses or rapid transit systems. However, too often public transport is becoming a 'poor relation'

with under-used double decker buses, for example, adding little to people's pleasure in going to town.

9.14   Going to town has also been made easier for many who would otherwise have greater difficulties through initiatives for the disabled, such as the establishment of mobility centres that can include dial-a-bus, shop-mobility and reserved disabled parking. New surface car parks have been developed on the sites of cleared buildings and many

---

Middlesbrough: providing quality open space

Extensive public space has been created in the centre of Middlesbrough by the local authority, which has transformed the centre. Housing clearance, and the failure to attract major office development on a central site, led to the design of a new space linking the shopping and civic cores of the centre with the surrounding residential business and business areas. Since 1986, a lake, miniature canal, amphitheatre, gardens and new public walkways have been created just one block from the central street. These have provided an attractive setting for new offices and workspace that has included new Crown Court buildings, a small business centre and two offices for the Inland Revenue. There has also been new build housing along the edge of the gardens. The scheme has now incorporated a major new work of public art, a metal sculpture, called "a bottle of notes", which was commissioned from an eminent international team of sculptors. Its cost of some £130,000 was raised from many different sources. However, there is still a need to increase usage of the area, which may come about through proposals for developing an arts centre and library extension.

have been integrated into shopping centres or other developments, while a growing number of multi-storey car parks have been upgraded. 70% of industrial towns have adopted programmes for improved car parks and 24% propose so doing.

Swansea: turning waste land into assets

Few industrial areas had greater dereliction to tackle than Swansea, and the City also suffers from being on the 'end of the line' from London. The response was a strategic plan in the 1970s which proposed a series of 'parks' with different themes. The start was turning the old docks into a Maritime Quarter. 20 years later the vision has become a reality. Not only has the 'urban village' around the 600 berth marina of over 1,000 residential units brought more people to live on the edge of the town centre, it has also given the city an exciting visitor attraction. The Maritime Quarter is memorable because of the high standard of design and the extensive use of public art.

The Maritime Quater now contains a mix of uses, including a museum, hotel, pubs, restaurants, and shops, together with a theatre and a display centre for the visual arts. It is linked to the centre by a highly successful leisure centre. The Maritime Quarter together with the Regional Sports Park and Enterprise Park have transformed the look of the city, and have helped to attract investment and jobs, to date some £72m investment in the Maritime Quarter alone. The completion of Britain's first barrage marks the next phase in making the most of the City's natural assets. The strong civic drive helps explain why Swansea is successfully promoting itself through initiatives such as being City of Literature in 1995.

Quality public spaces

9.15   In many towns an extensive programme of cleaning and lighting buildings has revealed the original character of the centre. This has often been achieved through the Urban Programme, sometimes with some contribution from property owners or occupiers. For example, Newport has used Town Scheme Funding to grant aid the repair of a significant number of Victorian buildings in the old market area and has accompanied this by extensive pedestrian priority schemes. For a number of years the district council has employed a sculptor and several major pieces of public art have been introduced into the shopping areas, one of which gives a memorable first impression to those arriving by train. Similarly in Bradford, a Civic Trust award was secured for a pedestrianisation scheme that used high quality materials (basically York Stone) and a few imaginative touches, such as ornamental iron gates, poems set into the paving and attractively painted Victorian-style light columns. But it is still rare to find an extensive network, with quality materials, street furniture and fine trees where pedestrians can wander without fear. Tree planting and water features are particularly effective in softening the image of industrial towns and making them feel friendlier.

9.16   'Enveloping' programmes for town centres in the West Midlands have been shown to be cost-effective (DoE 1988) 72% of industrial towns have adopted programmes for environmental improvements and 65% have programmes for frequent cleansing. For example, Bolton has adopted an environmental strategy which sets targets for street cleansing, litter collection and ensures that streets, street furniture, car parks, public toilets and other parts of the public realm are regularly maintained and repaired, complementing its elegant signs. Some towns are using environmental trusts, such as

Groundwork, to undertake large numbers of small-scale greening projects (Davidson 1988). Occasionally new open spaces have been created which act as a catalyst for surrounding development, by making it attractive to live near the centre. As industrial towns grew-up around canals and docks, there are opportunities to promote a waterside renaissance. In some cases such as Salford and Swansea, the docks have become attractive places to live and visit, though we have a long way to go to match American achievements in using water to create new parks (Breen 1994, Hoyle 1993).

9.17 Public spaces can provide ideal venues for events, from markets to street theatre and festivals. These help to promote the town centre as somewhere special. They can also involve ethnic minorities in celebrations as in Bradford and Leicester, and help attract visitors in the process.

Bradford: organising a city wide festival

Initiated in 1986 as a three day event to draw attention to the refurbishment of an historic industrial area close to the city centre, the festival has grown into an annual event, over 17 days, that covers the whole city, but with its main emphasis in the centre. A wide range of street events, including a major parade, are combined with the use of city centre pubs, theatres, cinemas, halls and other buildings to provide concerts, plays, events, and exhibitions. A particular feature is the involvement of many of the city's ethnic communities in staging special events, including a weekend *Mela* or Asian festival that attracts hundreds of thousands of people. Originally run and largely paid for by the City Council, but with Urban Programme input, the festival has for some years been organised by a company limited by guarantee established for the purpose. This employs a core full time staff with two directors and many temporary staff in the period running-up to the event. Funding is now a combination of ticket sales and extensive private sector sponsorship which is financially supported by the local authority.

Coventry: making the streets safer

Faced with problems of growing street crime, a working party was established in 1984, headed by the Chamber of Commerce. This led to a by-law restricting the consumption of alcohol in public places. A survey found that 12% of visitors to the city had been affected by abuse and were deterred from using parts of the city centre. The alcohol ban has been accompanied by identification cards for young people in pubs, available through schools, as well as improvements to lighting and subways, with funding through the Safer Cities Programme. 53 CCTV cameras have been installed, and a special graffiti team ensures immediate removal which has had the effect of virtually dominating it from the centre. Initial surveys show that crime has fallen in the centre at a time when it has been rising elsewhere.

Safer cities

9.18   As in many US cities, improving security is a crucial part of improving the appearance and amenity of a town centre. 34% of local authorities in industrial towns have adopted programmes on crime prevention initiatives and 36% propose so doing. In Newport, the main club and pub area, a regular focus for trouble, has now been illuminated by modern, bright but relatively vandal proof standard lights. 41% of responding industrial town local authorities have adopted policies on lighting. Many centres such as Slough have introduced Closed Circuit Television (CCTV), while partnerships that involve the local authority, police, town centre businesses and often representatives of licensees have been established as Business, Shop or Pub Watch schemes. The Safer Cities programme has produced significant reductions in crime (a 16% drop in Birkenhead town centre for example), and has recently been extended to a further twenty locations. There are some useful guides to improving security which emphasise the importance of deterring crime through a concerted programme, which includes providing positive options for young people, and designing spaces so there is natural surveillance (Crime Concern 1993). Good urban design, particularly through appropriate lighting aid materials, should be used to improve the town's image, rather than stressing defensive measures, and there is plenty of scope for imagination (RFAC 1994).

9.19   Living over the shop and infill housing schemes would be particularly valuable to revitalising industrial towns, but the economics may not always be favourable. It is, therefore, particularly important to retain uses like hospitals and to encourage students and others to live in town, for example through sheltered housing schemes. Over time many industrial towns need to consolidate their centres, and housing on the periphery of the town centre is an excellent alternative use. But the first step is creating an environment where people would want to live.

Leicester: Living over the Shop

A major problem for most industrial towns is keeping the centre alive at night, and also tackling the problem of vacant property on the edges. Leicester has adopted a 'green' policy, which has removed or calmed traffic in most of the city centre. As a result the centre now looks extremely attractive.

The success of a number of housing associations new-build schemes in the centre encouraged National Westminster Bank, who have been one of the principal backers of Living Over the Shop, to undertake one of the biggest ever projects, over a large branch in Granby Street. This was undertaken in association with Coventry Churches Housing Association. The branch provided a 30 year lease and put in £100,000, while the housing association invested £600,000. It provides some 26 flats for rent in what was a former office block. Banks are consolidating their office functions, and a third of their buildings are listed or in Conservation Areas, so finding new uses is a challenge. The scheme was made possible through City Grant, and also by the National Westminster's appointment of someone in their head office to act as a 'champion' for that kind of project. The flats have been taken by single people, often elderly. While securing housing over new shopping centres has proved impossible because of legal, insurance and financing difficulties, turning complete post-war office blocks into housing is actually easier. Leicester also boasts examples of a cinema and a church which have been turned into ingenious flats.

---

10 suburban centres

- Suburban centres typically have a Victorian legacy, competing centres with confused identities, a poor environment and over stretched public transport, cosmopolitan communities, and out-of-centre competition.

- Shopping centres with surplus space need to be turned into proper town centres by diversifying their attractions, for example through cultural activity zones.

- Use of public transport should be encouraged through well-designed interchanges, but short stay parking is also essential.

- The public realm should be upgraded so that people want to stop and look around.

'...houses sprang up as if in a single night; streets in a month, churches and chapels in a quarter'

South London, Sir Walter Besant

10.01 Of the 36 responses relating to London and Suburban Centres, 8% said that they were vibrant, 31% improving; 33% stable, and 28% declining. This was the highest percentage of declining centres in any of the five categories of centres.

Common features

10.02 **Victorian legacy:** The suburban centres are most prevalent in London, but are also found around the other major cities, and have special features and characteristics that distinguish them from industrial towns or the market towns that some of them once were. The reasons lie in the way British cities grew in Victorian times, and can best be understood by contrasting them with the continental experience of Paris. During the middle of the 19th century, as the population expanded rapidly, the middle classes moved to the suburbs, which then developed their own town centres (Fishman 1993). They moved to escape smoke, to find rural bliss in a front garden, and to keep wives and children away from immorality. The move was financed by small builders, land owners who commissioned plans for sub-dividing their estates, and tradesmen who provided for their families through renting out houses. It was made easier by investment in trams, suburban railways, and in London the extension of the underground. The Metropolitan Railway, for example, led directly to the development of the 'Metroland' suburbs of north London.

10.03 In contrast, in Paris the middle classes took on aristocratic tastes for theatres, restaurants and ball-rooms, and the city centre remained fashionable. Napoleon III, in a bid to make Paris look an imperial centre, backed Haussman's plan for great boulevards. The poor were squeezed out to the periphery, and the rich were housed in new apartment blocks. Churchill said 'we shape our buildings and they shape us'. Undoubtedly the differences in form have had a profound long-term influence, long after smoke and immorality went away, and the 'evangelical movement' lost its influence.

10.04 **Competing centres, confused identities:** All suburbs have to face competition from similar centres immediately adjacent to them. London has over 100 centres, of which some 30 were classed as strategic in the Greater London Development Plan. Residents of a suburb may well work in the city centre or in a neighbouring suburb. Equally they may shop, seek entertainment or use any of the other facilities offered by that centre. This is often made easier by direct public transport links to the city centre.

10.05 The proximity of other centres makes a declining centre particularly susceptible to a rapid loss of spend from its catchment population as alternative centres are readily available. Most of the largest drops in ranking in *Shopping Centres of Great Britain* have occurred in suburban centres. Brixton, Peckham and the Fulham Road in London, Wythenshawe in Manchester, Kirkby in Liverpool, and Smethwick near Birmingham. All have lost ground substantially over the thirty year period of occasional surveys. There are, however, great contrasts between the inner suburbs (where many people are without a car) and the outer areas. Surprisingly perhaps, because of the density of population, there is still considerable purchasing power in the inner areas; it has been calculated that there is more comparison spending available within one mile of Dalston than Wimbledon or Kingston, which are both more successful (PMA 1989). However, even though there are 50% more households within six miles of Woolwich than Bexleyheath, it has not stopped Woolwich losing out to Bexleyheath.

10.06 The overlapping catchment areas, in many cases the lack of correspondence between the suburban centre and a local authority district, and the lack of distinctive features for many centres have led to a lack of clear identity. A number of those designated as strategic centres are little more than shopping centres, and do not offer a range of cultural facilities, which for example, may be located in smaller centres. Even where the rail, tube or metro station might be 'on the map', non-residents often have little idea of what the centre has to offer. Equally, many suburban centres have high volumes of traffic, but much of it is through traffic and there is often little to identify the centre unless it shares a name with the district or borough council.

10.07 **Poor environment, over-stretched public transport:** Most inner areas suffer from through traffic - in Inner London 51% of residents used public transport and only 30% use cars to get to work (the figures are reversed in Outer London). In many instances the high volumes of traffic passing through a suburban centre, contribute directly to an environment that is not welcoming to shoppers or families. Where pedestrianisation has occurred it has sometimes led to evening security problems. A survey in London found that 63% of women avoid going out on their own at night (Bowlby 1985). Traffic fumes and the extent of underground cabling and pipework have in many cases inhibited greening or environmental improvements. Where improvements have occurred, lack of revenue funding has in some instances resulted in inadequate or no maintenance.

10.08 The trends towards dispersal and to increased car usage at peak times are making it more difficult for public transport to cope where there are not reserved bus lanes. Despite proposals for extending underground and light rail systems, complaints continue to mount about London's public transport system. There has been a steady decline in bus services which is putting pressure on other modes, even though buses are doing better than in the shire counties. New employment centres on the periphery may relieve the numbers entering the city centre, but do not contribute towards maintaining a quality public transport system. A city dominated by car users may simply not be viable. Polarisation also creates inequalities and conflicts which can lead ultimately to violence, which then intensifies the vicious circle.

10.09 **Cosmopolitan communities:** Large numbers of people from around the world were attracted to work in the major cities and to live in some of the inner suburbs such as Cheetham Hill in Manchester or Spitalfields in London. As these communities prospered they often moved out of their original area to be replaced by a new community. Many of the inner suburbs have substantial ethnic minority communities, often from a number of backgrounds. In some cases these communities have become the focus of the town centre, with specialist shops, markets, clubs and restaurants developing and community carnivals and events becoming a major source of local cultural identity as in Southall and Brixton for example. However, many of the traditional multiple retailers in the suburban high street are not providing goods that these communities want and may, therefore, be losing nearly half of the potential local spending power. Yet independent traders sometimes find it hard to secure positions in the centre.

10.10 The gentrification of parts of the inner suburbs and the developments in areas, such as London's Docklands and Salford Quays, have provided residences for the more affluent. As money gives a choice of where to live, it also offers a choice of where to shop and spend recreational and leisure time.

Many of the inner suburban centres need now to serve both the poor and the distinctly affluent if they are to improve their position.

10.11 **Out-of-centre competition:** The substantial catchment population and the availability of large areas of derelict industrial land within the major cities has led to a spate of successful planning applications for out-of-centre retail developments. Though London has lagged behind other cities, there are outer areas, such as Brent and Barnet, where retailing has replaced industry. The growth of out-of-town retailing has led to in-centre schemes falling through, not just

---

Bexleyheath: A suburban success story

Bexleyheath has become a highly successful town centre, contrasting with other centres in south east London. It provides over 800,000 sq ft of floor space (ranking 14th in London) 57% of which is comparison shopping. In terms of its score on the yield/rental index it comes 130th out of 400 centres, significantly higher than Woolwich or Dartford for example. In terms of numbers of multiples it moved from 184th in 1971 to 126th in 1989. Figures on footfall were 109,000 a week in the covered shopping centre (in January 1986), and the nearest available comparison is 150,000 for the Lewisham centre (in June 1987), which is roughly the same size in terms of floor space.

The growth since the 1970s reflect the local authority's vision, strategy and commitment to creating a major centre for the borough. The new council felt they 'lacked a heart, soul, and some muscle' and appointed an insurance company as development partner after a limited competition. In 1975 when the developers wanted to pull out because of the property slump, the Council took an equity stake and guaranteed the rentals, as well as using its CPO powers to make the site available.

Subsequent developments have included an edge-of-centre superstore, a ten pin bowling alley, and a four star hotel. Office developments have included attracting the headquarters of the Woolwich Building Society and a new police headquarters. Bexleyheath has prospered because it has made the centre highly accessible, with ample surface level parking, which has attracted the more affluent customers and also those moving into expanding areas such as Thamesmead. Pedestrianisation is following the completion of a relief road. A former Co-op store is now a thriving specialist shopping centre of stalls around a cafe.

The Council's Chief Executive attributes success to three factors, being patient, backing up wishes with action, and having the right team, with all party support. However, the next phase of the centre is uncertain. The decision to give planning permission for a competing out-of-town regional shopping centre near Dartford, together with difficulties in compulsorily purchasing the remaining land, set back proposals for attracting a department store, and without tenant confidence, it may not be possible to attract further significant investment.

Belgrave Road, Leicester: serving the needs of an ethnic community

What was twenty years ago a run down shopping centre with a high level of vacancy has been transformed into one of Europe's leading Asian retail centres, through the efforts of the City Council and the local community. With the arrival of many East African Asians, the Council undertook extensive housing renewal schemes in surrounding streets and deliberately limited retail use, except in traditional corner shops or along the Belgrave Road. Shop front improvement grants and design advice were provided by the Council, who saw the development of an Asian shopping centre as a positive way to secure revitalisation. More businesses were attracted to the area and today there are numerous Asian restaurants, jewellery shops, saree centres, tailors, gift shops, sweet and spice centres, and various Asian service outlets, including Indian banks, travel and estate agents.

A former church has been converted into a Neighbourhood Centre which, as well as providing a valuable community resource for all ages, also acts as a venue for weddings and major celebrations with over 15,000 users a month. The City is looking at how it can help the area consolidate its specialist retail role, and has assisted the conversion of a large former factory to create a retail arcade and off-street parking in a scheme promoted by an Asian entrepreneur. It has also introduced traffic management policies include the limited use of residential side streets for short-stay parking. Environmental improvements and residential parking schemes are now planned on what remains a busy arterial road. The Council and local businesses have together sponsored the annual Diwali Festival of Lights in October, which over ten years has developed into a major event. A study by Aston University found that the shops were used by customers from all over the country and there is a growing international trade.

in declining centres like Woolwich, but also successful centres such as Bexleyheath. The prospect of Bluewater Park, a new regional shopping centre in a chalk quarry near Dartford, has caused private sector proposals for the next stage of Bexleyneath's town centre development to be deferred. Intriguingly this £500 million scheme stresses that 'there will be a sense of the High Street and well-established permanence'.

10.12 The major emphasis in this section is on initiatives undertaken by London centres. They provide the largest concentration of suburban centres and therefore we looked in detail at two London centres which are both near neighbours and similarly ranked on the 1989 multiple retailer ranking, Bexleyheath and Woolwich. We have, however, also considered the experience of a number of suburban centres in Manchester and the very interesting example of Belgrave Road in Leicester. Some lessons are also drawn from suburban centres in Nottingham and Sheffield, where we undertook case studies on the city centres. The guidelines for good practice include promoting a cultural activity zone, co-ordinated local transport, and designing friendlier streets.

Cultural activity zones

10.13 One of the main assets of a great city is its cosmopolitan population, which can be used to make centres more diverse and broaden their roles (Bianchini 1988). It can also help create a distinctive identity and provide one of the best sources of new enterprises and new attractions, as well as reusing surplus space. The most obvious way is through places to eat, and there are many examples where parades of secondary shops have been turned into lively places through ethnic restaurants and specialist shops. One key to success, apart from

Islington, Upper Street: establishing a cultural activity zone

Over a period of at least twenty years, one of London's oldest shopping streets has turned into a significant visitor attraction, while the surrounding area has become 'gentrified'. The process started with the growth of Camden Passage Market as an antiques centre. An old pub was turned into a successful small theatre, while the 'Screen on the Green' was one of the first cinemas to reverse the decline of audiences through imaginative programming.

A local businessman achieved his dream of turning the old Agricultural Hall into the Business Design Centre, providing both permanent display and marketing space and changing exhibitions and events. These attractions in turn helped sustain a growing number of wine bars and restaurants, which received a further boost from the development of major new offices. The area has now attracted the Crafts Council, with its gallery, and a new Tourist Information Centre. Discover Islington, one of the English Tourist Board's Tourism Development Action Programmes, is seeking to promote the area's attractions to a wider market. The local tube station has undergone extensive refurbishment including the provision of a new entrance on Upper Street. During this period, the Council has assisted through enabling changes of use and improving the environment, as well as financial support for the Business Design Centre.

flexibility in planning and licensing, is being able to drive by and park locally in an evening. Only 28% of suburban centres responding to our survey have adopted programmes to encourage cafes and restaurants in the town centre and 19% have adopted them for specialist shops. It appears that the more popular programme for suburban centres is to encourage multiple retailers, which has been adopted by 47% of authorities.

10.14 What matters however, is whether there are enough attractions to exert a pull in people from outside the immediate area. That is why the concepts of critical mass and linkages are so important. Thus, a centre like Woolwich, which appears to offer a variety of attractions, in fact does not have a critical mass of places to eat and drink to justify people spending time in the town in the evening. The leisure centre, which is a major attraction, with over a million visitors a year, is so cut off from the town centre that it fails to act as a draw for the shops. The university does not seem to have much impact either, perhaps in part because most of the centre is owned by one financial institution and therefore is let to

Harrow: a well-linked town centre

Harrow, like most outer London centres, has to reconcile the demands of affluent car owning households with the need to make the centre attractive and enable access for all groups. The opening of the new bus station in 1993 marked the culmination of an ambitious partnership between the London Borough of Harrow and the developer Laings which has created one of the most successful centres in London, and which began in 1980.

The attractions come largely from a large choice of stores, with three department stores including Marks & Spencer, and the latest phase, the St Anne's centre, which was opened in 1989, added a further 200,000 sq ft of retail in a covered mall. The mall stretches from the station (British Rail and Underground), which adjoins the bus station, through to a pedestrianised street. The street itself has kiosks and entertainment so that it feels very lively. This runs into traffic calmed streets on the edge.

Access is excellent, with a number of short stay surface car parks as well as a 950 space multi-storey, and these are intensively used because there are also a number of offices and cinemas, which help to keep the centre occupied at all times. 22 bus routes converge on the town centre, and these are brought together in a new covered bus station. There is first-class information, including a manned enquiry point. As a result going by bus is a pleasure.

multiples who have not adapted what they sell to meet changing local demands. Yet in Rusholme, Manchester, there are now over 30 Asian restaurants, three of which are mentioned in the Egon Ronay guide. Together with a range of Asian shops, these have formed the basis for a three strand initiative to revitalize the area through business help, environmental works and promotion as one of Manchester's tourist attractions.

10.15 One of the best ways of generating vitality is through a market, and the changing population needs to be reflected in the provision of new markets and additional licences. The classic instance is Camden Lock, which has helped turn Camden Town from a declining district centre into a place that is on the national map. A third of suburban centres have programmes to encourage distinctive markets and a further 17% are proposing to do so. As an example, Peckham's Rye Lane, which has lost many of its multiples, is finding a new role as a place for good value, and Southwark Council has extended a street market using funds from the Urban Programme. Similarly in Deptford, the market has been a great success, and new traders are being supported through a training programme.

10.16 Cultural activity can also be stimulated through public facilities, such as libraries and educational centres which can help draw in children (and their parents too). 36% of suburban centres have adopted programmes to encourage libraries and museums in the town centre and a similar number have programmes for encouraging cinemas, theatres, arts centres or cultural zones. A good example is the redevelopment of Croydon's library, one of the corner-stones of their programme for promoting a new image for the town centre, which has included an exhibition of visionary architectural ideas.

Co-ordinated local transport

10.17 The fact that a centre is well served by public transport routes and good road connections to adjacent centres can mean that unless there are quality attractions within the centre, they take people away rather than bring them in.

Strong attractions need to be combined with good local accessibility, providing effective linkages between the centre and surrounding residential areas.

10.18 Improving accessibility depends on making it as easy as possible to use public transport, so that people are encouraged to leave cars at home. As rail systems are fixed, the main scope lies in making better use of buses, though it may be possible to make more intensive use of existing rail tracks for local services as the Manchester Metro does to Bury and Altrincham. There is scope for far more imagination in terms of routes and services, for example using 'Hoppa' buses that pick people up wherever the bus is hailed as is done with the service between Hampstead Garden Suburb and Golders Green. To be popular they must be frequent. There is plenty of potential for these to serve peripheral estates that are often relatively isolated. Well-designed interchanges can also encourage better utilisation, and convey the idea of a town centre as a communications hub. Half the of suburban centres say they have adopted programmes to establish transport interchanges. The most difficult problem to deal with is parking, and here concern for residents needs to be balanced with provision for shoppers. 69% of suburban centres have programmes to improve car parking. There is no perfect solution, but allowing short-term parking through meters or pay-and-display is one answer, making use of side roads when residents are at work. It is usually better to have a number of small car parks than one big one, and here the inclusion of a superstore at the edge of the town centre could work to a centre's advantage.

Harlesden: building confidence through a car park

Harlesden, in the London Borough of Brent, is one of many suburban centres that has lost out to neighbouring centres. There are still over 300 retailers in the centre, mainly independent, but by 1992 many had become apathetic and depressed by falling turnover and lack of progress in improving the centre. A survey found that the main problems were perceived as parking and cleanliness. To boost confidence at an early stage, a derelict site was converted into a car park, with a prominent sign saying "Welcome to Harlesden" as the first step in a comprehensive strategy. Brent was successful in its City Challenge bid for the area, and a major food store is now interested in developing the site where previous plans had come to nothing.

Friendlier streets

10.19 The heavy through traffic common to many suburban centres often makes stopping difficult. It therefore requires extra effort both to encourage people to disrupt their journey and to ensure that local people make the most of their nearest centre. Rather than see a polarisation between outer centres which depend entirely on car-borne customers and inner centres that are only served by public transport and foot, centres need to find ways of reconciling the different modes.

Wood Green: taking action to improve public spaces

As part of an initiative to improve one of London's major shopping centres, an Urban Design Action Team spent a weekend brainstorming possibilities with local people in Wood Green. One result was a project to transform the area in front of the library and next to the new radio station. Funded through the Urban Programme, a set of steps is now an inclined open area, used as a 'speakers corner' at weekends. New signs welcome people to the library and an arcade of shops within it, which are floodlit at night. Instead of standard street furniture, the planters were surrounded by colourful 'bookends' while trellis surrounds were designed for the main columns to deter flyposting. The concrete balconies were made friendlier through trailing plants. A neglected corner has becoming a popular space, and provides another reason for visiting Wood Green.

A good place to start is by creating a positive first impression (Hillman 1988).

10.20 Occasionally well-designed new centres and offices can change the image of a centre, as in Wimbledon or Ealing. More often reliance must be placed on improving the public realm. As diverting traffic is often impossible, attention needs to be focussed on measures such as tree planting, wider pavements, and pedestrian crossings, as well as removing clutter and improving standards of urban design, as in Westminster. Landscaping and public art can sometimes be used to create somewhere memorable, as in Lewisham, where the upgrading of the shopping centre is being signalled by the involvement of an artist in landscaping the new by-pass. Public art can help to create a sense of identity, like the large black cat outside the Catford Centre in South East London.

69% of centres say they have adopted programmes for environmental improvements.

10.21 Several surveys of businesses in London centres have found that the most common concerns are to improve cleanliness, and make parking easier (URBED 1990). Nearly two thirds of centres have programmes for frequent cleansing in the town centre. Before promoting anything more complex, it is essential to check that a good standard applies. There is probably scope for copying some of the US techniques for tackling 'crime and grime', which in some cases involves recruiting unemployed people in smart uniforms to help boost confidence, rather than relying on technical fixes such as CCTV to overcome fear (see example of Philadelphia page 133).

10.22 The challenge for many centres, in the light of limited scope for expansion, is how to make what they have more attractive. The problems are greatest for the centres that were redeveloped in the 1960s and which are showing their age. While redevelopment may not be financially viable, a great deal can be achieved through refurbishment. Sometimes all that can be afforded is a facelift, as at the Elephant and Castle in Southwark where an interim programme to paint the building pink and to let out market stalls managed to fill the centre for almost the first time in its history and helped increase rental levels. Combined with the improved subways at a busy traffic route and with developments such as South Bank University's Technopark, a joint venture with a financial institution, the area is becoming a friendlier place.

10.23 Sometimes more fundamental changes are needed and here the problem is financial resourcing. The sale of the Council-owned freehold to a property company can provide the security to justify refurbishment. Sometimes schemes can involve not just upgrading shops, but also providing additional housing, though the collapse of the property market has reduced the numbers of substantial developers. There are also examples of specialist developers or development trusts taking on the difficult task of packaging the commercial and non-commercial elements, as with projects in Deptford town centre, though the numbers are still small.

Lewisham: promoting a distinctive image

Like many inner London town centres, Lewisham has suffered from the domination of traffic, and an unappealing 1960's shopping centre. Concern about the centre's decline led to the Council launching Lewisham 2000, described as a '£35 million project to transform the town centre'. The first step was to upgrade the shopping centre, which the Council sold in 1989, thus providing the incentive for a public/private development consortium to upgrade the facilities, with for example a children's central play area and a cafe, as well as modern shop fronts and much more natural light.

The second major investment was in building a relief road to allow the High Street to be pedestrianised. Market research with group interviews was used to gauge reactions to proposals, and a working party comprising retailers and community representatives, meets every six weeks, while newsletters and a local office is used to keep everyone informed. A multi-disciplinary team is based there, including engineers and landscape architects, coordinated by a planner.

The next stages include a new cinema and an hotel, and the site was marketed through the Government's Private Finance Initiative. Importantly, in attracting investment, it is now possible to show real improvements, as well as firm plans for extending the Docklands Light Railway. One of the distinctive features of Lewisham 2000 has been the employment of a town artist, so that items like street furniture are beginning to make the centre look different. It is no coincidence that Citybank, a major US company, decided to relocate and is expanding its offices there. However, this work did not stop the centre's main department store closing down, with the intention of moving to a new out-of-town development.

11 metropolitan cities

- Metropolitan city centres tend to have a multiplicity of roles, characterised by the dominance of offices, a low residential community, and a vulnerability to dispersal.

- More people should be able to live near the city centre, for example, by converting former commercial buildings and promoting mixed uses or urban villages on redundant industrial sites.

- Superior public transport should be provided, with an emphasis on a frequent and reliable bus system integrated with faster forms of transport.

- Distinct quarters should be promoted, linked by a network of pedestrian streets, where a 'night time economy' can be encouraged.

'The building of the cities was a characteristic Victorian achievement, impressive in scale but limited in vision, creating new opportunities but also providing massive new problems.'

Victorian Cities, Asa Briggs.

11.01 Though we have only identified ten Metropolitan Cities in England and Wales, their size makes what happens in them of significance on a far wider scale. We received replies from eight of these centres and of those 38% were vibrant 25% improving and 37% stable. None was declining and a number provide models for what can be achieved through positive planning.

Common features

11.02 **Multiplicity of roles:** Metropolitan cities have a range and depth of functions that places them almost at the summit of the urban hierarchy, and lead to comparisons being made with international cities like Barcelona or Amsterdam (Civic Trust 1993a). All functions are present to a substantial extent. They are some of the largest shopping centres in the country, with some of the highest retail rents. They are substantial employment centres and major places to learn; there are four universities close to the centre of Manchester for example and 25,000 students living in Nottingham.

11.03 The centres have long provided places to meet and be entertained with pubs, clubs, theatres and concert halls and there are now also specialist conference and exhibition facilities. They provide hospitals and other health facilities and extensive sports facilities. Most of them have developed visitor attractions, in some cases building on their industrial heritage, and they have developed as major transport hubs, often with city centre motorway access, inter-city rail stations and links to ports and airports. The concentration of activity, which 20th century planners saw as a drawback, is also the factor which enables cities to generate a sense of vibrancy, a quality appreciated by US writers like Lewis Mumford and Jane Jacobs, but only recently by their British counterparts.

11.04 **Dominant offices:** Though developed on the back of industry, the metropolitan cities became major trading centres in the 19th century. Corn, wool and cotton exchanges were built and formed the base for today's extensive financial services operations, including international bank branches, major building society headquarters and stock exchange representatives. Leeds along with other major cities is involved in a network of European cities to develop these activities further. The cities are also substantial administrative centres both for national and local government and for many private sector companies as well as being major centres for professional services. It is estimated that there is some 20 million square feet of commercial office space in Manchester and about 7 million in Sheffield. The Inland Revenue is moving its headquarters to Nottingham, whilst the Department of Health's headquarters is now in Leeds.

11.05 Tourism is developing as another major service sector employer in the metropolitan cities, attracting both British and overseas visitors. As well as hotels, pubs, restaurants, theatres and the like, the cities have developed specialist sports facilities and major historic attractions, benefiting from the spending power of their working population as well as their visitors. In 1991 Birmingham and Manchester were fourth and sixth respectively in UK centres visited by staying overseas visitors.

11.06 **Low central residential community:** Unlike many continental cities, very few people live in the heart of the major English cities. Instead people have moved or been moved to the suburbs, as large scale commercial development took place. Commercial demand and the resultant high land values ensured this continued until the 1980s. As a result, the city centres generally do not cater for a residential community

'The urban centre is in fact a theatre... a place in which the social heritage is concentrated, and in which the possibilities of continuous social intercourse and interaction raise to a higher potential all the complex activities of men.'

Lewis Mumford, The City in History

131

and have few food shops, though some 'basket' supermarkets, such as Tesco Metro, are now opening.

11.07 With the vast majority of people living some distance from the centre, traffic and parking demand outstrips supply and so investment has been required in updating and improving public transport services into the centres, both at peak daytime periods and in providing adequate evening services, along with evening parking.

11.08 **Vulnerability to dispersal:** The size of the metropolitan cities, and the high central land values has resulted in pressures for development on the peripheries of the cities, where direct motorway access can be provided. Business and retail parks have opened at motorway junctions or near airports around the cities, sometimes with leisure facilities such as multi-plex cinemas and bowling alleys. The peripheries of the cities are now attracting planning applications from US-style warehouse clubs. The centres are potentially vulnerable to regional shopping centres, such as the Metro Centre in Gateshead and Meadowhall in Sheffield. Metropolitan cities, therefore, have to work hard to keep their centres attractive, through policies such as promoting a positive image, mixed uses, superior public transport, and distinctive quarters.

A positive image

11.09 Twenty years ago, the centres of most of the metropolitan cities were seen as unattractive places, dominated by traffic, with drab and redundant buildings, and neglected canals and rivers. Comprehensive redevelopment schemes made the centres dead at night, the Arndale Centre in Manchester being a classic example. British cities compared poorly with most continental ones.

Sheffield: seeing its centre decline

Sheffield city centre has always suffered somewhat from its development on a number of hills, which has resulted in parts of the shopping centre being physically separated from each other, as well as from the rail and bus stations. The decline of Sheffield's traditional industries had a major effect on the city centre. Rising unemployment and reduced spending power combined to threaten the viability of the centre. Although a number of initiatives promoted by the City Council, including the use of redundant buildings on the edge of the centre, to create a "cultural industries quarter", the centre's viability was further threatened by the development of the Meadowhall regional shopping centre, some four miles away. This was originally perceived as being one anchor of the redevelopment of the Don Valley, with the city centre forming the other anchor. However, despite a number of proposals for major schemes by the private sector in the city centre (including the Canal Basin development, which would have created over 400,000 sq ft of office space as well as residential and leisure shopping uses) very few proposals have been implemented.

Since the opening of Meadowhall, surveys have shown that retail turnover in the city centre has declined. Many stores have responded by cutting staff or by offering more regular sales and discounting. A 1992 study commissioned by the City Council, amongst others, has now recognised the growing problems of declining attractions, relatively poor access and a generally mediocre standard of amenity in the centre coupled with a lack of co-ordinated action. This has proposed a number of initiatives to take advantage of developments, such as the soon to be launched supertram. They are aimed at developing a "Vision of Quality" for the centre that will see a diversity of activities in an improved and more accessible environment.

11.10 Over the last ten years most cities have sought to change this image, and today the results are apparent. Cities have competed fiercely to attract new investment and jobs, setting up substantial marketing offices, as in Cardiff, for example. Both private investors and Government departments

Philadelphia: fighting crime and grime

The city's downtown had lost much of its retailing and was perceived as a particularly run-down part of the city. The establishment of a Business Improvement District, raising revenue from local property owners, led to the setting up of a central management organisation.

Through the Business Improvement District, the management company raises almost $7 million each year, largely through a 4.5% surcharge on the property tax paid by the owners of some 2,000 properties within the District. Its initial priority was to tackle problems of cleanliness and security through what has been termed a "grime and crime" initiative.

56% of the first two year's budget went into a clean-up and maintenance regime and 34% on public safety initiatives. This goes to employ over 100 extra cleaners and 40 community service reps, all in smart uniforms. A number of rangers were recruited to undertake improvements, including fifteen who had previously lived on the city's streets. Some became part of a system of increased security, through regular patrols that provide information and through personal radios report crime problems before they escalate. These early actions prepared the way for a more intensive programme of events and activities, including a "make it a night" campaign that deliberately sought to create a special atmosphere, with over 800 participating outlets, street entertainment, and cheap parking and transport for late night shopping once a week.

have been heavily lobbied to relocate to the major centres. Central Government and European grant aid has been used to undertake extensive infrastructure and environmental improvements. The commitment of local businesses has been enlisted for new visions of the centres, through bids for major events such as Sheffield's World Student Games. Undoubtedly, also, measures to support the arts, like Birmingham securing Sadlers Wells and the D'Oyly Carte Opera and developing its Symphony Hall, have helped in persuading office workers to relocate and young people to stay when they leave college. Birmingham's development plan noted:

'To a large degree the prosperity of the whole city will depend on the city centre. Entertainment, culture, leisure and recreation have an increasingly valuable role. Indeed, they represent the very essence of a large metropolitan international centre'.

11.11 However few British cities have gone as far as American cities in promoting a positive sense of pride through visible policing and maintenance.

Mixed uses

11.12 Many city centre buildings were erected by the Victorians at the peak of the city's prosperity. Whether commercial or civic, each city centre had a legacy of redundant buildings in the early 1980s. Many of these were listed or in conservation areas and were very much part of the identifiable fabric of the city, and of its image. Their continued vacancy both undermined that image and had detrimental economic consequences.

11.13 With few people living in the city centres, there were traditionally large parts of every day when the centre was devoid of life or underused. This is now changing, partly as a result of initiatives to develop city centre housing, but also through the encouragement of the city centres as places to visit, learn, meet and seek entertainment. The needs of visitors have created attractions and facilities, such as hotels, restaurants and museums, that are open at weekends and evenings and make the centre a more attractive place to be, effectively an ' urban village '(Aldous 1992). A good example is Castlefield Park in Manchester which is now a major tourist attraction. A leading example of regeneration through housing is Glasgow's Merchant City, where over 1,000 new homes have been created, mainly in refurbished commercial buildings, and assisted both by Government grants and by the City making buildings available on economic terms.

11.14 Universities also have an increasingly important role to play, not just in bringing people into study, but in supporting knowledge based industry, the Aston Science Park in Birmingham being a good example. Centrally-situated universities, as in Sheffield and Liverpool are more popular than out-of-town campuses. Increasingly city centre housing is being developed

---

Manchester: restoring life to the city centre

Manchester is one of a number of cities, including Glasgow with its Merchant City and Leeds with its riverside, where the city centre now houses a rapidly growing residential population. In Manchester the focus has been on what is called 'the Whitworth Street Corridor', a group of massive warehouses. Using City Grant, the Central Manchester Development Corporation has succeeded in persuading a number of private developers to follow the lead set by the Northern Counties Housing Association in their conversion of Mantra House. There are now some 1,000 flats, and the presence of more people close to the city centre is helping Manchester in its aim to create a lively evening economy.

Environmental improvements, such as public art, have helped to generate positive publicity and change traditional images, a good example being a 'public art umbrella' in one town centre alley. The Castlefield Park area, Britain's first urban heritage park, has transformed the environment of the canal, which, together with a whole range of museum and visitor attractions, has brought a dead area to life. Urban rangers, influenced by American experience, are used to keep the place looking attractive.

---

for these students above shops, in converted buildings and in new build developments. In many cities, factories, warehouses and wharf buildings have been converted to provide workspace for small businesses, often managed or targeted at particular sectors, such as media or design. Other uses have included specialist shopping as in Leeds, where the prominent Corn Exchange was refurbished by a private company, and a growing number of examples of housing, often facilitated by City Grant.

Superior public transport

11.15 As traffic and parking is a major problem for all metropolitan cities, public transport must be the best available. Over half of the users of Nottingham city centre arrive by this means. To compete with the car, it is essential that it is both efficient, reliable and accessible. Bus deregulation in 1986 had a profound effect on cities such as Sheffield, where a previously heavily subsidised bus system operated. With many operators seeking to develop routes, Sheffield's central streets were often nose to tail with buses of all descriptions. A recent estimate indicates that the bus seats available in the city increased by 25% following deregulation, but the number of shoppers arriving in the city centre by bus fell from 49% in 1980 to 34% in 1989 (Foley 1992). In response, Sheffield has sought to integrate its bus and rail stations by creating a transport interchange and has largely refurbished both. This has included improving access to the city centre. The city's new light rail metro system will also link to the interchange.

11.16 Light rapid transit services connecting the city centre and suburban centres already exist in Newcastle and Manchester, and are proposed for Nottingham. Manchester's metro system uses existing rail lines to outlying suburbs and then runs through the city centre streets to link the main railway stations and key shopping areas. Both Sheffield and Manchester are publicly-financed schemes, but the proposed Nottingham metro system, that is currently awaiting parliamentary approval, involves an innovative public/private partnership. Despite the strides that have been taken recently, British cities still lag behind their European counterparts in the quality of public transport they offer, and hence in persuading people to leave their car behind. This involves more than reintroducing

Birmingham: promoting distinctive quarters

A strategy for the city led to a number of distinct quarters being established. An example of what has been achieved is the Jewellery Quarter, one of a series of areas around the city centre, which now have distinct identities. A strategy commissioned for this 100 acre area divided it into a number of zones. The 'industrial middle' now includes several business centres. Access to the City Centre has been improved while the convention centre is linked by a canal side walk. Housing has been developed in what is now a 'smart area' with wine bars and restaurants by St. Paul's Square. A Discovery Centre has been set up in another area, designated "the golden triangle", where there are now many jewellery retailers, as well as manufacturers. The City Council worked closely with a local economic development initiative, Jewellery Quarter Action, funded by the Government and the private sector. Support from local businesses was mobilised through a Jewellery Quarter Association.

trams, however attractive. A frequent, modern bus system with priority in congested areas and good interchange facilities, can often achieve more for less cost.

Dusseldorf: developing public transport

In most German cities, such as Dusseldorf, public transport has become a fashionable alternative to using the car, and people leave their cars behind when they go into town. As a result even though car ownership is higher than in Britain, usage has not risen as rapidly. The reasons lie in the quality of the German public transport system and the way different services are integrated.

Dusseldorf, which has one of the best public transport networks in Germany, combines trams, light rail and buses. Trams have priority at traffic lights, and interchange with fast suburban trains at the main railway stations. The timetable allows for 10 minute and in some cases even 5 minute intervals, while off peak public transport runs every 20 minutes.

As in other German towns an 'environmental ticket' has been introduced covering the entire Ruhr area. Students are obliged to buy a public transport ticket when they register, as are the employees of many large organisations, which then reduces the cost of a parking space, (which has led to an increase of 25% in public transport passengers over the last 3 years).

Distinctive quarters

11.17 Most of the Metropolitan Cities have invested in restoring their heritage of redundant buildings and watersides. Canals and rivers have been cleaned and towpaths and new foot bridges introduced. Interpretive signs and leaflets have been produced to explain the historic significance of sites and buildings. Areas with high ethnic minority populations have been encouraged to develop a distinct character, as in Manchester's central Chinatown where the City Council changed its planning policies to allow neon signs and banners on listed buildings and the Chinese community contributed to an archway and street furniture that gives the area a distinct identity.

11.18 The rich legacy of industrial heritage left in many cities has also been used as a visitor attraction and to create areas of the city centre that are attractive to certain kinds of businesses. In Bristol Docks, a warehouse was turned into a media centre, and the example has now been followed in many other centres. In Nottingham, the Lace Market, an area adjacent to the city centre with many listed buildings, was designated as an 'Industrial Heritage Area' and buildings were cleaned and restored, paviours replaced tarmac and a former church was converted into a combined museum, lace shops, and cafe. With distinctive signage and interpretation panels, the area has become a popular location for professional firms.

11.19 However, it is as places of entertainment that city centres have made some of the most rapid developments. Experience shows that this needs to be part of a strategic approach. Though Sheffield has successfully restored the Lyceum Theatre at a cost of some £12 million and provided secure car parking, most users appear to drive in and out of the centre, simply for the performance. In Nottingham, in contrast, the Theatre Royal and Concert Hall have become part of a *cultural quarter* with many wine bars, restaurants offering pre and post production meals and drinks, with *well-lit and easily-accessible car parks* surrounding the area. This area is separated from the more entertainment-orientated part of the centre that caters mainly for younger people. Police estimate that up to 40,000 young people are in the city centre on a Friday and Saturday evening.

Nottingham: making visitors more welcome

Though Nottingham is a smaller city than Sheffield (with which it compares in many ways) and has a lower socio-economic rating, it had twice as many shops before the opening of Meadowhall, and has been relatively unaffected by out-of-town competition. One of the reasons for Nottingham's success has been the range of non-retail attractions, from the Robin Hood Experience to the town centre itself. As a consequence it was given the highest satisfaction rating by shoppers in a survey of Northern cities.

Nottingham has succeeded in conveying the image of a continental city through an extensive pedestrian network, one of the largest in the country. This has linked fringe areas, like the Lacemarket, with the two main shopping centres and the Castle, thus helping to convey a very distinct image and identity.

Nottingham has sought to improve accessibility and car parking in the city centre. Radio announcements keep listeners informed of parking spaces available throughout Nottingham's 22 car parks. City Centre Management has encourage private sector and City Council car parks to introduce a series of security improvements such as information points and patrols, which has dramatically reduced car crime by 50% in key car parks (in a city which had a high level of recorded crime). The highly successful Park and Ride service has been extended including a new £1.5 million state-of-the-art site on the main approach from the M1. Major improvements to public transport are also underway including a new high-tech information system, high quality shelters and an upgraded central station which are all part of a customer welcoming strategy. To ensure that newly pedestrianised streets are kept in prime condition a Considerate Contractors Code has been introduced and a City Centre Ranger provides a rapid response to frustrating maintenance problems. Nottingham has a wide variety of specialist and alternative shops which are promoted in a free shopping guide. A comprehensive shopping directory is also available for visitors to browse through at a series of reception points including the City Information Centre. All this is done on a shoe-string budget, through the Town Centre Manager using his influence to persuade organisations, like the bus companies and car park operations to work together for the good of city centre (from which they all then benefit).

12 resorts and historic towns

- Resorts and historic towns share a changing pattern of visitors, heritage assets and liabilities, residents on limited incomes, and conflicts over roles.

- The ongoing priority is to make the centres of resorts and historic towns attractive to the people who live and work in them.

- Fresh attractions and periodic promotion can make the most of the town's special heritage to draw visitors and help avoid over-concentration in particular areas.

- Visitors can be made more welcome and less intrusive through visitor management policies, such as 'park and ride' and good signing.

- Comprehensive schemes, such as 'conservation area partnerships', should encourage private owners to restore their buildings, while improving the public realm, using quality design and a mix of uses to make places feel safe.

'Our research reveals that England's heritage is a popular motivation in people's choice of destination either on holiday or a day trip. This is even more evident when looking at the choices made by visitors from abroad. Resorts must react to such trends if they are to widen their appeal and begin to win back market share'.

John East, Foreword to 'Turning the Tide'.

12.01 46 Resorts and Historic Towns replied to our survey, 4% of which were vibrant, 37% improving, 37% stable, and 20% declining. However, 29% of resorts were declining compared with only 12% of historic towns. With the English Tourist Board looking at how the heritage of resorts can be marketed, it would appear that there are lessons that can be learned from the experience of historic towns.

Common features

12.02 **Changing pattern of visitor:** Although those who live in the town sometimes seek to deny it, the local economies of both historic towns and resorts depend to a great extent on visitors. We have taken the definition of an historic town to be one where more than 20% of visitors to the town come from beyond its immediate catchment area. A broader definition would be any town that succeeds is being known as a place to visit for example by being included in one of the standard guides such as Town Tours in Britain (Readers Digest 1990). The relative success of the historic towns compared to most resorts reflects the increasing discrimination of the visitor. The traditional holiday by the sea has largely gone, possibly to the Mediterranean, with a devastating effect for those resorts that have not developed alternative attractions or a conference trade. For example, by 1992, the amount of visitor accommodation available in Margate was only 5% of that available in 1939 (URBED 1993). Day trips and short breaks have replaced the two-week holiday for many Britons, whilst a record 18.5 million overseas tourists visited the UK in 1992.

12.03 For many seeking short breaks, and particularly for the overseas visitor, heritage is an important appeal. Brighton and Hove was the only resort to be in the top ten of towns stayed in by overseas visitors in 1992, though it was behind historic cities such as Oxford, York, Cambridge and Bath. Historic towns also attract conferences, which in many cases complement their role as university towns.

12.04 **Heritage assets and liabilities:** In many historic towns heritage is seen as a major asset. The cathedral, castle, city wall, spa or the Victorian and Regency terraces are major attractions and are largely in a restored condition. This is not always the case in the resorts, where the piers, large hotels, winter gardens, lido and theatres may be deteriorating or vacant. Even when restored, such features need continuing maintenance and protection from the large numbers of visitors and volumes of traffic that they can generate.

12.05 As in market towns, many of the buildings in the town centre may be listed or in a conservation area and uses or additions, such as shutters or closed circuit television cameras, may be prevented. New development is often restricted for the same reason. The historic streets are often unsuitable for modern traffic volumes. The main streets are usually pedestrianised or have other restrictions imposed.

12.06 **Residents on limited incomes:** Though attracting visitors who spend money, many resorts and historic towns have large numbers of residents on limited incomes. They have long been seen as attractive places to retire to. As interest rates have fallen, many of the retired residents have seen their incomes decline. In recent years, resorts have also attracted people on Social Security who have often taken space in former hotels. A 1993 report by SAGA, who organise holidays for the elderly, said that Social Security tenants were often their main competition for hotel accommodation in English seaside resorts. In many seaside resorts there is only a limited season when visitor-related employment is available and there has been little diversification to offer other jobs. Many visitor-related jobs such as hotel, restaurant or pub work are anyway poorly paid. In many of the historic towns, a large student population exists, with many on limited incomes.

12.07 **Conflicts over roles:** Although tourism is a major contributor to the local economies of most resorts and historic towns, it also brings problems. Traffic, parking, litter, noise, and public order are all issues that feature regularly in letters to local newspapers and councils wherever large numbers of visitors are attracted. Conflicts can arise over the image created by visitor attractions, with many residents objecting to the apparent down-market appeal of seaside facilities such as amusement arcades and fast-food outlets. Some businesses in historic towns complain about buskers and others seeking money from visitors in the street. Restaurants, bars and shopping areas are often perceived as crowded with visitors, thus restricting use by residents.

Multiplicity of attractions

12.08 Faced with a dependence on attracting visitors from outside the area, successful towns have adopted policies for promoting a multiplicity of attractions, visitor management and heritage enhancement.

12.09 The historic towns and the more successful seaside resorts know the importance of a variety of attractions. These provide a longer 'visitor experience', thus encouraging visitors to spend more money in the town through needing to eat, drink or stay. They also help to spread the influx of visitors to different locations. Traditionally theme parks, such as Black-

---

Margate: changing customer base

Like many seaside resorts, Margate has seen a substantial change in the habits and make-up of its customers over the last few decades. Where once families came to its many hotels for a fortnight, now most visitors are day trippers, or perhaps older people on coach tours. The number of hotels in the town is now about one tenth of what it was in the 1950s. This drop in staying visitors has resulted in many of the smaller hotels being converted for residential use, in some cases as accommodation for those on Social Security, whilst some of the larger hotels have become vacant. Demand for sea front attractions and shops has also fallen, resulting in an extended period with little fresh investment, apart from the area immediately adjacent to the central beach, railway station and Dreamland Amusement Park. This has seen the development of numerous amusement arcades, cafes and souvenir-type shops offering a limited range of goods and catering for the day visitor. The area is not well regarded by many residents, including those who have retired to the town. Proposals to develop visitor facilities in other parts of the town often meet with numerous objections from residents.

The town centre has suffered from both a drop in visitors and a loss of local trade to Canterbury, a reviving Ramsgate and out-of-town retail parks. It has also been affected by a number of unfortunate schemes implemented in the 1970s and a lack of co-operation between the various parties in the town. A new initiative, Thanet 2000, has now been launched to bring together the various interests in the town. A project team has been put in place working to implement a strategy, developed by consultants, that incorporates economic, social/cultural and environmental programmes.

---

pool Pleasure Beach, have sought to keep people on-site for as long as possible (the Pleasure Beach now has on-site bank machines) and to draw them back by offering the promise of new or improved features. More town centres need to adopt a similar policy. York is a classic example of revitalising an industrial railway town as a historic city through visitor attractions that interpret the city's distinctive history, such as the Jorvik Viking Museum. Similarly Bath was for many years largely abandoned by visitors who went to the seaside instead. Now as well as being a World Heritage site, Bath has some 17 museums, theatres and galleries that attract both visitors and residents, the latest being a Chinese gallery and an architecture centre.

12.10 The bigger resorts, such as Bournemouth and Brighton, have developed conference and associated facilities that prolong the visitor season and bring visitors to the towns for

reasons other than holidays. This in turn creates trade for higher-class hotels, providing en-suite accommodation and offering quality restaurants, bars and other facilities. Many historic towns have proved attractive to both major multiples and a variety of specialist shops, as shopping has increasingly been seen as a leisure activity.

12.11 Resorts have long been venues for events such as veteran car runs from neighbouring major cities or summer carnivals. On the whole there were additional attractions for people already in the town. However, events and promotion

---

York: Rediscovering its unique heritage

Thirty years ago, York was as well-known for its industry, particularly railways and chocolate, as for its historic character. In 1968 a report by Lord Esher provided a new vision for the future of the city that looked at new development as well as conservation. The Council established a tourism department in 1969 to attract staying visitors and in 1975 the National Railway Museum was secured for the city. York has been a pioneer in excluding traffic.

Car access to the historic core of the city centre was first restricted in 1973 and an area-wide traffic management study followed. In 1978, the Great York Travel study set out proposals for pedestrianisation and learning from the experience of continental cities. Although many of these proposals raised objections and the process was slowed, a £3 million scheme was undertaken in 1987 following a public inquiry. This included a network of short and long-stay car parks serving central "footstreets" where traffic is excluded during the day. A warden and manager were appointed to manage the streets and ensure effective maintenance. Licenses have sought to encourage street activity. Park and ride schemes include provision at a Tesco superstore on the city's fringes, with a 5 minute service at peak-time, and the service diverts approximately 15% of the traffic arriving from that side of the city.

The creation of a quality environment has been accompanied by the continued development of new attractions, including the Coppergate shopping centre, which was developed on a site marketed by the City Council through design and tender bids. One of the most successful initiatives is the Jorvik Viking Museum, which developed in the heart of the city using imaginative interpretation methods and rapidly became one of the country's most visited museums.

Exeter: Combining accessibility with amenity

After Exeter lost two-thirds of its centre through bombing in 1942, the City implemented a comprehensive plan which included a partially completed inner ring road. However by 1974 road proposals were dropped in favour of traffic management, and Exeter was one of the first British cities to go for traffic calming. The City and the County collaborated on a Traffic and Parking Plan, which included a park and ride scheme which saves 8-900 cars a day entering the city, linked traffic lights, advance message signing to the multi-storey car parks, special shopping and tourist car parks including an award winning multi-storey residents parking schemes, traffic calming, car sharing and bus priority schemes and cycle routes.

In spite of the 1950s architecture, traffic calming in the High Street has produced a very popular and highly accessible centre, with a continental feel. The frequent mini-buses add to the bustle, without dominating and attract people to leave their car behind. Significantly perhaps the major out-of-town schemes have now been dropped. The City has also turned its Quay and Riverside into a popular visitor attraction. This complements the city centre, thus helping to boost tourism and provides significant extra housing within walking distance. Exeter has succeeded in turning itself into an historic city that draws visitors and investment.

are increasingly being used to bring people into the town. Resorts have also tried to attract visitors out side of the peak summer months. Perhaps the most successful example is Blackpool Illuminations, which actively extends the season into November and is a major attraction for many of the 16 million annual visitors to the town. Arts and culture have been promoted as draws by historic cities, the classic example being the Edinburgh Festival. Smaller towns too have used festivals to restore confidence and raise their profile. An example is Hay-on-Wye, which in turn inspired the people of Sandwich to organise their own festival, when they heard about it at a symposium.

12.12 Attractions do not have to be large, and can include imaginative uses of buildings; for example in Lancaster, a redundant Methodist chapel is now a thriving Indian restaurant, and former mills have been turned into student housing.

Visitor management

12.13 Often seen as a priority by those who live or work in the town, visitor management has in many centres been under-resourced. Increasingly it is being seen as an essential requirement if conflicts are to be avoided and the town is to remain an attractive place to both live and visit. Many historic towns, and some resorts, have followed the example of York and established park-and-ride services (York, 1988). There are now some 20 year-round and 40 seasonal systems in place and another 30 being actively considered. Many of these are operated in historic towns or resorts. The English Historic Towns Forum has published a Good Practice guide on the subject (EHTF 1993). In planning for pedestrian movement it is also important to design routes where cyclists can ride safely.

12.14 Other arrival points can be equally crucial. Bus and coach set down points and parking are another significant factor for both kinds of town as in many places restrictions on stopping have been introduced. Equally, car parking and pedestrian access to major attractions, including provision for queuing, have become significant factors. Brighton has introduced a new signing policy that both reduces the previous multiplicity of signs at many junctions and uses a series of readily identifiable symbols to attractions and other facilities.

12.15 Following a government Task Force study in 1990/91 on the *Impact of Tourism on the Environment*, a three-year national pilot project on visitor management in historic towns was launched in Stratford-upon-Avon, in November 1992. The main priority of this initiative, which brings together local authorities, retailers, transport operators and representatives of major attractions in the town, is on 'maintaining the balance'.

12.16 The central location of many attractions, the daily influx of visitor and, in many cases, the historic street pattern, have all contributed to congestion and conflict between vehicles and pedestrians. A useful English Tourist Board report illustrates the range of transport management options:

'The impact of visitors in cars and coaches can be managed through such means as signposted routes, sophisticated traffic control systems, traffic calming techniques, parking strategies, park-and-ride schemes, promotion of public transport, facilities for walking and cycling, traffic restrictions and pedestrianisation schemes.'

Tourism and the Environment: English Tourist Board

Brighton: broadening the economic base

Brighton developed as a fashionable Georgian watering spot and has again become an attractive and lively location for residents and visitors. While the traditional two week holiday has gone tourism remains very important, with 2.5 million day visitors, 1 million staying visitors and 200,000 conference attenders a year supporting some 11% of local jobs. The town has also found new roles as an educational centre, with 27,000 students and 3,500 staff, and a as financial and administrative centre with American Express among others. The Council built the Brighton Centre in 1977 and Brighton hosts some 1200 conferences a year worth an estimated £63 million to the local economy. Above all it has become an attractive place to live.

Brighton has made the most of its heritage, such as the picturesque Lanes, and has some 1900 listed buildings and 27 conservation areas. These attract younger and more affluent visitors. Only two streets lack people living in them so they are alive at all times. As a consequence of both the residents and the visitors there are 400 restaurants (the largest number of places to eat outside London), and a very lively night-time economy. Three distinct shopping areas exist in the town, providing a variety of retail outlets and a considerable overall floorspace. There are problems, however, with links between the three areas, and with one of the centres.

Brighton provides an excellent example of how a resort can find new roles by making the most of its heritage. It is now taking action to reduce the impact of traffic and make the centre a more pleasant place to shop. The Transport and Environment strategy *"Putting People First"* is tackling a situation where traffic has been rising at 2-3% a year and bus usage has halved. The councils are striving for `accessibility for all, rather than mobility for some' by making walking and cycling safer and ensuring that buses offer an attractive alternative to cars, including park and ride. Some £2 million has been spent on creating an improved shopping environment, landscaping, pedestrianisation and bus priority in the central area. A further £1 million is being spent on improving the seafront and improving links to the shopping areas.

Eastbourne: building bridges to better business

Eastbourne has a population of around 86,000 and a reputation of being an old person's town, though this is changing. A town centre management partnership was set up following an initiative from key local businesses, who came together as Business in the Community.

The focus is on promoting the town as an all year round shopping centre. There have been three day open aid festivals with a French theme. A series of courses have been run from retailers with backing from the Training and Enterprise Council. These covered language, statutory requirements, customer care, and product display, and drew over a hundred participants, mainly small businesses, in the first year. A consultancy report led to the setting up of the Eastbourne Marketing Group, concerned with promotion and events, which has attracted support from a number of agencies.

12.17 In many towns pedestrianisation has been coupled with the provision of peripheral car parks, and increasingly the use of park-and-ride buses. Thus, in Bournemouth, the two pedestrianised arms of the shopping area have recently been linked by the creation of a new garden feature replacing a busy round-about that now only allows bus access. In all cases the pedestrianised streets have allowed for the incorporation of new street furniture, and other features that reflect the quality of the historic environment. Pedestrianised space allows street cafes, kiosks and events. However, there is a continued need to monitor such developments to prevent them creating additional blockages.

Heritage enhancement

12.18 Heritage and the quality of the environment is one of the principal attractions of historic towns, and has increasingly been seen to be an important potential attraction in seaside resorts. After years of decline, investment is being proposed for refurbishing many of the seventy traditional nineteenth century promenades in seaside resorts. In some cases this has been done through a *Tourism Development Action Programme* (TDAP). Thus, a partnership between the English and West Country Tourist Boards and both the county and district council led to a series of initiatives in Torbay, including the repaving of Torquay sea front, pedestrianisation of shopping streets and investment in signage, lighting and street furniture, as well as investment in shop front improvements. Places like Saltburn, with its railway station, Hastings with its Old Town and Shrewsbury, with its hospital, show how attractions in smaller towns can be enhanced through restoration and adaptive reuse of key buildings. Useful reports have been produced based on the experience of cold water resorts, and on proposals for Weston Super Mare that draw on local initiatives.

12.19 Wherever pedestrianised areas are created, there are security implications. With no traffic, retail streets can become very quiet at night and thus may encourage vandalism or crime, that in turn leads to demand for shutters on shops. Full shutters enhance the feeling of insecurity and are often out of keeping with the historic nature of the centre. In some instances CCTV has been introduced, but ultimately security is created by usage. However, it is often the nature of this use that is key. Many resorts, and some historic cities, have experienced problems caused by rowdy groups of young people. In Bath, the City Council used a bye-law to ban

Oxford: Leaving the car behind

Having started in 1973 Oxford has gone further than most cities in park and ride, but the level of traffic in the centre has remained almost constant. There are 3,000 spaces available, with usage up 27% on five years ago of which 40-45% are shoppers, but only 10% of car-borne visitors and tourists use it. All of the four sites have CCTV, bus shelters and telephone kiosks.

A comparison with the similar city of Freiburg in Germany found that the entire old city has been pedestrianised and that most people live close to a bus or tram stop, or use bicycles (27% compared with Oxford's 12%). The reasons for the differences were attributed to a greater political consensus in Germany, but also more funding for public transport, (which is cross-subsidised from surpluses on municipally owned utilities). Oxford City Council is now promoting a £17 million plan to ease congestion over five years. This involves investing in public transport, including experimental electric buses in partnership with Southern Electric and bicycle lanes, and reducing car access in the centre to try to match European standards.

out-door drinking except in designated sites, still allowing for continental-style cafes that encourage people to sit down and survey the street. In Rochester the traffic-calmed streets have excellent lighting and improved shop fronts to help make the centre look inviting at all times.

12.20 Many pedestrianisation schemes have been spoilt by poor quality materials and detailing. An English Heritage leaflet recommends local authorities to 'carry out less, in phases and to a higher standard rather than to compromise on overall quality and appearance' (EH 1993). Commenting on the 'discordant and inharmonious impact' of using too much inter-locking brickwork in historic areas, the guide calls on authorities to depart as little as possible from original materials and details. It also points out that 'there is increasing recognition that in some historic areas, the total exclusion of traffic can create sterile precincts, particularly at night'. Canterbury provides a good example of allowing cars in at night. Historic towns have achieved a great deal and their experience should be of interest to most town centres.

12.21 Good design does not mean simply building replicas of the past. Some of the most successful places have interwoven the new and the old, by using first-class architects. Good instances are Carlisle, Norwich and Chesterfield, not normally perhaps regarded as a historic town. (Aldous, 1990).

Norwich: a positive approach to security

A survey on crime undertaken by the Forum of Private Businesses in Norwich City Centre produced an 80% response from the 150 members and highlighted many of the concerns felt by those running businesses in a busy centre. The main worry related to vandalism and not planned burglary and there was a strong demand for an increased police presence, or failing that the introduction of CCTV. Increasingly retailers were responding to problems by installing shutters, often on historic buildings or in Conservation Areas. The Council took action against 14 properties. New security guidelines were drawn up and published which stress the need for a balanced approach and the use of deterrents such as reinforced stall risers rather than full length glass windows.

Perhaps more importantly the central population rose by over 40% in the decade to 1991 which leads to more people on the streets in previously quiet periods. 9,000 people now live within the city walls, an increase of 75% of households in the last 15 years. Most of them are in-fill schemes by the Council, by private developers and housing associations. There has also been a long running 'Living-over-the-Shop' programme. Norwich undertakes a survey every five years of the condition and use of all its historic buildings to target buildings at risk. It then uses grants under a town scheme with English Heritage, and invests in the buildings it owns, to ensure that buildings under threat are brought back into use. A stress is placed on interpretation, including interactive computers in the Tourist Information Office and a couple of shops, to help visitors and local people appreciate the city's history.

Saltburn: establishing a partnership for conservation

The Victorian planned seaside resort of Saltburn had become quite run down by the early 1980s. Langbaurgh-on-Tees Borough Council has taken a number of initiatives to bring about the town's revival. Encouraged by a Borough-wide tourism study which recognised the unspoilt potential of the town, a comprehensive package of projects were put in place. The town's 125th anniversary in 1986 saw the launch of the now annual Victorian Week festival which involves both special events and much use of nineteenth century costumes. A major programme of environmental improvements and restoration works have enhanced the Victorian character. The cost of the programme has been met through a partnership approach between the Local Authority, the Private Sector, English Heritage and the DoE and the European Community. The old station site has been redeveloped through a mixed use scheme that involves a bistro, small retailers and the tourist information office being situated in the station buildings, a new-build Gateway store and the conversion of the station hotel to provide flats. A new-build sheltered housing development on part of the site will complete the project. A themed 'Smugglers' visitor experience has been provided adjoining the historic Ship Inn in association with a brewery.

The local community has played a major part in backing the revival. A 500 Club raises money to enhance the town, through initiatives such as jumble sales for funds for the Christmas lights and even selling off the geraniums that were being dug out from a Council summer bedding scheme to pay for a strimmer to keep roadside borders tidy.

13 conclusions and recommendations

- Local authorities should keep the health of their town centres under review

- Strategies should seek to improve attractions, accessibility and amenity by applying a number of basic principles

- Higher standards of town centre management should be promoted

- Investment in key sites should be encouraged through positive planning

- Improvements to public transport should form part of town centre strategies

- National organisations should offer technical assistance

- A positive climate for investment should be created and local businesses should be actively involved

- Answers should be found to the longer term problems of resourcing town centres.

'If we are to make British town centres liveable and the envy rather than the poor relation of their European counterparts, we need renewed commitment, a change of public attitude and the local community working in a spirit of partnership towards a long term vision and a comprehensive approach to quality management of town centre. Town and city centres need to be celebrated and enhanced by all sections of society rather than half-heartedly tolerated as a necessary inconvenience.'

Liveable Towns and Cities. Liverpool John Moores University, Civic Trust

13.01 This research project has revealed a number of important findings concerning the state of town centres in England and Wales. Town centres are at the heart of communities, and it is their diversity of roles which makes them special. While the recession and the threat of out-of-town superstores has put town centres on the planning agenda, the problems they face are far more fundamental. Like the inner cities, town centres have to cope with strong pressures for dispersal, fuelled by the growing dependency on the car and changing patterns of work and lifestyles. Some centres, in expanding market towns as well as contracting old industrial and suburban areas, are felt to be declining. Some of these are at a tipping point where they could lose the basic attractions that keep them vital and viable.

13.02 This report has put forward ways of analysing town centres in terms of their performance and the factors influencing their health. It suggests some key quantitative indicators in terms of changes in yield and pedestrian flow, combined with various other measures, such as changing space in use and vacancy rates. We have proposed a sequential process for looking at the underlying factors which we have termed the four A's - attractions, accessibility, amenity and action.

13.03 Despite the warning signs the overall message of this report is positive. Though depressing comparisons can be made with American cities, we should be able to avoid the dangers of excessive dispersal before it is too late. Some British towns are already drawing on the lessons from the US experience in creating public private partnerships where the different interests work together to promote improvements. Others are copying Continental towns, creating liveable places by applying policies such as traffic calming to create neighbourhoods where people want to live and where it is safe to walk or cycle.

13.04 This report shows that we can now also take inspiration from many places in Britain. Amongst our greatest success stories are the historic towns. Not only have these attracted many people to live and work there, but they also draw enough visitors to support a higher standard of public facilities. Places like York, Norwich, Exeter and Worcester have all undergone a renaissance, and resolved the problems of regenerating run-down areas and attracting investment. The quality of their new developments has helped to reinforce what makes them special. The same is true in the centres of many of the metropolitan cities, such as Cardiff, Birmingham and Nottingham. More surprisingly, perhaps, there are now excellent examples from industrial towns such as Halifax, Preston and Wolverhampton, that are attracting people and have changed their image in the process. There are also promising signs of progress in many smaller towns, from Beverley and Horsham to Saltburn and Witney, some of which are fighting back by emphasising the traditional qualities of a real town, for example, friendly service, coupled with easy access and a pleasant environment.

13.05 Our research suggests the most serious threat to the future of town centres is not just the competition from out-of-town retailing, but neglect - the institutional inertia that stops some places from responding to changing needs and competition until it is too late. Yet despite limited local authority powers and resources, many places have shown what is possible, by applying some of the same practices as managed shopping centres in terms of monitoring performance and responding to consumer needs - what the North American International Downtown Association calls "Centralised Retail Management". We have therefore concluded that strengthening planning policies alone is not enough. The priority is to unleash a positive approach to planning and town centre management of the kind exemplified by the terms 'pride of place 'or' civic pride'.

13.06 The menu of possible initiatives is extensive, and resources will always be limited. It is therefore essential to prioritise, and to concentrate efforts where they will produce tangible results. We put forward a variety of innovative ideas culled from practical experience, from 'rangers' to undertake instant maintenance to 'cultural quarters' or entertainment zones. But what really matters is not the number of ideas but the capacity to turn visions into results.

13.07 We therefore look at resourcing town centres before putting forward a series of recommendations for what should be done at a local level using the existing planning system. These provide a summary or check-list of the main findings. We also set out some ideas for creating a more positive climate for the future of town centres at national level, addressed particularly at those who control the bulk of investment funds. These could form an agenda for making the most of the assets of our town centres. While these recommendations are intentionally general we have focussed particularly on proposals which apply to areas that are declining. These proposals are intended to build on the work currently undertaken by local authorities in drawing up local plans and exercising development control. In many cases there is also a need for greater involvement by the private sector in local initiatives for town centres.

Resourcing town centres

13.08 A central concern of many of the people we consulted was where the resources should come from for improving and maintaining town centres. Local authorities often say they lack the funds and staff time (and some town centre managers are struggling because there is no budget and no agreed plan). Retailers say they pay enough already in taxes. Financial institutions say they invest where the security and returns are greatest, and lack the management capacity to get involved in improving individual towns.

13.09 The system seems to operate very differently in other countries where there is more local control and involvement. However, just as town centres have succeeded in the past in mobilising investment in major new shopping centres, so it is possible, given the will, to focus efforts on improvements and on smaller development projects that involve diversification, for example through housing, education or cultural uses.

13.10 The main problem seems to lie in securing the involvement and commitment of national **financial institutions** - the property owners and investors, including insurance companies, banks and building societies, all of whom have considerable investments at stake but who tend to play a reactive role. Yet their international operations, as well as their branch network should put them in a good position to contribute positively if the topic were given serious attention at top management level.

13.11 There is the precedent of Michael Heseltine's Financial Institutions Group to draw on, which resulted in the secondment of senior managers to a task force. A number of companies have appointed Community Affairs Managers and Town Centre Support Managers, which have led to changes in mainstream practice as an indirect result. There are also a number of instances where town centre management initiatives are beginning to involve major property owners, and where City Challenge bids have brought the private and public sectors together.

13.12 There is therefore a major challenge for financial institutions to join with local communities in making it easier for new uses to occupy the space that is being vacated, and in providing the investment funds for diversification and improving the attractiveness of town centres. If that does not happen voluntarily there could be a case for learning from the Americans and introducing a system like the **Business Improvement District** (or Special Services District). This enables property owners to be locally levied for an additional contribution towards higher standards of environment, security and promotion, and for improving the facilities of the town centre.

Town centre focus

13.13 The most successful places are ones which receive continued care and attention from the local authority and where the different interests work together for the good of the town over a period of many years. All local authorities should ensure, as part of the planning process, that the health of their main town centres is kept under review by:

- forming multi-disciplinary town centre **management groups**, which bring together the departments concerned, including transport, environment, leisure and cultural services, planning, economic development and property services;

- periodically reviewing the situation in some kind of **forum** with the main interests, including not only

relevant officers and councillors and representatives of other departments and public agencies, but also the private sector, key retailers, the Chamber of Commerce or Traders Association, important property owners or their agents, and community groups such as amenity societies;

- collecting and analysing basic information, every one or two years, on population, economic growth and expenditure trends, and the **profile and performance** of the main centres, including changes in pedestrian flows and the yield on prime shops, and also indicators of changing health in terms of attractions, access and amenity;

- preparing **reports** approximately every two years on how the town centre is doing;

- participating in **study tours and conferences** to learn from other's experience, and;

- publishing **promotional material** on the town centre's position and vision.

Town centre strategies

13.14 Our research suggests that the complex nature of town centres means that there is a need to go further than conventional land use plans and this is particularly important where a centre is declining or at risk. The process of turning a town centre around starts with a realistic understanding of the situation - the town **profile**. There needs to then be a positive **vision** of where the town would go that is shared by the key interest. A **strategy** then needs to be devised with action programmes covering pilot as well as flagship projects. Such a process can provide confidence or guidance to all those interested in the town as well as setting a clear agenda for action. Use should be made of techniques that encourage a creative and multi-disciplinary approach. There is no general answer, and strategies must be geared to the type of town and what makes it special. However the basic principles for good practice include:

- **creating welcoming gateways**: first impressions endure; towns need to review their car parks, bus and railway stations, and the signing to them, to ensure they project the right image or identity for the town and that visitors are encouraged to return. Similarly public toilets or mother and toddler changing rooms all provide signals as to whether customers are welcome;

- **providing appropriate parking**: the way the car is handled has a major bearing on how well town centres perform. There are many options from upgraded multi-storeys to short-stay on-street parking with disks. What is required depends on the primary role the shopping centre is playing - comparison, convenience or specialist - as well as the other functions the area is intended to perform, such as housing or entertainment;

- **making public transport a more attractive option**: local authorities need to work with public transport operators to give buses priority, including park and ride, and improving interchange facilities. A first essential is to provide good information;

- **designing quality streets**: requirements for access need to be balanced with considerations for amenity. People should be able to walk safely and pleasantly to the centre from all the main gateways. The linkages should be as direct and level as possible so they provide access for all. Policies for traffic calming and exclusion at busy times can make centres attractive places to linger. A good choice of materials, landscaping and lighting can make town centres feel attractive most of the time and encourage private owners to improve their property too;

- **ensuring a feeling of security:** people have growing concerns about both crime and personal safety. A view held particularly among women, is that streets need to be busy and overlooked if they are to feel safe. This may be through encouraging more people to live in or near the centre or through good urban design. It can also be helped by improved maintenance and visible policing to revive confidence, as well as sensitive lighting and landscaping, and places where after hours activities can flourish without conflict;

- **safeguarding key attractions**: a major priority is to hang on to what the town already possesses. Planners need to identify the particular uses or stores that act as anchors and work with those businesses to ensure they stay and prosper. Environmental improvements and other efforts need to be focussed on maintaining a critical mass of attractions. Local authorities can sometimes use their ownership of land to mobilise private investment, and,

- **encouraging diversity**: real town centres involve far more than just shops. There are major opportunities to re-use empty shops and under-utilised property in ways that will make the town centre more distinctive and create complimentary attractions. As more people need to live in town centres housing should be a priority, with its own special strategy and action programme, together with educational, health and cultural uses.

Town centre management

13.15 Securing improvements is always complex as it involves co-ordinating the activities of many different interests. While the scale of the town will affect the level of staffing that is feasible, towns need to adopt appropriate methods for implementing town centre strategies, including:

- drawing up **action programmes** and budgets for the short, medium and longer terms;

- establishing **management teams** or town centre managers and working with business and community organisations, such as chambers of commerce and amenity societies so that local people can play a full part;

- generating **ongoing funding**, for example from car parking receipts, licensing market stalls and other uses of public space, promotional events, and agreements with property owners and developers, and;

- collaborating with **networks** of similar towns at county, regional or international levels to raise standards.

Positive planning

13.16 Local authorities should encourage investment in sites that present opportunities for development and diversification, including vacant or under-utilised buildings by:

- identifying **key sites** where development is possible;

- devising and publishing **planning briefs**, for example to provide new housing, cultural facilities or specialist shops;

- considering the use of techniques such as securing **outline planning consents**, or in some cases introducing Simplified Planning Zones in very restricted areas that have high levels of vacancy

- encouraging owners of prominent vacant property to allow **interim uses** where leaving the space vacant would damage the centre;

- where space has been vacant for several years, using **compulsory purchase** powers to bring land back into use by the private sector for schemes that are in accordance with the development plan, and particularly for housing, and;

- channelling financial contributions from new developments to help implement initiatives such as improved public space that form part of an approved town centre strategy, where possible routed through some form of **development trust** or public private partnership.

Public transport review

13.17 Transport is such an overriding issue that it needs to be given special consideration. Although in most centres providing for cars is a key priority, attractive alternatives should form part of an integrated package of town centre improvements and a sustainable transport policy. Public transport operators and local authorities at district and county levels should consider ways of:

- improving traffic management with schemes such as bus priority lanes and precedence at traffic signals;

- co-ordinating and extending public transport routes into residential areas;

- creating better bus/rail/car interchanges with, for example, places to wait in comfort;

- providing attractive fare structures, for example through travel cards;

- introducing friendlier and more efficient bus services;

- providing priority measures for cyclists through, for example, cycle routes and secure parking and above all creating more pedestrian friendly streets and networks.

Technical assistance

13.18 The work of organisations concerned with town centres such as the English Historic Towns Forum, and the Association of Town Centre Management, confirm the value of sharing and documenting experience. Many of the smaller authorities have only limited experience and expertise and could usefully draw on national organisations or their regional counterparts to provide town centre liaison and support. This would involve:

- spreading good practice through English Heritage and the English Tourist Board, and their Welsh equivalents to historic towns and resorts, and through the Rural Development Commission to smaller market towns;

- encouraging the new Government Integrated Regional Offices, and the Single Regeneration Budget to assist industrial and suburban town centres to prepare strategies, particularly those that would formerly have received Urban Programme funding;

- involving bodies like the Housing Corporation and the Regional Arts Boards in the task of diversifying the roles of town centres;

- tapping the Training and Enterprise Councils for town centre management programmes that encourage small businesses to set up or to improve their standards, for example through training in customer care.

Local business involvement

13.19 Many of the above proposals depend for their success on the involvement of the business community. Town centres serve a range of interests, and their well-being requires a spirit of partnership. The experience of successful towns shows that a range of ways is possible including:

- participating in a forum or **working groups** to assess problems and opportunities and to monitor progress;

- joining a **town centre management company** or steering group;

- **sponsoring** events, greening, street furniture, publicity material or promotional or management campaigns, both in cash and in kind;

- supporting **security initiatives** such as Business or Shop Watch schemes, and ensuring adequate mainte- nance of their own property including allowing temporary uses of vacant property and collaborating with the local authorities over issues such as signage, shutters and lighting.

A positive climate for investment

13.20 The most important change required is a change of attitude, so that town centres generally, not just historic ones, are fashionable again as places to live and enjoy. However, the trends have been towards the concentration of ownership and control away from town centres. There is therefore also a need for new initiatives at the national level. At present there are large numbers of bodies with some interest in town centres, including voluntary organisations like the Association of Town Centre Management the British Urban Regeneration Association, and the Civic Trust, professional institutes like the Royal Institution of Chartered Surveyors, and the Royal Town Planning Institute and trade associations like the British Retail Consortium, the British Property Federation, the British Council of Shopping Centres and the Association of British Chambers of Commerce. All from time to time organise events, produce reports, and engage in lobbying. But what is lacking is a mechanism that harnesses the interests and resources of those with most at stake, namely the property owners and investors and the retailers and leisure operators whose income depends on the success of the High Street, plus the building societies and insurance companies who could provide the finance for diversification.

13.21 There have been calls for a campaign on the part of the Association of Town Centre Management, and for an urban equivalent of the Countryside Commission on the part of the Civic Trust. Without wanting to prescribe the mechanism, there does seem to be a need at regional or national level for some kind of equivalent to the International Downtown Association or National Main Street Program that can bring practitioners together across sectoral and professional bounda- ries, and progressively promote improvements in standards.

13.22 Most people are convinced by what they see, and by the knowledge that they are not acting alone. We therefore suggest that a valuable first step would be for representatives of the various organisations involved to join some kind of **town centre task force** to take forward the ideas in this and other reports, with particular regard to:

- standardising ways of **collecting and exchanging information** to enable town centre health to be monitored cost-effectively, with particular regard to retail turnover and living in towns;

- encouraging private investment by **publicising success stories** and examples of positive action on the part of private as well as public organisations;

- **disseminating good practice** through publications, conventions, training programmes, and a central pool of information eg awards schemes;

- ensuring that **policy research** is undertaken into unresolved issues, such as the impact of superstores on market towns, and the effect of different forms of pedestrianisation on levels of trade in larger towns.

13.23 This report has explained how towns can adopt an approach that is pro-active, through the creation of local partnerships. It proposes a process for drawing up profiles, visions, strategies and action programmes, and applying good practice from around the country. Rather than advocating uniform standards, our research argues for an 'holistic' approach, related to the type of town and its situation. The approach should be rather like a good gardener's responses to local conditions and attention to ongoing maintenance. We suggest focussing on attractions, access and amenity, through appropriate and realistic strategies that reflect the particular circumstances of the town. We propose giving consideration to the economic and social as well as physical dimensions of a town centre, and the range of seven or eight roles it plays.

13.24 In conclusion, many town and city centres are at a turning point. PPG6 calls for planning to provide a positive lead. This report shows what can be done to make town centres the viable and vital hub of lively communities. But like mending a leaky roof, the time to act is before the rot sets in.

APPENDIX A ● MEASURING THE RETAIL PERFORMANCE OF TOWN CENTRES

Appendix A: Measuring the retail performance of town centres

Concepts

The performance of the shops in a town centre can be measured in a number of ways, which can be divided into retailing criteria and property criteria. Retailing criteria cover indicators of both size and success. Size can be measured by factors such as number of shops, total floorspace, presence of key multiples, level of retail sales etc. Success can be measured in terms of factors such as sales per square foot, profitability etc. Property criteria deal with the value of shop property as expressed in terms of rental value (the amount of rent which retailers pay) or capital value (the open market value of a freehold or long leasehold).

For the purpose of this research, it was decided to develop a simple single indicator of retail performance using values. Values have a number of advantages. Firstly, there are in existence data sets covering all towns of significant size on a comparable basis over time. Data of this regularity is less readily available for most of the other retailing indicators.

A second advantage of value as a measure of performance is that it in many ways reflects and encapsulates retail success. The level of rental value for shop property reflects the level of demand by retailers to occupy shop premises. The capital value reflects the desirability of that property (and the value placed on the rental income) by investors. For these reasons it was decided to attempt to develop an indicator of retail performance using valuation data.

Data

Rental values of shop property, comparing one town with another, are commonly quoted in terms of rent per square foot Zone A in the 100% pitch. Zone A is the front part of a shop and is a device developed to enable shops of different shapes and sizes to be compared on a like for like basis. The 100% pitch refers to the highest value area within a town centre. This is an area of some 50-100 yards long in the most accessible and heavily used part of the high street, and is typically occupied by shops selling fashion and other comparison goods. The 100% pitch may be found in a traditional high street or within a purpose built shopping centre, depending on the situation in each individual town.

The data used were the Hillier Parker Research database of open market rents and yields. This covers the top 700 towns in Great Britain at six monthly intervals since 1984. The analysis was limited to towns of major district centre rank or above, based on the presence of key multiples (1). This has produced data on 407 towns over an eight year period. The data were analysed in terms of rental growth and value.

Rental growth

The level of shop rents in a town centre is heavily affected by the size of that town, however measured. The correlation is far from perfect but the influence of town size on rent levels in sufficiently strong to make the level of rent itself an insufficient indicator of rental success. It was felt better to analyse the rate of growth of shop rents to see if this provided a useful indication of retail performance.

The period of analysis (May 1984 to November 1992) covered the major boom of the late 1980s and the following recession. In many ways, it was therefore an abnormal period. Analysis of rental growth by different categories of town showed an interesting pattern of cyclical variation.

The results can be summarised as follows. In 1984 recovery after the recession of the early 1980s was well under way. Small prosperous towns had started to experience rental growth in the period 1982 to 1984. Recovery of the more depressed towns came through later in the mid-1980s period. In the boom period from 1986 to 1988 rental growth occurred most rapidly in the most prosperous southern towns. This was followed by a sharp reaction as the economy moved into recession, with the South experiencing greater levels of rental decline than the North.

The effect of the boom and recession on rental growth by town type is summarised in Table 1. This shows the 407 towns divided into eight categories as used by the OPCS in the presentation of census data. Five of the eight categories saw average rental growth in the period 1984 to 1988 run ahead of the national average. The following period, 1988 to 1992, saw the exact mirror image of this pattern. For example, shopping centres within the London boroughs experienced an average rental growth above the national average in the first time period but below the national average in the second. Industrial districts, in contrast, having experienced below average rental growth in the first period, enjoyed above rental growth in the second.

We concluded that this method of analysis was not appropriate to provide an indicator of retail performance which would indicate the basic underlying success of a town as a retail centre.

TABLE 1

RENTAL VALUE GROWTH IN BOOM AND SLUMP BY TYPE OF TOWN

Shop Rental Growth greater (+) or less (-) than national average

		1984-88	1988-92
1	London Boroughs	+	-
2	Metropolitan Districts	-	+
3	Non-Metropolitan Districts	-	+
4	Industrial Districts	-	+
5	New Towns	+	-
6	Resort, Port, Retirement	+	-
7	Other, mixed	+	-
8	More remote, mainly rural	+	-

Sources: OPCS Classification of Local Authority Districts. Hillier Parker data on shop rents in November of relevant year for 407 towns.

Value

Because each property is individual and different, property values are compared by means of the yield. Yield shows rental income as a percentage of capital value. Thus, the higher the yield the lower the rental income is valued, and vice versa.

The level of yield for a town is, in many ways, a good indicator of retail success. There are, however, two issues which arise in using this method. Just as the level of rent tends to rise with the size of town, so does the level of yield level which produce a coefficient R = 0.79. This is a fairly strong correlation which suggests that approximately half the variation in yields can be 'explained' by the level of rent.

For the purpose of this research it was decided to standardise yield by the rent level. Yield was therefore regressed against rent using 398 town centres for which data were available. Analysis was then made of the residuals. In this way it was possible to compare the actual level of yield against the level of yield which might be expected given the level of rent.

The second issue to raise in using yields as a method of analysis concerns the question of shopping centre development. The analysis was undertaken for May 1992. This is a date coming at the end of a very intensive period of town centre shopping development. Several towns (for example Watford, Bromley, Kingston, Worcester) were still experiencing the effects of major retail development. Retail development affects both rental levels and rental values. Research on the effect of development on rents (2), suggests that the long-term effect is fairly minor but there is a significant short-term effect. The results of the analysis for towns which had recently experienced major development may therefore be misleading.

A further factor is the longer term effect of retail development on a town centre. The results of the analysis showed similar scores for Walthamstow, which has experienced a major shopping development, and Woolwich which had not experienced development. Town centre development does not necessarily lead to higher rents or lower yields. The results of the analysis, therefore, need to be regarded as a simple, somewhat crude single indicator of retail

performance which needs to be used in conjunction with other indicators and analysis, set out in Chapter 5, before any firm conclusions should be reached.

Results

Tests of the residuals suggested the use of a single simple curvilinear function:- $Y = a - b\,1/x$ where y = yield, x = rent, and a and b are constants. Residuals were tested for skew and the results were satisfactory. The 398 towns were ranked by their residual running from Barrow where the yield expected from the level of rent was 7.9% compared with the actual yield of 11%, to Newbury at the other extreme where the expected yield was 7.3% compared with an actual yield of 5.75%. Table 2 shows the top and bottom ten in the ranking.

The results were analysed according to the OPCS Classification of Local Authority Districts and by standard regions. These showed (see Table 3 and 4) a preponderance of high valued towns (with negative residuals, ie where yields are lower than expected) in non-Metropolitan cities (category 3) and in resorts, ports and retirement districts (6), other urban and mixed urban rural district (7) and remote mainly rural districts (8). Values were low in Greater London and the Metropolitan districts. The regional pattern showed the South West region with the highest valued towns and the Northern region with the lowest.

The results tend to reflect the general level of prosperity, and might be expected. The full results, which are not reproduced, have been used in order to compare groups of towns which are similar with respect to their affluence, size or special functions.

Summary

Having studied various alternative methods of producing a single simple indicator of retail success, we concluded that property value, despite a number of drawbacks, was the best one to use. The advantages lay in the tendency of values to reflect the diverse components of retail performance, and also because a detailed and up-to-date database was available. It was decided to use the residual level of yields, that is the difference between the actual yield and the yield expected given the level of rents in any given town centre.

The results generally tend to favour the more affluent Southern towns. There appears to be no strong pattern favouring towns of different size or specialist type. It is therefore possible to use the analysis as an initial method of providing a preliminary measure of retail performance. Town centres which are similar in non-retail terms, for example, size, affluence or specialisation, can be compared, as a first step, using this method of analysis of their retail performance.

TABLE 2

RETAIL PERFORMANCE FOR TOWN CENTES

Top and bottom towns ranked by shop property value May 1992

RANK	TOP	BOTTOM
1	Newbury	Barrow
2	Weybridge	Wallsend
3	Bridgwater	Workington
4	Chippenham	Ashington
5	Inverness	North Shields
6	Durham	Gateshead
7	Ashford, Kent	Grimsby Freeman Street
8	Worcester	Cwmbran
9	Sevenoaks	East Ham
10	Lichfield	Holloway

(1) A New Classification of Shopping Centres in Great Britain using multiple branch numbers, Reynolds J and Schiller R, Journal of Property Research Vol 9, No2, 1992.

(2) Investors Chronicle Rent Index Research Report No 4, 1979.

TABLE 3

Total Number of Towns within each quartile

OPCS Category	1	2	3	4	5	6	7	8	Total
Quartile 1	25	18	8	23	10	3	6	7	100
Quartile 2	13	17	9	16	4	13	16	12	100
Quartile 3	13	11	9	15	3	9	23	16	99
Quartile 4	0	5	13	8	2	12	41	18	99
Total	51	51	39	62	19	37	86	53	398

* Q1 = Positive Residuals, Q4 = Negative Residuals

KEY FOR OPCS CATEGORIES

1	Greater London Boroughs
2	Metropolitan Districts
3	Non-Metropolitan Cities
4	Industrial Districts
5	Districts including New Towns
6	Resorts, Ports, Retirement Districts
7	Other Urban, Mixed Urban-Rural Districts
8	Remoter Mainly Rural Districts

TABLE 4

Percentage of Towns within each quartile

OPCS Category	1	2	3	4	5	6	7	8	Total
Quartile 1	49	35	21	37	53	8	7	13	25
Quartile 2	25	33	23	26	21	35	19	23	25
Quartile 3	25	22	23	24	16	24	27	30	25
Quartile 4	0	10	33	13	11	32	48	34	25
Total	100	100	100	100	100	100	100	100	100

APPENDIX B • INDICATIVE HEALTH CHECK SURVEY

Appendix B: Indicative health check survey

The following appraisal is designed to be undertaken by a Town Centre Manager, local authority planning officer or an external consultant. In each case we would recommend that it draws on the views of others with an interest in the town centre.

Under each main category, a description is given of the attributes of a **good** and **poor** town centre. This is then followed by a series of questions that provide an indication of how particular aspects of a centre are performing. These are not intended as a scoring mechanism with a pass or fail rate, as the variation between centres means this is not possible. Rather they are intended to draw attention to possible weaknesses and to indicate areas needing action.

Whilst each question can largely be answered by personal observation and through information possessed by many local authorities, we have also indicated a source of additional information where applicable.

1.   ATTRACTIONS

A good town centre is one where there is a variety (**diversity**) and good choice (**critical mass**) of shops and services to draw people on a regular basis in both the day and evening throughout the year.

A poor town centre is one where the variety and number of attractions has only a limited appeal to those whom the centre should be serving resulting in restricted use of the centre and its facilities.

We have identified a number of factors to take into consideration when assessing the attractions in a centre. Each of these should be ticked under one of three categories. When undertaking this appraisal, special attention should be paid to the comparison used in each case.

1.1   How would you rate the quality of the **retail provision in the town centre**?

	Good	Average	Poor	Source
Number of multiple retailers				Multiple ranking
Number and variety of independent shops				Goad
Number and range of specialist shops				Goad
Frequency and variety of general market				Brit Mkt Survey
Reputation and frequency of specialist market				Tourist Board
Appearance and condition of shopping centres				

1.2   How would you rate the quality of **arts, culture and entertainment provision in the town centre**?

	Good	Average	Poor	Source
Variety and reputation of pubs/bars				Police
Number and range of places to eat				Goad
Number and variety of social clubs				Thompson Local
Frequency and breadth of cultural events (plays/concerts/festivals/other events)				Tourist Board
Availability of sports and leisure facilities				Thompson Local

1.3   How would you rate the quality of **service provision in the town centre**?

	Good	Average	Poor	Source
Range and choice of financial services (banks, building societies, insurance etc)				Thompson Local
Number and variety of health care facilities (Doctors, dentists, health clubs, clinics etc)				Thompson Local
Size and variety of educational facilities				Education Dir

1.4   How would you rate the **business space provision in and immediately adjacent to the town centre**?

	Good	Average	Poor	Source
Quality and variety of retail space				Property Agents
Amount and quality of small business workspace				TEC/Ent Agency
Range and availability of office space				Property Agents
Variety of other business space				Ent Agency

1.5   How would you rate the provision of **residential accommodation in and immediately adjacent to the town centre**?

	Good	Average	Poor	Source
Quality and availability of sheltered housing				Social Services
Availability of single person accommodation				Estate Agents
Amount and quality of family accommodation				Estate Agents

Compared to NEIGHBOURING centres....

1.6   How well do the attractions in the centre **serve the needs and wants of the local population**?

	Very	Adequately	Barely

Source: survey

1.7   How well do the attractions in the centre **draw in people from outside its immediate area**

	Very	Adequately	Barely

Source: Tourist Board, surveys

In OVERALL terms...

1.8   How would you say the **variety and number of attractions** available in the centre **has changed**?

	Improved	Same	Declined
Previous year			
Previous three years			
Previous five years			

2. ACCESSIBILITY

A good town centre is one where access to the centre (**mobility**) is available by a range of means and is of sufficient ease and quality to encourage visits and provide a positive welcome to all, and where movement within the centre (**linkages**) is easy, pleasurable and comprehendible for everyone.

A poor town centre is one where access is restricted either through a limit as to the means available, or through obstacles or conditions that make arriving in or moving through the town centre unpleasant or unsafe.

Factors to be taken into consideration are:

Compared with SIMILAR centres....

2.1   How would you rate the quality of the experience of **arriving in the town centre on foot or by bike** from the surrounding area?

	Good	Average	Poor	Source
Quality, well lit pavements/cycle routes				Environ. Audit
Readily usable crossing points on major roads				
Easily negotiatable routes for all people (push chairs, wheel chairs, with children etc)				Disabled groups
Adequate and secure cycle parks				

2.2   How would you describe the quality of the experience of **moving around the town centre**?

	Good	Average	Poor	Source
Well signposted routeways and good local maps				Environ. Audit
Little traffic/pedestrian conflict				
Easily accessible to all				
(with push chairs, people with disabilities etc)				Disabled groups

Compared to NEIGHBOURING centres....

2.3   How would you rate the quality of the experience of **arriving in the town centre by car**

	Good	Average	Poor	Source
Accurate and informative directional signs				Environ. Audit
Accessible and ample varied period car parking				
(in town or in well served park and ride)				Survey
Well-lit, safe feeling car parks				Environ. Audit
Free parking or user-friendly machines				
Helpful maps, information and signs at parking				

2.4   How would you rate the experience of **arriving in the town centre by bus, rail or LRT**?

	Good	Average	Poor	Source
Frequent and reliable service				Bus user surveys
Central dropping-off/pick-up points				
Passenger friendly stops/stations				
(well-lit, covered, maps, timetables)				

In OVERALL terms....

2.5   How well does the centre **serve the access needs of local retailers and businesses**?

Very   Adequately   Barely

Source: retail survey

2.6   How has the quality of **access to the town centre changed** in

	Improved	Same	Declined
Previous year			
Previous three years			
Previous five years			

2.7   How has the quality of the experience of **movement within the centre changed** in

	Improved	Same	Decline
Previous year			
Previous three years			
Previous five years			

3. AMENITY

A good town centre is one which is regularly cleaned, well-maintained and gives a welcoming impression that encourages people using the centre to explore and linger (**identity**) and which feels and is relatively safe for both users and property owners (**security**).

A poor town centre is one where the general appearance is one of lack of care, investment or effort and which feels or is threatening or unsafe.

Factors to be taken into consideration are:

Compared to SIMILAR centres....

3.1   How would you rate the **overall appearance of the public space in the town centre**?

	Good	Average	Poor	Source
General cleanliness of shopping streets				Environ. Audit
General cleanliness of access streets				
Overall condition of street surfaces				
Extent and variety of appropriate planting				
Amount and appropriateness of public art				
Impact of vacant sites and buildings				

3.2   How would you rate the **overall appearance of privately owned buildings and space in the town centre**?

	Good	Average	Poor	Source
General condition of prime retail buildings				Environ. Audit
General condition of secondary retail buildings				
General condition of other buildings				
Quality and appropriateness of building signage				
Extent and appropriateness of floral displays				
General condition of vacant sites and buildings				

3.3   How would you rate the **distinctive character of the town centre**?

	Good	Average	Poor	Source
Identifiable and welcoming gateways				Environ. Audit
Distinctive but practical street furniture				
Informative and appropriate maps/signs				
Quality and appropriate street treatments				
Displaying a unique feel				

3.4   How would you describe the **perception of security in streets and public areas**?

	Good	Average	Poor	Source
Well-lit and maintained main streets				Environ. Audit
Safe, pleasant access routes				
Busy, bright stations/dropping off points				
Appearance of shop front security measures				
Absence of threatening groups				
Effectiveness of security measures				Police
(Police/security presence, CCTV)				

Compared to NEIGHBOURING centres...

3.5   How would you describe **actual crime rates**?

	Good	Average	Poor	Source
Public order offences				Police
Offences against the person				
Vehicle crime				
Theft from shops				
Offences against property				

3.6   How has the **perception of security in the centre changed** in

	Improved	Same	Declined
Previous year			
Previous three years			
Previous five years			

APPENDIX C • SOME EXAMPLES OF GOOD PRACTICE

Appendix C: Some examples of good practice

The report has described many examples of good practice. This appendix brings together some towns and cities which illustrate one or more of the aspects highlighted in the report as contributing towards vitality and viability.

It should be emphasised that this section does not provide an exhaustive list of good practice or of towns that are doing things well. Many other centres could have been included. Instead it reflects centres visited by the study team in the course of the project. To that extent it is a subjective assessment, though some of the centres listed have received general praise for their initiative, possibly in the form of some of the many awards now available.

The towns and cities have been chosen to present a wide geographical spread and it is hoped that neighbouring centres considering an initiative will be able to learn from centres that exemplify good practice. Two symbols have been used in the charts, a solid circle may be 'worth a visit', while a hollow circle is 'interesting'.

If there is enough interest among local authority officers and others involved in town centre initiatives, it may be that a more comprehensive listing could be produced on a regular basis as a guide for those proposing actions in town centres. This will depend on the level of enthusiasm and finance available.

	ATTRACTIONS				ACCESS				AMENITY				ACTION	
MARKET TOWNS	Retailing	Business space	Arts, cult & Ent	Residential	Car	Public transport	Foot/cycle	Special needs	Townscape	Streetscape	Public space	Private space	Strategy	Management
Beverley, Humberside	●			●			●		●	●		●	●	
Bury St. Edmunds, Suffolk	●		●		●		●		●	●	●			
Carlisle, Cumbria	●		●				●		●	●				
High Wycombe, Bucks	●		●		●	○	●	●	○	●	●		●	●
Horsham, E. Sussex	●	○		○	●	○	●		●	●	●		●	○
Kendal, Cumbria	●		●	●			●		●	○	○			
Maidstone, Kent	●	○			●	●	●		○	○			●	●
Newark, Notts	●	○			●	○	●			●	●	●		
Petersfield, Hants	●				●	○	●		●	●	●		●	●
Shrewsbury, Salop	●		●	○			●	○	●	○	○			
Tunbridge Wells, Kent	●		○				○		●	●	○		●	●
Witney, Oxon	●			●	●		○		●	○	●		●	

INDUSTRIAL TOWNS

	ATTRACTIONS					ACCESS				AMENITY				ACTION	
	Retailing	Business space	Arts, cult & Ent	Residential		Car	Public transport	Foot/cycle	Special needs	Townscape	Streetscape	Public space	Private space	Strategy	Management
Bradford, W. Yorks		●	●			○	●	●		●	●	○		○	○
Bury	●						●		●	○			●	○	
Halifax	○	●	●				○	●	●	●	●	●		●	●
Middlesbrough		●	○	●		●		●		●		●		○	
Neath	●		○	○		●	●	●		○	○			●	
Newport, Gwent	○		●				●	●	●	●	●		○	●	○
Preston, Lancs	●	●	●	○		●	○	●		○	●	●	●	●	●
Swansea			●	●				○		●		○	●	●	○
Wakefield	●		○			●	●	●		○	●	●		○	
Wolverhampton	○	●	●			●	●	●		●	●	○		○	●

SUBURBAN CENTRES

	ATTRACTIONS					ACCESS				AMENITY				ACTION	
	Retailing	Business space	Arts, cult & Ent	Residential		Car	Public transport	Foot/cycle	Special needs	Townscape	Streetscape	Public space	Private space	Strategy	Management
Bexleyheath	●	●					●	○			○		○	●	●
Belgrave Road, Leicester	●	●	●				○						○	●	
Brixton	○		○				○				○				
Camden Town	●		●				○		●	●			●		
Holloway, Nags Head	●		○				○				●			●	●
Ilford	●					●	●			●	●	○		●	●
Islington, Upper St.	●		●				●			●	●			○	
Lewisham	○		○			○	○				○	○	●	●	●
Wimbledon	●	●	●				○	○		○	●			○	

METROPOLITAN CITIES

	ATTRACTIONS					ACCESS					AMENITY				ACTION	
	Retailing	Business space	Arts, cult & Ent	Residential		Car	Public transport	Foot/cycle	Special needs		Townscape	Streetscape	Public space	Private space	Strategy	Management
Birmingham	●	●	●	○				●	●		●	●	●		●	●
Cardiff	●		●				○	●			○	●	●		●	○
Leeds	●	●	○	●		○	○				○	●	●	●	●	
Leicester	●		○	●		○		●				●	●	●	●	○
Manchester	●	●	●	●			●	●	●		●	●	●	●	●	○
Newcastle	●	○	●				●	●			●	●	●	●	●	●
Nottingham	●	●		○		●	●	●	●		●	●	●	●		
Sheffield			●				○		●		○	○	●	●	○	○

RESORTS AND HISTORIC TOWNS

	ATTRACTIONS					ACCESS					AMENITY				ACTION	
	Retailing	Business space	Arts, cult & Ent	Residential		Car	Public transport	Foot/cycle	Special needs		Townscape	Streetscape	Public space	Private space	Strategy	Management
Bath	●		●	○		●	●	●			○	●	●	●	●	●
Bournemouth	●							●				●	●			
Brighton	●	●	●	○		○	○	●			●	●			●	
Cambridge	●					○		○			●	●	○		●	
Exeter	●	●	●	●		●	●	●	○			●	●		●	
Norwich	●			●		○	○					●	●	●	●	
Oxford	●		●	○		●	●	●	○			●	●	○	○	
Weymouth	●		○								○	●				
Worcester	●	○	○			●	●	●	○		●	●	●	●	●	○
York	●		●	●		●	●	●			●	●	●		○	○

BIBLIOGRAPHY

Bibliography

Aldous, T., (1990), *New shopping in Historic Towns: The Chesterfield Story*, English Heritage, London.

Aldous, T., (1992), *Urban Villages*, Urban Villages Group, London.

AHF, (1993), *Annual Report*, Architectural Heritage Fund, London.

ATCM, (1992), *Working for the Future of our Towns and Cities*, Association of Town Centre Management, London.

ATCM, (1994), *The effectiveness of Town Centre Management*, report by Donaldsons and Healey and Baker, Association of Town Centre Management, London.

Bernard Thorpe, (1990), *Who Runs Britain's High Street: A Research Report examining the Occupation of Britain's Town Centres by Multiple Retail Companies*, Oxford Institute of Retail Management and Bernard Thorpe, Oxford.

Besant, W., (1899), *South London*, Chatto and Windus, London.

Bianchini, F., and Fisher, M., (1988), *City Centre, City Cultures*, The Centre for Local Economic Strategies, Manchester.

Bianchini, F., and Parkinson, M., (1993) *Cultural Policy and Urban Regeneration: the West European Experience*, Manchester University Press, Manchester.

Bowlby, S., (1985), 'Planning for Women to Shop in Post-War Britain', *Environment and Planning*, Vol.2 pp179-199.

Breen, A., and Rigby, D., (1993) *Waterfronts: Cities Reclaim their Edge*, McGraw Hill, New York.

Briggs, A., (1990), *Victorian Cities*, Penguin Books, London.

Brown, J., (1986), *The English Market Town*, Crowood, Marlborough.

Browning, H.C. and Singelmann, J., (1978), 'The Transformation of the U.S. Labor Force: The Interaction of Industry and Occupation', *Politics and Society*, Vol.8 nos. 3-4, pp481-509.

Breheny, M., (1989), Rating Places, Built Environment Vol 14, No2, Alexandrine Press, Oxford.

Burke, G., (1975), *Towns in the Making*, Edward Arnold, London.

Burke, G., (1976), *Townscapes*, Penguin Books, London.

CACI, (1993), *Acorn Users Guide*, London.

Cantacuzino, S., (1989), *Re-Architecture: Old Buildings/New Uses*, Thames and Hudson, London.

Carr, J., (1990), Out of Town Shopping: Is the revolution over?, *Royal Society of Arts Journal*, Vol 138 No 5403, February 1990, London.

Champion, A.G., et al, (1987), *Changing Places:Britain's Demographic, Economic and Social Complexion*, Edward Arnold, London.

Champion, A.G., and Townsend, A.R., (1990), *Contemporary Britain: A Geographical Perspective* Edward Arnold, London.

Chase, M., and Drummond, P., (1993), *Shopping after the Millennium*, Proceedings of Town and Country Planning Summer School, Donaldsons, London.

Calvino I., (1974), *Invisible Cities*, Secker and Warburg, London.

City of Worcester, (1993), *Annual Retail Monitor*, City of Worcester.

Civic Trust, (1994), *Liveable Towns and Cities*, Liverpool John Moores University.

Civic Trust and English Historic Towns Forum, (1993), *Traffic Measures in Historic Towns: An introduction to good practice*, Civic Trust and English Historic Towns Forum.

Comedia, (1991), *Out of Hours: A Study of Economic, Social and Cultural Life in Twelve Town Centres in the UK*, Gulbenkian Foundation, Comedia, Stroud.

Comedia, (1993), *Borrowed Time? The Future of Public Libraries in the UK*, Comedia, Stroud.

CEC (Commission of the European Communities), (1992), 'Green Paper on the Urban Environment', Eur 12902, Commission of the European Communities, Brussels.

Crime Concern, (1993), *A Practical Guide to Crime Prevention for Local Partnerships*, Home Office, HMSO, London.

Davidson, J., (1988), *How Green is your City? Pioneering Approaches to Environmental Action* Bedford Square Press, London.

Davies, R., (ed), (1988), 'Planning for Retail Change: International Comparisons,' *Built Environment* Vol 14, No 1, Alexandrine Press, Oxford.

Davies, R., (1989), *Retail and Commercial Planning*, Croom Helm, Beckenham.

Department of the Environment, (1980), *Urban Renaissance: A Better Life in Towns*, HMSO, London.

Department of the Environment, (1987), *Re-using Redundant Buildings: Good Practice in Urban Regeneration*, HMSO, London.

Department of the Environment, (1988), *Improving Inner City Shopping Centres: An Evaluation of Urban Programme Funded Schemes in West Midlands*, HMSO, London.

Department of the Environment, (1992a), *The Effects of Major Out-of-Town Retail Development*, by Building Design Partnership and Oxford Institute of Retailing Management, HMSO, London.

Department of the Environment, (1992b), *This Common Inheritance: Britain's Environmental Strategy*, HMSO, London.

Department of the Environment, (1992c), *Developing Indicators to assess the Potential for Urban Regeneration*, HMSO, London.

Department of the Environment and Department of Transport, (1992d), *Reducing Transport Emissions through Planning*, by ECOTEC, HMSO, London.

Department of the Environment / Welsh Office, (1993a), *Planning Policy Guidance (PPG6): Town Centres and Retail Developments*, HMSO, London.

Department of the Environment, (1993b), *Merry Hill Impact Study*, HMSO, London.

Department of the Environment, (1994a), *Sustainable Development: The UK Strategy*, HMSO, London.

Department of the Environment, (1994b), *Planning Policy Guidance (PPG13): Transport*, HMSO, London.

Department of Transport, (1989), *National Road Traffic Forecast*, HMSO, London.

Department of Transport, (1991), *Transport and the Environment*, HMSO, London.

Department of Transport, (1992), *Bypasses*, HMSO, London.

Design Council and the Royal Town Planning Institute, (1979), *Streets Ahead*, Design Council, London.

Distributive Trades Economic Development Committee, (1988), *The Future of the High Street*, HMSO, London.

Donaldsons, (1992), *Retailing in Historic Towns*, English Historic Towns Forum, Bath.

DTA, (1994), *Directory of Development Trusts*, Development Trust Association, London.

DTZ, (1993), *Index of Retail Trading Locations: Special Report*, DTZ Debenham Thorpe, Property Managers Associates, London.

Edward Erdman Research, (1990), *Traffic Free Shopping*, Edward Erdman, London.

EHTF, (1993), *Bus-based Park and Ride - a good practice guide*, English Historic Towns Forum, Bath.

EH, (1993), *Street Improvements in Historic Areas*, English Heritage, London.

ETB, (1989), Jones Lang and Wootton, Retail, Leisure and Tourism, English Tourist Board, London.

ETB, (1991a), *Maintaining the Balance: Report of Historic Town Working Group*, English Tourist Board, London.

ETB, (1991b), *Tourism and the Environment*, English Tourist Board, London.

ETB, (1993), *Turning the Tide: a heritage and environment strategy for a seaside resort*, English Tourist Board, London.

Falk, N., (1993), 'Regeneration and Sustainable Development', in Berry, J. et al (ed), *Urban Regeneration, Property Investment and Development*, Spon, London.

Fishman, R., (1993), *Bourgeois Utopias: The Rise and Fall of Suburbia*, Basic Books, Inc., New York.

Foley, P., and Lawless, P., (1992), *A Vision of Quality*, University of Sheffield/Sheffield Hallam University

FOE, (1992), *Less Traffic, Better Towns*, Friends of the Earth Trust Limited, London.

Garreau, J., (1991), *Edge Cities: Life on the New Frontier*, Anchor Books, New York.

Gershuny, J.I. Prof., (1987), *Lifestyle, Innovation and the future of work'*, From the series, "Re-inventing the place of work: Proceedings", *Journal of the Royal Society of Arts*, pp492-502, London.

Glancey, J., (1993), 'The Supermarkets that are Eating Up Stroud', *The Independent*, 18 August 1993, p15.

GOAD Plans, (1994), Chas. E. Goad, Old Hatfield.

Greater London Council, (1986), 'Tesco, Neasden: A Study of Retail Impact', GLC/Brent LB/Tesco plc., London.

Greater Peterborough Master Plan, (1970)

Guy, C., (1994), *The Retail Development Process*, Routledge, London.

Hall, P., et al (1973), *Containment of Urban England*, Allen and Unwin, London.

Hall, P., (1988), 'Planning for Retail Change: International Comparisons', *Built Environment*, Vol.14(1), Alexandrine Press, Oxford.

Hass-Klau, C., (1990), *The Pedestrian and City Traffic*, Belhaven, London.

Hass-Klau, C., (1992), *The Impact of Pedestrianisation and Traffic Calming on Retailing: A Review of the Evidence from Germany and Britain*, Environmental and Transport Planning, Brighton.

Hayward, R., and McGlynn, S., (1993), *Making Better Places:Urban Design Now*, Butterworth Architecture, Oxford.

Hertfordshire County Council, (1989), 'Guidance Notes on Town Centre Enhancement', Hertfordshire Technical Chief Officers Association, Town Centre Panel, Hertfordshire County Council, Planning & Estates Department, Hertford.

Hillier, B., and Hanson, J., (1984), *The Social Logic of Space*, Cambridge University Press, Cambridge.

Hillier Parker, (1991a), *Shopping Centres of Great Britain: A New Classification*, Hillier Parker, Chas E. Goad Ltd., Oxford Institute of Retail Management, London.

Hillier Parker, (1991b), *Shopping Schemes in the Pipeline*, Hillier Parker, London.

Hillman, J., (1988), *A New Look for London*, A Report for Royal Fine Art Commission, HMSO, London.

Hillman, J., and Mayer, (1991), *One False Move: A Study of Children's Independent Mobility*, Policy Studies Institute, London.

Howard, E.B. and Davies, R.L., (1990), 'Trading at the Meadowhall Shopping Centres: the First Results', *OXIRM Research papers Series D7*, Oxford Institute of retail Management, Oxford.

Howard, M., (1989), *Britain in 2010: Future Patterns of Shopping*, Out of Town Shopping: Is the Revolution Over?, Royal Society of Arts Symposium, London.

Hoyle, B., (1993), *European Port Cities in Transition*, Belhaven Press, London.

Institute for Retail Studies (IRS) (1991), *Distributive Trades Profile 1991: A Statistical Digest*, Institute for Retail Studies, University of Stirling.

ICE, (1993), *Tomorrow's Towns: An Urban Environment Initiative*, Institution of Civil Engineers, London.

IDA, (1993), Centralised Retail Management, International Downtown Association, Washington.

IPD, (1993), *Annual Review*, Investment Property Databank, London.

Jacobs, J., (1969), *The Economy of Cities*, Random House, New York.

Kay, W., (1987), *Battle for the High Street*, Piatkus, London.

KCC, (1993), *Town Centre Management: Building and Working in Partnership*, Kent County Council.

KCC, (1994), *Review of the Town Centre Intiatives in Kent*, Kent County Council.

Kostof, S., (1991), *The City Shaped: Urban Patterns and Meanings Through History*, Thames and Hudson, London.

Lee Donaldson Associates, (1991), *'Shopping Centre Appeals Review 1991'*, Research Paper, Lee Donaldson Associates, London.

Lloyd, D., (1984), *The Making of English Towns*, Gollancz, London.

LPAC, (1994): *High Accessibility and Town Centres*, report by URBED with Donaldsons and Halcrow Fox, London Planning Advisory Committee, Romford.

Maidstone Town Centre Management Steering Group, (1993), *Strategy for Action*, Maidstone Town Centre Management Initiative, Kent.

Marks and Spencer PLC (1992), *Retail Impact on the Vitality and Viability of Town Centres: The Experience of Marks and Spencer*, Marks and Spencer, London.

McNulty, R. H., et al (1985), *The Economics of Amenity: Community Futures and Quality of Life*, Partners for Livable Places, Washington.

Michell, G., (1986), *Design in the High Street*, Report for the Royal Fine Art Commission, Architectural Press, London.

Ministry of Transport, (1963), *Traffic in Towns: A study of the long term problems of traffic in urban areas* by Colin Buchanan and Partners, HMSO, London.

Mumford, L., (1961) *The City in History*, Harcourt Brace, New York.

NEDO, (1988), *The Future of the High Street*, Distributive Trades Economic Development Committee, National Economic Development Office, HMSO, London.

NTHP, (1988), *Revitalising Downtown 1976-1986*, U.S. National Trust for Historic Preservation Urban Institute, Washington.

NTHP, (1992), *'Main Street'*, Main Street News No.78, June 1992, The National Trust for Historic Preservation Urban Institute, Washington.

OPCS, Social Survey Division (1990), *General Household Survey 1990* No. 21, HMSO, London.

Oxford Retail Group, (1990), *Retailing Issues for Development Plans*, OXIRM, Oxford.

Oxford Institute of Retail Management (OXIRM), (1986), *The Health of the High Street*, Research Paper, OXIRM, Templeton College, Oxford.

Oxford Institute of Retail Management (OXIRM), (1993) *The Shopping Centre Industry 1993, Thirty Years of Growth*, British Council of Shopping Centres, Reading.

Parkinson, M., et al., (Aug 1992), *Urbanisation and the Functions of Cities in the European Community*, A report to commission of the European Communities Directorate General for Regional Policy (XVI), European Institute for urban affairs, John Moores University, Liverpool.

Pedestrians Association, (1993), *Our Kind of Town*, Pedestrian Association, London.

Peiser, (1989), *The Changing Face of Retailing*, Fuller Peiser, London.

Petherick, A., and Fraser, R., (1992), *Living Over The Shop: A Handbook for Practitioners*, University of York, York.

Piauchaud, D., (1974), *Do the Poor Pay More*, Poverty Research Series 3, Child Poverty Action Group, London.

PMA (Property Market Analysis), (1989), *Greater London Retail Market Assessment: 1989 Review*, LPAC, London.

Powell, D., (ed), (1987), *Quiet Revolution: The Tesco Papers, 1975-1987*, Hallam and Mallen, London.

PSI Research Team, (1991), *Britain in 2010*, Policy Studies Institute, London.

Reader's Digest, (1990), *Town Tours in Britain: A Walker's Guide*, The Reader's Digest Association Limited.

Reynolds, J., (1992), and Schiller, R., *A New Classification of Shopping Centres in Great Britain*, Journal of Property Research Vol 9., No 2, 1992.

RFAC, (1994), *Lighten our Darkness: lighting our cities, successes, failures and opportunities*, Royal Fine Arts Commission, London.

RICS, (1991), *Shaping Britain for the 21st Century: A Land-use and Transport Planning Strategy,* Discussion paper prepared under the auspices of the Planning and Development Division of the RICS, The Royal Institute of Chartered Surveyors, London.

Royal Borough of Kensington and Chelsea, (1987), *Kensington High Street Action Plan,* RBK&C, London.

RTPI, (1992), *Town Centres and Retail Development - observations on PPG6,* Royal Town Planning Institute, London.

Schiller, R., (1986), The Coming of the Third Wave, *Estates Gazette,* 16 August 1986,

Peter Shearman Associates, (1993), *Peckham Town Centre Shopping Provision and Prospects,* Report prepared on behalf of J. Sainsbury PLC, Peter Shearman Associates, London.

Sherlock, H., (1990), *Cities are Good for Us,* Paladin, London.

Simmie, J., Penn, A., and Sutcliffe, A., (1993), *The Death and Life of Town Centres,* Bartlett School of Planning, University College, London.

Solesbury, W., (1990) *Reconstructuring National Urban Policy for the 1990s,* Economic and Social Research Council, Swindon.

Stabler, E., (1989), *Centralised Retail Management: A Brief Introduction and Organising Principles,* International Downtown Association, Washington.

Stansbury, M., (1989)*The Survival of the Town Centre: A Practical Approach to its Management and Development,* London Borough of Redbridge.

TCPA, (1989), *British Towns and the Quality of Life: 1989 Annual Conference,* Town and Country Planning Association, London.

TEST, (1987), *Quality Streets: How Traditional Urban Centres benefit from Traffic-Calming,* TEST, London.

TEST, (1989), *Trouble in Store: Retail Locational Policy in Britain and Germany,* TEST, London.

Thorpe, D., (1990), 'Retailers Strategies in the 1990s', in RTPI *Retail Development Conference,* RTPI, London.

Tibbalds, F., (1992), *Making People-Friendly Towns: Improving the Public Environment in Towns and Cities,* Longman Group, Essex.

UDQ, (1994), Involving People in Urban Design, UDQ, Issue 49, Jan 1994, Urban Design Group, Didcot, Oxon.

URBED, (1987), *Re-using Redundant Buildings: Good Practice in Urban Regeneration,* HMSO, London.

URBED, (1988), *The Highbury Initiative: Proceedings of the Birmingham City Centre Challenge Symposium,* URBED/DEGW, London.

URBED, (1990), *Wood Green: A Strategy for Revitalisation,* URBED, London.

URBED, (1992), *Sandwich Looks Forward: A Strategic Plan for the 21st Century,* Urban and Economic Development Group, London.

URBED and LDR International Ltd. (1993), *Reviving the Heart of Margate: A Strategy for Economic Regeneration,* URBED, London.

Whyte, W., (1988), *Rediscovering the Center City* Anchor Books, Doubleday, London.

Wilcox, D., (1988) *Creating Development Trusts,* Department of the Environment, HMSO, London.

Worpole, K., (1992), *Towns for People,* Open University Press, Milton Keynes.

Worcester (1993), Annual Retail Monitor, Technical Service Department City of Worcester.

York, (1988), MVA Traffic and Parking Study, City of York.